WHO REALLY KILLED NICOLE?

O. J. Simpson's Closest Confidant Tells All

NORMAN PARDO

Skyhorse Publishing

10 9 8 7 6 5 4 3 2 1

Library of Congress Cataloging-in-Publication Data is available on file.

ISBN: 978-1-5107-6845-1
eISBN: 978-1-5107-6848-2

Cover design by Brian Peterson
Cover photograph by Vinnie Zuffante/Archive Photos/Getty Images

Printed in the United States of America

Contents

Introduction

It's the greatest crime story ever to play out on national television—the murder of Nicole Brown Simpson, the thirty-five-year-old ex-wife of famed pro football star O. J. Simpson, and Ron Goldman, a twenty-five-year-old restaurant worker and friend of Nicole, who were brutally murdered by an unknown assailant outside Nicole's home in Brentwood, California, on the evening of Sunday, June 12, 1994.

Charged with the murders, O. J. Simpson underwent a nationally televised murder trial in October 1995 that lasted nearly nine months, ending in a dramatic acquittal that was watched live by over one hundred million people—one of the largest audiences to ever witness anything in the history of television. It was called the "trial of the century." But people still want to know what really happened that summer night when Nicole Brown Simpson's and Ron Goldman's lives were literally cut short.

I know secrets about that murder that have never been made public. I possess evidence of that horrific crime that took me years to uncover—evidence that this book is sharing with the public for the first time. Some names have been changed to protect the innocent, and the guilty.

Who am I and how do I come to possess such intimate knowledge of O. J. Simpson?

I, Norman Pardo, was O. J. Simpson's right-hand man, his confidant, and the keeper of his secrets. For nearly twenty years, I was O. J. Simpson's business manager. I traveled with him daily, arranged his professional appearances, spent countless days in cars and on airplanes accompanying him and videotaping him so constantly that O. J. became unaware that his words and actions were being recorded.

This book exists to show you the proof for the first time ever—the back-up for the claims I made in a two-hour documentary film I produced to disclose startling revelations O. J. Simpson made in exclusive footage I took and possess. O. J. Simpson can be heard to say clearly in that video footage, "You know in certain situations, I think that just about anybody is capable of doing just about anything."

What exactly did O. J. mean? Read this book, examine the evidence, decipher the clues, and solve a murder mystery that even today, over twenty-five years after the fact, keeps people guessing. Who did it? Who killed Nicole Brown Simpson and Ron Goldman? For the first time ever, you will now have what you need to discover the motive behind this hideous crime. In these pages, the mystery unravels.

While I believe I know who killed Nicole, I am going to share the evidence with you the reader and I am going to invite you to solve the crime. I have constructed a companion web portal with useful clues and hours of exclusive videos of O. J. Simpson behind the scenes, raw and uncensored. I believe I can say there is no person who knows more about who killed Nicole than the killer or killers themselves.

But my dilemma is that I cannot prove anything for certain in this book. Why can't I prove anything for certain? The answer to that question is simple. O. J. Simpson cannot be put on trial for those horrific murders again. Determining guilt or innocence can only be done in a criminal trial before a jury of your peers. So, in all honesty, what I am about to present to you in this book are some allegations I consider serious, backed up by years of painstaking investigation.

I have spent hundreds of thousands of dollars of my own money tracking down every living person who knows something of value to solving this mystery and digging up every bit of documentary evidence—going so far as to correspond with a notorious serial killer who as this book is being written is confined to prison, awaiting execution. In this book you are going to find evidence you've never seen before: new leads, new suspects, and a whole new perspective on the Nicole Brown Simpson and Ron Goldman murder mysteries.

My final decision is to leave the "solving" of this great mystery up to you, the reader. Presented here for the first time with evidence that has never before been made public, you will have the opportunity to be a detective on a par with the greatest detectives of all time. You have a chance to come forward with a solution that will not only have to be ingenious but will have to connect the evidence in a way even O. J. Simpson would have to agree solves the crime.

The clues given in this book will link to information that I intend to present over the next few months in a companion website. There, I will also archive important videos from the seventy hours of videotape that I made of O. J. Simpson being O. J. Simpson in his most outrageous self in all those years that I rode with O. J., traveling to events all over the country with him as his business manager.

Once I tell everybody everything I know, it will be over. I can end this within myself. At that point, I can live without the weapon I have legally carried for ages to protect my life. I won't have to worry about the police chasing me or the FBI breaking into my offices. The drug smugglers angry at me, O. J. angry at me. The only way I can be free is really to say what's on my mind.

By writing this book and laying it all out on the line for you the reader, I can finally plan to live in peace. Once I tell my story, it's over—no more asking me what do I think happened? I'm going to turn the entire world into investigators. I'm going to give you all the clues, all the answers to everything you're looking for, and all you have to do is put them together. You will find that everything I am telling you is true, but nobody has ever put these clues together like I have. So, by doing this, I can sleep at night.

People are going to complain that I am making a whole lot of money off this O. J. Simpson thing, all this promoting. But a lot of people don't know that I've never made any money off O. J. Simpson since I started doing this. It's never been about the money. It's always been about whether I can solve something in my own head so I can go to sleep at night and feel I've figured it out—O. J. is a murderer, or O. J. is not a murderer.

Everybody has a different idea about whether O. J. is a murderer and I wanted to know. But it isn't about the money. I didn't need the money. O. J. knows I never needed the money. I've done this strictly to find out what happened. By taping O. J. on film, I was able to hear his stories, take the truth from his stories, and that's exactly what I did.

Almost everyone involved in this O. J. saga is either dead or in prison. And I have always had to pack a gun in fear of that. So, to free myself, I want to say what's on my mind. For the first time in almost twenty years, I am going to tell everybody in the world what O. J. told me. I am going to tell everybody in the world what we took out of what he told me—the truths and the falsehoods—and show you what we've come up with and what we've concluded.

So, I've decided to share with you, the reader, the documents, the research, the revelations from private videos, as well as the personal stories O. J. shared with me.

It's not going to be pretty. It's not something O. J. Simpson wants me to say. It's not something the Goldmans want me to say. It's not something the police want me to say. The Kardashians are going to be unhappy and the family of Dodi Fayed would probably prefer this book never be written.

But I'm going to show you the evidence because I don't want the responsibility anymore. I've had the responsibility ever since I first met O. J. Simpson in 1999 and now, I'm passing it to you, the reader. Everything I know, you're going to know. Good or bad. O. J. won't speak to me after this. A lot of people won't speak with me after this. But it doesn't really matter because I don't really care. I'm done.

Over the last two decades, I've researched every living person, every single detail to come to the conclusion. This is not my notion. I didn't start with any preconceived conclusion. I just wanted facts. Now, I want to give those facts to you, the reader, and let you deal with it.

So, here's the deal—in my opinion, this is what happened . . . .

The 911 Phone Call and the White Bronco Crawl

O n October 25, 1993, Nicole Brown Simpson made a 911 emergency telephone call to the police.

Never-Released 911 Transcripts

This was the section Norman Pardo's audio technicians transcribed that directly pertained to the murders. The media promoted O. J. Simpson's voice was inaudible.

> **Dispatcher:** Um-hum, OK.
>
> **Nicole:** He wanted somebody's phone number and I gave him my phone book or I put my phone book down to write down the phone number that he wanted and he took my phone book with all my stuff in it.
>
> **Nicole:** What?
>
> **Dispatcher:** What is he saying?
>
> **Nicole:** What else. (Sound of police radio traffic)
>
> **O. J.:** For a flipping $100.00 they're going to hurt you like a God damn Kennedy. I ain't doing that. I asked you tonight. I want your phone book, all the dealers you know, everything about brothels.
>
> **Nicole:** O. J. O. J.!! The kids are sleeping. (More yelling)

O. J.: You didn't give a shit about the kids when you were sucking dick in the living room while they were here, and you didn't care about the kids then. Oh, it's different now. I'm talking. You're doing fine, now you go, shake your head, you're doing fine, Nicole. Now think about that!! (Sarcastically) It's all ok, Nicole, just keep thinking that.

Dispatcher: Is he upset with something you did?

Nicole: (Sobs) A long time ago. It always comes back.

That is the never-published part of the 911 call that is key to getting down to the truth. But the media's goal is not to tell the truth but to make money and nothing made more money in the 1990s than the story of a famous athlete, O. J. Simpson, a black man, who went into a jealous rage and murdered his young, beautiful, white ex-wife in a horrific fashion, while their children were asleep in their beds.

Add to the drama that the out-of-his-mind black athlete did not stop there. He also slit the throat of the handsome, white, Jewish young waiter who was doing a good deed, bringing Nicole the eyeglasses her mother had left at the restaurant where Nicole had eaten her last dinner with her children.

The media's profit reward would be realized in a multi-million dollar feeding frenzy if O. J. could be framed as the murderer and Nicole as the victim. After all, aren't women entitled as mature adults to fulfill their sexual needs equally with men? So, what if Ron Goldman were a lover?

In the aftermath of Nicole's murder, the old 911 tape was one of the first pieces of "evidence" the media dug up. With O. J. framed as the enraged jealous lover, no one had ever constructed a better tale since Shakespeare wrote *Othello*.

But what was the truth? That was the question that interested me.

Why Was O. J. Upset? What's the Truth?

I decided to work with O. J. not for the money—truthfully, I never took a penny from O. J.—but because I was on a quest to find out what really happened and solve the "who-done-it" mystery with the truth.

With this never-before-published transcript of the 911 transcript published here, the true transcript, we can see what the media hid.

This true transcript makes clear that O. J. Simpson wanted Nicole to hand over to him her address book, complete with the telephone numbers of the people she knew and was dealing with. His concern was that Nicole was involved in drugs—dealing drugs, most likely, but certainly buying drugs and using them combined with open, possibly adventurous or even wild sex with her "friends."

In the transcript, O. J. says enough to make it clear he was also concerned that Nicole was also having frequent sex, with multiple partners, casual sex he did not want his young children hearing or maybe even seeing as it happened. O. J. was especially concerned drugs being used were criminally illegal.

This was clearly not the type of home atmosphere that O. J. felt was appropriate for young children Nicole assumed were asleep or otherwise oblivious to what was happening.

The bottom line was that O. J. had reached the point of exasperation and he was indignant at Nicole's lack of responsibility as a parent. He felt out of control. He wanted to get ahold of Nicole's address book so he could put an end to what rightly could be judged as Nicole's irresponsible, reckless, and most likely illegal activities.

He had concluded correctly that Nicole was openly combining sex and drugs with her "friends" in her Brentwood living room while his young children were upstairs in their beds asleep. It appears he was concerned that his children needed a healthy home environment so they could grow up into mature and responsible adults themselves.

And, as we shall see, O. J. had also been paying Nicole's drug debts with sums that demanded tens of thousands of dollars.

Here's O. J.'s Take on the 911 Tape

"Everybody who listened to that 911 tape dogged me when they heard me yelling on that tape," O. J. explained to me. "What am I saying on that tape? I got criticized because I told Nicole I don't want this. I wasn't living with Nicole. She wasn't my wife. But I was telling her

I don't want my kids in this house with these drug people and these hookers hanging around my kids."

That was the point: O. J. was concerned about the welfare of his children given his wife's indulgence in illegal drugs and her involvement with prostitutes.

"But I became the bad guy yelling on that tape," O. J. continued. "But what am I yelling about? Nobody argued in any of these cases that I was arguing about hookers and drug pushers. I know they were hookers because three of them that I'm speaking about in that tape were specifically named in that book, *You'll Never Make Love in This Town Again*[1] published about a year and a half after this incident, proving I was right. They were call girls."

O. J. got angry when one of the girls working with him told him about what was going on at Nicole's house while they were on the set of the *Naked Gun* movies that he was filming in 1993. O. J. played the character of Officer Nordberg in the *Naked Gun* movies. O. J. left the set to go to Nicole's home to solve the problem. He wanted to get her address book so he could identify the drug people. O. J. had enough and he wanted the names and phone numbers so he could get rid of the drug people and the prostitutes himself.

"America made me the 'dog of all dogs,' the poster boy for abuse, because I'm pissed off that drug people and hookers are hanging around the house that my kids are in," he stressed. "I don't get it. You explain that to me."

The White Bronco Chase

The night of June 17, 1994 was a big sports night in America. That evening, the Eastern Conference champions New York Knicks were scheduled to play the Western Conference champions Houston Rockets in Game 5 of the NBA Finals. The Knicks were up 3 games to 2 games and the crowd at Madison Square Garden in New York City was looking forward to taking the lead in the series. The match-up featured two of basketball's most celebrated centers of

---

1   Terrie Maxine Frankel, Joanne Parrent, and Jennie Louise Frankel, *You'll Never Make Love in This Town Again* (Newstar Pr, 1996).

all time—Hakeem Olajuwon for the Rockets and Patrick Ewing for the Knicks. These two players had a history. In 1984, Olajuwon was with the University of Houston when Ewing was with Georgetown University. In the NCAA Championship game, Georgetown beat Houston 84-75.

Then, at 6:45 p.m. Pacific Time, 9:45 p.m. Eastern Time, television around the nation was interrupted as a white Ford Bronco believed to be carrying O. J. Simpson led a squad of police cars, blocking all lanes as they followed in a chase along the famed multi-lane interstate highway system in Los Angeles.

With the Bronco driven by O. J.'s best friend and former teammate Al Cowlings, O. J. rode in the back seat as the nation watched that white Bronco drive out front of the police cars in a sixty-mile, two-hour, low-speed pursuit through Southern California. Al "A.C." Cowlings was one of O. J.'s oldest friends. They grew up together in the projects, in Potrero Hill, a poor neighborhood outside of San Francisco, both members of a local gang known as the Persian Warriors.

News helicopters with live cameras hovered overhead to broadcast the dramatic chase mile by mile. Drivers on the other side of the interstate stopped their cars in the lane closest to the other side to get out of their vehicles and watch as the Bronco carrying O. J. was followed by the squadron of police cars. Crowds formed on overpasses to cheer O. J. on with shouts and signs. All broadcast channels across the nation and CNN covered the O. J. white Bronco chase live.

On one side of the big screen in Madison Square Garden, the basketball fans Knicks battle the Rockets, while on the other side of the split screen they watched the white Bronco crawl slowly down the LA freeway heading south, with the police following closely in pursuit.

So, the 911 call, as published by the media, was spun to establish in the public mind that O. J. murdered Nicole in a fit of jealous rage. The media seized the opportunity to broadcast nationally on live television the Bronco "chase" as obvious evidence of O. J.'s attempt to run away. Why else would O. J. attempt to escape if he weren't the murderer?

But like everything else in the O. J. Simpson drama it was a lie—a media "narrative" shown on live television to captivate an audience addicted to a story that reeked of race, sex, and drugs.

That's why it took me twenty years to get to the truth. Was I the only guy in America who wondered why that phalanx of LAPD squad cars trailing O. J. in a slow-speed freeway crawl couldn't have figured out a way to get the Bronco to stop, especially if the police were really concerned O. J. might escape?

Was I the only guy to wonder why O. J.'s dramatic run to Mexico ended up with Al Cowlings driving O. J. to the driveway of his L.A. home, where the LAPD were waiting to arrest him?

But as the O. J. murder drama kicked off, the media story line that O. J. had killed his former wife and her supposed lover in a jealous rage, viciously cutting both their throats and leaving them to bleed out in front of her stylish L.A. home, was now topped off by what the media portrayed as obvious evidence of guilt.

Why would O. J. seek to steal away riding in the back seat of his white Bronco, concealed by the vehicle's tinted side windows, unless he was guilty of having committed this horrific double homicide?

Headlines announcing the double murder of Nicole Brown Simpson and Ron Goldman on Sunday, June 12, 1994, grabbed international attention. Then, five days later, on Friday, June 17, 1994, following one of the most watched and most dramatic television events in history, with the Bronco "escape," the mainstream media now began licking their chops at the prospect of televising what was certain to be the trial of the century.

That's why I agreed to be O. J.'s manager. I was on a quest to find out who O. J. was and what really happened that tragic night in the trendy Brentwood section of Los Angeles.

I'm now giving you the clues that I found after some twenty years of this quest, and I am inviting you to solve the mystery with me.

Chapter 2

How I Started Working with O. J., Witness #1, and the L.A. Nightclub Drama

L et's get this straight.
I, Norman Pardo, came onto the scene a few years after the Brentwood murder happened. I met O. J. in 1999. Actually, it was because of a bet I had with my attorney. You see, I had just purchased a flight training school in Miami, Florida. We had helicopters and a couple of airplanes and flight training simulators. I found out later it was the same training school that trained the 911 terrorists.

So, we were sitting there, me and my attorney. I was just goofing with him, saying that I could market and promote anybody on this planet, I don't care who they are. And he laughed.

How I Met O. J. Simpson

Then, a week later, he wanted to meet me at the airplane hangar, and he brought O. J. over. He called me on my bet. And I said, "Wow, that's a big one, you've got me there, a pre-conceived murderer and all-around bad guy."

Truthfully, I was surprised to see O. J. in person. He could barely get out of the passenger seat of the Lincoln Navigator that drove him. He limped up to us with a smile on his face. He stuck his hand out to shake my hand as he got out of the car some six paces before he got to me. Really, O. J. looked all crippled up. It was kind of pathetic.

And I'm saying to myself, "Hey, you mean that's O. J. Simpson?" I don't know what I was expecting. Maybe that O. J. Simpson would be seven feet tall. O. J. swore about his bad knee from football days. I came right then to understand O. J. swore, a lot—almost as part of his regular speech.

But it didn't faze me. I'm not easily impressed one way or the other. I'm not going to say, "Oh, that's O. J. Simpson." Don't expect me to drop down to my knees and say O. J. is the master, like everybody else did.

So, after we met at the airplane hangar, we took O. J. for a ride in one of the helicopters. Then, to get away from the crowd that had assembled, O. J. and I decided it might just be better that we met alone, so we went to a restaurant, a sports bar called Tony Roma's. He and I drank—a lot. I mean, he would drink a drink, I would drink a drink, and I asked him, "Did you kill all those people?" That's what I really wanted to know. Was O. J. the murderer?

He looked at me and said, "Norman, what do you really want from me?" He thought I was up to something. But the more we drank, the worse it got.

Finally, he said to me, "I didn't kill those people, but you don't want to know what happened. Let it go."

We drank so much, all I could remember was that we walked out of the sports bar, he peed on the tire of my car in the parking lot, and somehow, we got home.

A Win-Win Proposition

So, while I met O. J. in 1999, it was two years later, in 2001, that I decided I would work with him. What I did in those two years was to begin researching the Nicole Simpson and Ron Goldman murders. That's when I began the research that I have continued for the last twenty years. That's when I began to realize working with O. J. might be a win-win proposition.

Somehow, I found I liked O. J. He told me he was ostracized as a kid. I understood that. I was ostracized as a kid too, but that's a long story that maybe I will tell a bit later. O. J. explained he was getting bored with golfing and watching golf all the time.

In 2001, O. J. was ostracized after the murder trial because most people just figured O. J. was the murderer. But O. J. was still a celebrity, and I came up with the idea of booking O. J. at Hip Hop events where he could be the emcee and people would want to meet him in part because he had this reputation as a bad guy—the famous acquitted murderer—that was his rap in the popular culture, then and now.

The "Birthday Bash"

So, let's talk about "Our Tour"—that's what O. J. and I called it.

In 2001, when I started doing my magic, I made a few phone calls to some friends of mine and we put on a "Birthday Bash" with a radio station. It was incredible—seven thousand people chanting out O. J.'s name, holding up cigarette lighters. "Juice, Juice, Juice, Juice." The chanting wouldn't stop, the crowd was actually still chanting "Juice, Juice" when Wyclef Jean went on the stage, so O. J. had to go back on and he did a duet with Wyclef and worked him in. Remember Wyclef wasn't a huge star at that time. The people loved O. J. and he loved them back. The media said it couldn't be done. O. J. said it couldn't be done. But I did it and it was great—better than even I expected.

The event was at the TECO arena in Estero, Florida, just south of Fort Myers on the Gulf coast, on August 24, 2001. It was a hip-hop concert headlined by the Haitian rapper Wyclef Jean and others like Foxy Brown. The Clear Channel radio station sponsored the event and we featured it as "The First Damn Birthday Jam." It was a great success.

The planning of that event was amazing. So, after I met O. J., I watched him for two years. O. J. at that time was living south of Miami and I would see O. J. around South Beach, on the beaches, in the restaurants and clubs. I watched the people around O. J. and his reaction to them. I noticed that if anything came out in advance, the media would have time to stir something up and make it a negative event.

In 2001, when I decided to do this, I told a good friend of mine, Big Mama, who had a very popular show on Clear Channel Radio, that O. J. would host the event, but the radio station could not announce that O. J. would be the emcee until the day of the event.

That wouldn't allow the media any time to put up a defense, to attack
O. J., or to demonize his appearance. He probably should have mentioned it to his higher ups—once they found out they were the first
company to bring O. J. back out, all hell broke loose. Clear Channels
stock took a dive when the media blamed Clear Channel Radio, and
DJ Big Mama paid dearly for helping me.

For two weeks in advance, the radio station promoted the event
by saying, "We've got a host coming. You're not going to believe who
is going to be the host. This is the biggest thing ever. This is going
to be the greatest thing on the planet. The guy hosting this thing is
unbelievable." The radio station did this every day, all the way up to
the event, and they were selling tickets like mad.

And then the morning of the event, the radio station announced,
"Here it is—the emcee is going to be O. J. Simpson." The ticket sales
went through the roof. The media came out, but they couldn't do
anything. The media interviewed a few people, but when the people
and groups like "NOW" said they didn't care, what was the media
going to do?

So, when I made that happen, it was the first time I saw O. J. break
down. O. J. got up on that stage and he felt the emotion of the audience. It was the first time I ever saw him tear up. He began crying.
And when he came off stage, he said, "Norm, I would never expect
in a million years for you to pull that off, especially after all the past
few years being called a pariah and murderer. You had seven thousand people in that arena, lighting it up with their cigarette lighters,
chanting my name. So, whatever you want, you've got it." That was
the moment that we began working together.

"All in the Planning"

My formula was all in the planning. It was like a chess game where
every piece has to be moved properly. If I moved a piece out of line,
they would get me. So, what I would do is I would move my pieces
just right.

Even at the TECO arena. When they announced that O. J. was
going to host that event, the owner of the TECO arena came out and
said, "O. J. is not getting out on my stage and doing anything."

I had to have one of my attorneys go back in the back with him where they had a little conversation. After that, the owner came out and said, "Okay, O. J. can get up there and host the event because basically O. J. Simpson has a contract and if O. J. Simpson does not get up there and host the event, I would have to refund all this money to all these people because I can't tell who came here because of O. J. Simpson or because of Wyclef Jean."

That first event was a big success and afterwards, we planned to go to an after-party. We were going down Interstate 75—I remember it like yesterday—and O. J. said, "Pull over. Pull over right here." We pulled over on the side of the Interstate because we had three cars with us. O. J. got out of the car and he got in this other car, and he said, "I'm going home. I'm not going to mess this night up. If we go to an after-party, something bad could happen, and I don't want to do that."

When he was back in prison, after that incident with the sports memorabilia dealer in Las Vegas, I'm sure O. J. looked back on that event. O. J. just had to think, "When I was out. I was a king."

In that event, I learned what it took to promote O. J. Simpson. We went from that event to probably thirty-five different cities across America, different events, and that's how we made this thing happen. Every city was a little bit different.

The "Godfather"

O. J. began working under the umbrella of my company, Spiderboy International. I would promote him, he would show up, host an event, and get paid. O. J. signed a contract with my company, Spiderboy International. Basically, he worked for me. That's why he and everyone around us called me his manager as he worked for me.

We went into Cincinnati in the Over-the-Rhine district where the riots were going on over the shooting by police of an unarmed black teenager. At that time, before his own legal problems, Bill Cosby joked, "I can't believe O. J. Simpson is going into the riots to promote peace." O. J. got into an argument with Cosby over that. O. J. couldn't understand why he wouldn't go into the riot for his people, to give the community entertainment. He just didn't understand that, even if there was a curfew. He wanted to see the family of the teenager who was shot by the police officers.

Spending countless hours traveling with O. J. to all these different cities, I filmed over seventy hours of video of O. J. Simpson and his interactions with others. I was always the guy in the back seat with the video camera. But it was never about the film. The filming was about keeping O. J. distracted. If you think I was there to film a documentary about O. J. Simpson, you're wrong.

When you deal with O. J. Simpson, you're dealing with a very special person who is really like a child who doesn't understand reality. When you see him with me and you watch the footage, you will see that he always gets out of the car asking, "Where are we going? What is this about? What are we doing?" Because I never told him. I would put him on a plane going to Connecticut and not tell him why. "We've got a gig," I would say. "That's all you have to know." Because if he knew, he would screw it up.

I learned from each event. We announced a week in advance we were coming to Hartford, Connecticut. That gave the ex-mayor time to come out and say, "O. J. Simpson is not going to appear on stage in this city." The ex-mayor would find some excuse. It was a big fight. The ex-mayor actually took away the permits for the event, claiming the bathrooms in the facility were too small to handle the crowd O. J. would draw. Whatever. Any excuse would do.

So, every event, the morning of the event, we could promote it. I developed a formula. We had to make sure that by the event that night we had certain things done—a radio show in the morning, a radio interview in the afternoon, a radio show in the evening, one television event of our choosing, a newspaper, and a magazine. The most important aspect was a good street team to go out and spread the word. As soon as we got that done, people knew we were there.

There was this one time we were in Philadelphia. I put O. J. in a Rolls Royce convertible, and we put him on South Street. I said, "We're just going to drive right down South Street. People will know you're here, and we're just going to see what happens." When we got in the convertible, we put the top down. O. J. sat there and told me he felt like Jack Kennedy, riding through downtown in an open limousine. "You know we're not going to make it through town like this." He laughed at me and shook his head.

Like always, O. J. sat in the front in the passenger's seat, and I sat on the driver's side in the back. It started out with two or three people coming up, wanting autographs. And when we got down South Street, there was a row of people for what looked like miles who were mobbing the car.

We got down to a real slow pace and the police started gathering around us; we had some ten or fifteen police officers around the car who were trying to keep people off the car. The police thought we were out of our minds for being in a convertible and they thought someone would kill O. J. on their streets . . . later that night we returned, and the police blocked us and made us put up the top, but the mob found us anyway and that got a little scary as we were unable to see out of the car, and they were all over it. The people weren't mad. They weren't saying, "Oh, O. J. is a murderer." We had one person who yelled, "Murderer," and that was it. Everybody else was just trying to get to O. J., to see if they could get an autograph. They wanted to touch O. J., they wanted to touch the "Godfather." O. J. became the guy that I was creating.

O. J.'s kids say that because I made him the bad guy, that's why he went to prison after the Las Vegas incident. The kids think that if I had left O. J. on the golf course, he still would have been golfing with his sports buddies and none of this would have happened

I started understanding that this was who O. J. had become. He was the "bad guy." The media had made him into the "bad guy," and they sold tons of newspapers making him the "bad guy." So, I figured I had to keep O. J. being the bad guy. And I did. I made O. J. so bad that he began thinking in his own mind that he was the bad guy. I don't believe that, but there's a lot more to the story before we get around to deciding whether or not O. J. is the bad guy, and I assure you, coming to a conclusion won't be easy—not easy for you, and not easy for me.

Bottom line was—and I hate to say this—but by the time I decided to work with O. J., I had just created a publicly traded company, Spiderboy International, that eventually grew into a $100 million corporation, and at that time, in 1999, I was buying and selling companies. I didn't need money and I didn't expect to get paid for what I did with O. J. Simpson. I didn't do it for the money. The only thing I didn't have was this—basically, a quest, to find out who killed Nicole.

So, let's get back to the murder mystery. Let me tell you about this informant, "Witness #1," who you are about to meet. We were at the AFM film festival in Santa Monica. This occurred after we began making our documentary film, "Who Killed Nicole?" We had a booth for the film and a woman came up to us and said she had a story to tell about Nicole that she had been afraid to tell for twenty years.

My film producer and I went to the bar with her, and we began taping her, in the dark, so her face could not be identified. I'm going to tell you right now what she said, in her own words. Her story was incredible. She was basically an informant and we agreed to keep her identity secret. Let's call her "Witness #1." In real life, she was black and clearly when she was younger had been beautiful. She told us that at the time she knew Nicole, she was working as a "super model."

Just so you understand, U.S. law provides the following definition: "A confidential informant is a person who provides information about criminal activity to law enforcement officers. The identities of these individuals are privileged in order to protect these individuals against retribution from those involved in crime." That definition comes from the Federal Circuit Court in the Sixth Circuit, Ohio, in 2009.[2]

A confidential informant is someone who provides information in exchange for remaining anonymous. The spectrum of why someone becomes an informant can be all over the place. Not all informants are bad people. Sometimes, people just have information, and they feel they need to provide it in the effort to help make a case, but they don't want their identity out there, or they don't want their safety endangered, or they're afraid. Sometimes for the players involved in big cases in which there is criminal enterprise, coming forward can be dangerous.

---

2   *United States v. Warman*, 578 F.3d 320 (6th Cir. Ohio 2009).

Here's Witness #1. Pay careful attention to what she has to say . . .

The Informant—Witness #1

Here is what the informant told us. This turned out to be a very important witness, as you will soon see. There are a lot of clues in what our anonymous Witness #1 told us.

We are going to give you her exact words, transcribed from the interview. As we said earlier, we are leaving it up to you to decipher the evidence, follow the clues, and solve the Nicole Brown Simpson and Ron Goldman murders without us biasing the evidence one way or the other.

This is not a book aimed at demonizing O. J. Simpson or arguing that he is innocent. This is a book aimed at allowing you, the reader, to sort through the evidence, decipher the clues, and uncover the truth."

Witness #1—How She Met O. J.

"What I'm about ready to say is the whole truth, as I know it, under penalty of perjury, and it's factual.

"I met Nicole, O. J., and Faye Resnick at the Harley Davidson Café in New York City. This was in December 1993, approximately six months before Nicole's death. It was the 'who's who' of all parties in New York. Pretty much, you had to be there. Donald Trump was there. The person who introduced me to O. J. was the heavyweight champion boxer, the famous 'Smoking Joe' Frazier."

Note: Faye Resnick is the television personality and author who socialized with Nicole. In June 1994, Resnick was visiting Nicole at her Brentwood home. Nicole and a group of friends intervened with Resnick into what had become a serious cocaine problem. Nicole and her friends convinced Resnick to go into drug treatment for cocaine abuse at the Exodus Recovery Center in Marina Del Rey, California. Resnick's 1994 book entitled *Nicole Brown Simpson: The Private Diary of a Life Interrupted* affected the O. J. murder trial by revealing shocking details of O. J. and Nicole's troubled relationship.

"At the same point in time, the singer Prince was doing the 'Most Beautiful Girl in the World' video. So, I flew out to California to be with my family, and it turned out my roommate flew out to be in Prince's music video. Everything was happening. Everything was smooth."

Witness #1, Dodi Fayed, and the Trip to London

"Then, a week before Nicole's death, we ended up going to a club called 'The Gate' on La Cienega Blvd. in Los Angeles. The Gate was a famous nightclub at that time. I was with my roommate, Julie. We went in and immediately went to the VIP section. You had to do a walk up to the VIP section. It was a very dark part of the club.

"Nicole sent a bottle of champagne to us. We were the 'It' girls of modeling. Then she came over and introduced herself saying, 'I'm Nicole, the ex-wife of O. J. Simpson.' I looked at my roommate and Nicole sat next to me—I had a blonde on this side, and a blonde on the other side, and I was the translator. I had told my roommate that I had met Nicole and O. J. in New York.

"It turned out that Nicole was there with Dodi Fayed and Dodi invited my roommate and me to go to London."

> Note: Dodi Fayed was the Egyptian eldest son of the Egyptian billionaire Mohamed Al Fayed, the former owner of the Harrods department store in London. Dodi was allegedly romantically involved with Princess Diana. On August 31, 1997, Princess Diana and Dodi were killed in a tragic car accident in the Pont de l'Alma underpass in Paris.

"Dodi told us the trip to London would be *carte blanche*—it wouldn't cost us anything. He said, 'Anything you want. You can go to Beverly Hills and pick it up, *carte blanche*.' He was being very discreet, and he meant it. He looked at us and Nicole said, 'Oh my God, you should go to London. It's a good opportunity.' But I wasn't sure. I told Dodi we would love to go but they had to check their schedules. Dodi said he had model agencies in London, and my roommate and I would both be able to work.

"But what got me was the words *carte blanche*. I had to put two and two together. I became the black Marilyn Monroe at that moment. Nicole was so sweet. She started interpreting for me. She said, 'You can go to any store. You can do anything you want. He's really an important person.'

"What really freaked me out is that we were supposed to leave for London on the day Nicole was killed. It was the same day. The night she was killed was the night we were all supposed to meet to go to London. That was the scariest part for me of the whole thing. It wasn't scheduled for the day afterwards, but that very night. That night was the night we were supposed to meet.

"But something happened that prohibited or caused a lot of problems for us, a lot of perplexities with the situation. One was the gentleman with Dodi sitting to his left, kind of faded in and faded out. But he was watching, he was observing everything.

Note: The man Witness #1 identified with Dodi turned out to be Glen Rogers, but more about him later. As a hint for what's coming, Glen Rogers has a history as a serial killer. He is in prison today, on death row, awaiting execution.

"He would have been the closest one to hear what Nicole was saying because he was sitting between Dodi and Nicole as she was talking. I remember that he had sandy blonde hair and that he seemed to watch intensely, but he didn't say very much."

What Did Drugs Have to Do with the London Trip?

"It was Nicole who was speaking about drugs. He just acknowledged the conversation. Nicole was very credible to me. I cannot say about her other involvements, but I can say that she told us she was going to go to Washington to pick up drugs. That was another thing. I didn't do drugs.

"Julie and I were getting ready to say our saving graces and excuse ourselves from the table. One of the reasons we were excusing ourselves was that we're good girls and we did not want to get into a compromising position.

"But there were two gentlemen standing over there with Dodi and they were scowling at us after we had been dancing. We didn't know how big Dodi Fayed was. We had no idea except that he was Nicole's friend.

"But we all of a sudden got the idea of exactly what was happening and exactly who Dodi was by the way they were treating us, like 'How dare you leave the table? How dare you go with another man?' But we didn't go with another man. We just went down to the dance floor and we were dancing.

"But at the same point of time this is what really happened. We got intimidated. At first, it wasn't scary, it was just intimidation. It was uncomfortable, right up to the point we began to feel our lives were in danger."

Dodi's Henchmen Manhandle Witness #1 and Her Roommate

"We wanted to leave on good terms, so we said, 'You know, we're getting ready to go. We have an early call tomorrow.' If one of us says we have an early call that was the password Julie and I had to leave, like signaling it was time for a get-out-of-jail-free card.

"We were beginning to feel uncomfortable, afraid, but we wanted to be gracious and we wanted to be professional. So, I said, 'Excuse us, but we have an early call tomorrow. It was a pleasure being with you. You've been so nice, and we will speak to you later.'

"I gave Nicole a hug and we got up to say goodbye to Dodi, who was acting as our host there. We also said goodbye to the sandy blonde guy sitting on his left.

"As we stood up to leave, the two guys, Dodi's henchmen, grabbed us. I was about 120 pounds, a total model, and Julie was five feet, seven-and-a-half inches tall, about 105 pounds at most—all curves, all model. They grabbed us hard, not a social 'just touch.' These guys were physically manhandling us and we were in plain view inside of this fancy L.A. nightclub."

"I'm not going to say there was a zillion people around, but it was a full nightclub. In the VIP section, less than about five or ten feet away, there were like five or ten people. When they grabbed us, it was the scariest thing in my life. It was like you swallow your throat. I looked at Julie and we were both in a situation—both of us were being taken hostage.

"Right there and then, we were being detained, forcibly. The only thing I could think of, because I knew Julie wasn't going to talk—you could just see it in her face that her whole voice was gone.

"The only thing I could do was ask myself who looked like they were in charge here. I didn't know Dodi Fayed, but I looked at him and he was the man who was predominately talking, who was really the schmoozer who was very sweet.

"So, I looked at him and I looked at the other guy, the sandy blonde guy, and he didn't say a word. It seemed clear to me. Dodi was the man. Dodi was in charge here.

"At the same time, these henchmen guys have us and they are not letting us go. I started talking to Dodi and I looked right into his eyes. I said, 'You know, you have a lot of money. I don't know exactly who you are, but we have to work.'

"I was going here by instinct, by what Nicole told me—that Dodi Fayed was a very rich man, a very powerful man.

"So, I used what Nicole told me and I said to Dodi, 'You already have your money. But we're just two simple working models. And we have to get up early the next day for a call. We have to work. This is how we work. We do fashion shoots; we do fashion shows. This is what we do.'

"Then I looked him even harder in his eyes, and I said, "Besides, we are going to see you again on the London trip. We're going to London.' I said this like the decision to go had been made and agreed to by everyone at the table.

"Right then, Nicole freaked out. She started jumping up and down, screaming, 'Oh, my God! Oh, my God!' It was too much for her and it was too much for us. 'Oh, my God! Oh, my God!' I was try-ing to figure out what was going on and the only thing I could figure is that it was like we had disrespected Dodi because we had danced with these other guys.

"Right at that moment Nicole Brown Simpson saved our lives. Nicole got the point and started saying very positively, 'That's right. We're all going to London.'"

This Was the Last Time Witness #1 Saw Nicole Alive

"Okay. That was the last time I saw Nicole Brown Simpson. It was that night, when she saved my life. The next time I saw Nicole Brown Simpson was on television. And then the story would be about the horrific fact of her murder, the fact that brought everybody's life to light in this tale.

"The problem with the truth is that I don't think the public really wants to know the truth. But what I'm telling you here today is the truth.

"There has been so much exploitation on this side. Why didn't we come forward earlier?

"O. J. Simpson was a mega-star. If he murdered his wife—a known mega-woman—what would they do to us? I've been on magazines, but you haven't seen my face, not really—it's not like I'm a well-known person. So, what would they do to us?

"And if this person, Dodi, put fear into Nicole, what would he have done to us? He didn't care that there was a whole nightclub full of people. That was the scary part for us.

"It's been a nightmare since the time of the escapade, Sunday, June 12, 1994, the night Nicole died. Hopefully, by me telling you now, I will be able to get this out all these years later, so that finally it stops haunting me. I don't care whether the public believes me or not. I don't care. What I care about is telling the truth."

Nicole Murdered the Night Scheduled for the London Trip

"So, Nicole was still talking to us about the London trip a few days before we were supposed to meet, wondering if it was worth going. Julie and I didn't think it was worth going. Finally, we all decided we wouldn't go to London, not with Dodi.

"So, the night we were supposed to meet to go to London, the night Nicole was murdered, we did not meet.

"The next day, when I found out Nicole had been murdered, that was one of the scariest days of my life. At that time, I was taking care of my handicapped father and I was modeling. I didn't know what to do after Nicole died. It kept coming into my mind that it was the day after the night we were supposed to meet to go to London. I keep wondering if that timing was coincidental, so does this have any correlation?

"When I heard about Nicole's death, I called Julie on the phone and I started sobbing, I was becoming frantic, both from shock and from fear . . .

> **Note: At this moment, relating the story, our Witness #1 began crying. Relating these memories to us clearly brought back the hysteria she felt that Monday, after learning that Nicole had been horribly murdered with her throat cut, the evening before, on Sunday, June 12.**

"I asked Julie, 'Did you see the news?' But I was afraid to talk on the phone. I went over to her place, where she was staying, the model's apartment on Fairfax.

"When I got there Julie—she's German—she was as white as a sheet.

"I said, 'We've got a problem.' This was a big problem, not the average person's problem. Certain people in life, things don't happen. Me, I stand on the street corner and everything comes by. This was the everything that came by."

Witness #1 Decides to Forget All About the Nightclub Drama

"And I looked at Julia and I said, 'Are we going to have to go to the police? We have to tell somebody." But Julia was in that model's apartment by herself, and she had nobody, I mean, not one person. At least, I had my father.

"Then all of a sudden, I put it behind me. I thought that maybe there's no way in heck they would accuse O. J. of this situation, especially with what I knew. I didn't think that they would. God is my witness.

"Plus, in New York, when I met O. J. through Joe Frazier, what most people know—what all of the world knows except for the public—the public has a different accountability that they only believe what they want to believe—O. J. is very narcissistic. O. J. loves O. J.—O. J. loved O. J. more than anyone. Most of Hollywood knows that. Most of Beverly Hills knows that. O. J. was not a killer.

"But even knowing that, I had a bigger problem. I never thought they would take someone who was innocent and color them evil. But if they killed Nicole, who was the high-profile wife of a big entertainer, what would they do to me? If they killed Nicole, what would they do to my friend?

"This was the quandary of what I was feeling, so I acted just like I just knew nothing, not about the nightclub, not about Dodi, not about his henchmen, not about London, nothing about Nicole and bringing back drugs."

The Prostitutes Enter the Story

"Hollywood is so small, and I met this lady, and her godmother was Norma, the woman known as the Beverly Hills Madam. So the day the police found Nicole Simpson's body, I went over there, and I was helping her water her plants. We were discussing her dietician because she has diabetes, and my father was diabetic.

"Norma looked like the average older woman. She didn't look like some super-lady. She was living right next door to Dolly Parton, and on the other side lived Diana Ross.

"So, I was dealing with Norma and all of a sudden, in comes the girlfriend of O. J. Simpson's son. That was also the night I spoke with Julie. I didn't speak with Julie until later on that night. I left Norma's house and went over to Julie's apartment to speak with her. I left Norma's after I heard what the girls in Norma's house were saying.

"This one girl she was just with O. J. Simpson's son and they were talking about the whole thing. And still, at the same time, I didn't know what to say. I didn't know what to do. I didn't know what kind of a cavalcade of a situation I found myself in. I didn't know it was going to be the biggest murder of the year, or of the century, or any-thing like that. I just knew that I was in hot water.

"I remember they were talking about O. J.'s son. There were about four girls, beautiful ladies, and we were all watching the tele-vision. I had just taken Miss Norma's breakfast into her because she wouldn't eat right to save her life. That was another situation where I got caught up again in another aspect of his life, or his son's life."

Witness #1 Calls the Judge and Contacts the FBI

"When they started the O. J. Simpson trial, Julie and I didn't know what to do. So, I started thinking we should say something because I didn't believe they were going to do anything to O. J.

"So, I remember leaving a message on Judge Ito's Santa Monica office letting him know exactly what I knew. I told Judge Ito that I had been given the business card of the gentleman (Dodi Fayed) and that I could get that business card to the judge. I told the judge that I believed this gentleman was the one who actually killed Nicole Brown Simpson.

> Note: Judge Lance Ito presided over the 1995 O. J. Simpson murder trial in Los Angeles Superior Court.

"At the same time, I was talking with another friend of ours who's daughter worked with the FBI. This was down the road some because we were talking about the baseball cards and Las Vegas and stuff. This is a woman whose son also works for the CIA.

> Note: On September 13, 2007, O. J. Simpson and several accom-plices entered the Palace Station hotel room of sports memorabilia dealer Bruce Fromong in Las Vegas and allegedly stole memora-bilia at gunpoint that O. J. Simpson believed had been stolen from him. On October 3, 2008, thirteen years after he had been acquit-ted for the murders of Nicole Brown Simpson and Ron Gold-man, Simpson was found guilty of thirteen criminal charges. On

December 5, 2008, he was sentenced to thirty-three years in prison with eligibility for parole in nine years. On October 1, 2017, after spending nine years behind bars for armed robbery, O. J. Simpson, then seventy-one years old, was released from prison on parole.

"I told my friend that I had a problem that I never really talk about but knew O. J. didn't kill Nicole. My friend asked why I was sure. After I told her, my friend explained she didn't believe O. J. killed Nicole either. She said there were too many strings to the case, and she believed there was another party who was there at Nicole's Brentwood home the night of the killing. She believed that was the person who killed Nicole and Ron Goldman, and this information was coming from the FBI.

"I told her that she was absolutely right because we were at this party and this guy there and all this stuff happened. He had these henchmen with him, and we ended up with bruises all over our arms. It felt they were threatening us, and they were out for blood. That's why we didn't go to London. Yes, a free ride to London, but a free ride to where? It looked like we were going to get killed, or get hurt, or have our passports taken if we went there. Sometimes free isn't free."

O. J. and Nicole Were Friends First, Lovers Second

"I met O. J. through Joe Frazier. I know stories of Nicole and O. J. going to parties in New York. They were friends—eclectic lovers, but not lovers to where O. J. was overzealously attached to Nicole Brown Simpson. The way the newspapers ran this was that O. J. couldn't get over the situation of his color with the love of a lady he once knew. Nicole and O. J. were friends, but O. J. was narcissistic, the most narcissistic person I ever met, even after meeting Donald Trump.

"After Joe Frazier introduced me to O. J., he asked me what I thought of him. I said, "O. J. is O. J." A very important person, Robert DeNiro, told me that you can't control the media. So, I've been afraid of the media because I knew the media would tear me up because I don't believe it was O. J. who killed Nicole.

"On the conspiracy theory regarding the FBI, the lady told me there's more people involved in the case than I knew. And as I listened to her as she talked, and she started mentioning Dodi Fayed because I told her his name. But I pushed all this to the back of the shelf because I had done everything I could do. O. J. Simpson was acquitted, so I didn't have to remember about it or think about it anymore."

Dodi Fayed, Back in the Picture

"You would think that chapter was closed, but no. Next thing you know, I see the guy who was sitting at the table, a part of my nightmare, and that was Dodi Fayed. How I remembered him was because of his eyes and how he looked. I'm thinking about that guy every other night. When you have a dream about somebody you don't ever want to meet again, I mean those guys at that table, you're afraid. But the next thing I know, I see Dodi Fayed with Princess Diana.

"That lady spoke with her daughter and her son. Later she told me I was right. She said Dodi Fayed had a private plane. Then it connected, how Dodi Fayed got through customs. Then little pieces began fitting together. This lady told me about Dodi's father owning Harrod's department store. All of a sudden, I was becoming afraid because two and two equals four.

"I remember when me and my dad were watching the O. J. trial on television and they said the bloody gloves came from Harrod's department store. I remember then that when Dodi stopped his henchmen, he had on a pair of gloves. I remember because it was weird, he had on gloves.

"And I remember the other guy, the sandy blonde hair guy who didn't say much. He had on pointed shoes, I saw them when the henchmen grabbed us because I was looking down and I saw the shoes. It was a different pair of shoes because the average guy has shoes with rounded toes. So, I looked and thought maybe those shoes and I thought those were special, expensive shoes.

"Every bone in my body tells me those were the guys that killed Nicole because of the way they treated us that night.

"That's another thing. Dodi Fayed's hands were small. Don't ask me why women look at hands, but I remember his hands. I'm telling the truth. His hands were small, and he had on gloves."

"I Know O. J. Did Not Kill Nicole"

"But that lady told me that her daughter in the FBI and her son with the CIA both said there was much more to the story than I could ever imagine.

"But I knew O. J. and Nicole. O. J. would walk into a room and there was bravado. He was "The Juice." He was a sex appeal guy. He would flirt with anybody and everybody in the room, young and old. He did not have his full allegiance to Nicole. But they were friends—they were best friends.

"I saw Nicole flirting with other people. In the court case, they said O. J. got mad at Nicole flirting. I didn't see any of that. Nicole was a lively, vivacious woman. Nicole flirted with everybody and O. J. flirted with everybody. That was part of their persona. They got a kick out of being special people. They got a kick out of being the "IT" people. I never saw anything that would give me a hint that fortunately or unfortunately were exclusive to each other, or that he was the kind of person who would go crazy like the media stipulated.

"But I did see, and I do know who killed Nicole and it was not O. J. Simpson."

"I Feel Good . . . "

"I feel good to get this off my chest because I've felt guilt for a long time for not saying anything.

"But everyone and their mother who didn't even have any idea what happened, you know, to possibly Nicole at that time spoke. Everyone and their mother made money off an unfortunate situation speaking hypothetically, even though they knew nothing about what really happened.

"They had no idea exactly who Nicole was hanging out with, what Nicole was doing, or why she was there at that time. Nobody knew why Goldman was involved. Me and my friends are the closest ones to knowing exactly what happened, or at least to give clarity so people can draw their own conclusions.

"So now you know what I know. A week before Nicole's death, we ended up going to a club. So, you had Dodi Fayed sitting at a table. You had Nicole sitting at the same table. The person who invited us to London was Mr. Dodi Fayed. Ironically, what was so scary about the whole thing and Nicole Brown Simpson's death was that Fayed asked us to leave for London on the same day that she was dead. That day, the day Nicole was murdered, was the day Fayed was supposed to pick us up for the trip to London.

"When we got up to leave, Dodi's two henchmen grabbed us. We were both almost taken hostage."

CHAPTER 3

Enter the Kardashians

We are going to start off this chapter with a video transcript, one of the many videos I recorded of O. J. over the years. As his manager and promoter I had full access to him 24/7 during our adventures. Let me set the stage for this video. The video starts after we have just picked up O. J. at the airport and he is riding in the front seat of the car as we are driving to Philadelphia, where we have a gig that evening. I'm in the back seat, videotaping O. J. on the early morning ride.

The night before, I flew into New York to pick up the crew for the event. That day we drove from New York to Hartford, Connecticut, to pick up the promoter. It was a blizzard all the way from New York to Hartford. The next day, we drove from Hartford to Philadelphia, where we picked up O. J. at the airport.

With me in the back seat is Del, one of O. J.'s entourage. The driver is the club owner in Philadelphia. We are headed from the airport into the club in Philadelphia, to get ready for the event that evening.

Transcribed verbatim, including the fast-talking, jive bad language. You might as well get a sense of the real O. J. Simpson. In all those countless hours we spent on the road, O. J. could be outrageous—ridiculously funny, making no attempt to be politically correct, or even proper. He could flash his gang personality, his football locker room bravado, always mixed with his jabbing at you, in both good humor and bad moods.

That morning, O. J. was tired, feeling put out that he had to get up so early. It was cold outside and I'm sure the arthritis throughout his body was giving him pain.

This is exactly how that ride came down. O. J. typically was trying to figure out where we were and what we were going to do. He knew we had a gig in Philadelphia, but I hadn't given him any details about it. O. J.'s words are reproduced here just like they sound on the video, including slang, missing letters, and general slang-talk. That's generally how O. J. talked when he wasn't on stage or at a microphone being interviewed.

Remember: I videoed O. J. not because I wanted to make a fortune producing a movie. The videos were a technique I used to distract O. J. Simpson, to keep him off what I was doing. I was on a quest to solve the murder mystery. What you get in this video is a sample of the real, unfiltered O. J. Simpson.

(VIDEO STARTS)

O. J.: What crack head puts me on a 5 a.m. flight! Man! We got
to the airport . . . he says, 'Juice, too early for you.' and I said,
'you the man.'
[O. J. looks back at the camera.]
O. J.: Filmin' us sittin' in the car. Normally I'm a happy mothafucka
. . . other than . . . some motherfucka was on crack that booked
me on a 6:40 flight to Ft. Lauderdale! I was on the road at 4:45
this morning to get to Philadelphia at 8:30 . . . what time is it?
Driver: 9:30.
O. J.: At 9:30 . . . ., tryin' to do something at, tonight.
[O. J. doesn't say what time the event starts.]
O. J.: Norm: See, that was a good plan.
O. J.: Whoever that crackhead is, I'll have Del, I can't kick his ass
no mo, but I'll have Del kick his ass.

Del: (with a Jamaican accent) You got this boy walkin' . . . hittin' walls.

> **[O. J. points back to me and Del, smiling.]**

O. J.: That Del . . . that's Norm. Call Norm "Spiderman." . . . "Spiderboy!"

> **[O. J. and Norm laugh.]**

O. J.: Even though he's an OLD mother fucka he's claimin' he's Spiderboy.

Norm: I'm in disguise.

(VIDEO OFF)

Even when he was joking or in a playful mood, I still took seriously everything O. J. said. Most investigators will get on the trail of something, and they will put blinders on. And so, those investigators never really solve the case because they've got a theory on what happened.

I never had a theory on what happened. That wasn't something I was focusing on. The story just started falling in place. All I did was investigate and then I would let it go.

Let's Go Back to the Beginning, to 1973

Most people don't understand the O. J. murder mystery goes back to 1973. Most people think the story started in 1994, that O. J. got jealous and decided to kill those people. But every murder has a backstory. There's always a reason somebody is killed. In this particular story, we have to go back to 1973, back to the era of the bell bottoms and the mini-skirts, back to disco and the Bee Gees—that's where it all started.

Truthfully, Robert Kardashian's history with O. J. Simpson goes back to the 1960s, the era of the Beatles, JFK, the civil rights marches, and the anti-war protests. These two first came across one another in 1967, when Robert Kardashian was a "water boy" for the University of Southern California (USC) football team where O. J. was a star running back. They later met playing tennis at the home of a mutual friend.[3] So, their association, although not deep or a close friendship at that time, dates back to long before the Kardashians came into national prominence with their reality television show, *Keeping Up with the Kardashians*, that started in 2007, long after O. J. won the Heisman trophy and became a National Football League superstar running back with the Buffalo Bills.

But in the 1970s, O. J. and Robert Kardashian got together seriously. In my opinion, Robert Kardashian is the man who made O. J. who he is today. He gave O. J. everything O. J. started with. Robert Kardashian brought O. J. into a trade publication company that started R & R, *Radio and Records*. Robert Kardashian and a guy named Bob Wilson had an idea and O. J. threw $50,000 into the venture.

Fortunately for Robert Kardashian and for O. J., R & R became the standard publication for radio stations playing popular music. R & R made its mark with a TOP 20 chart listing the top artists and songs that were trending nationally on radio each week.

In 1979, *Radio and Records* magazine sold to marketing consultant Harte Hanks for millions, yielding a large fortune for Robert Kardashian and a hefty capital gain for O. J. Simpson.

Robert Kardashian's relationship with Kristen Mary Houghton, his future wife, also goes back to the 1970s. Kris was only seventeen years old when she met Kardashian at a horse-racing track. At that time, Kris was involved with pro-golfer Cesar Sanudo, who was ten years her senior. In 1975, Kris and Robert's romance broke up. Kris started working as a flight attendant for American Airlines, living in a two-bedroom in New York City in Harlem. This first relationship with Kris reportedly broke up when Robert suddenly decided she was too young for him, and he needed a more mature mate for a serious relationship.

After breaking up with Kris, Kardashian allegedly had an affair with Priscilla Presley, who had divorced rock legend Elvis Presley. When

---

3   Rachel Chang, "A History of O. J. Simpson's Relationship with the Kardashian Family," Biography.com, June 16, 2000, https://www.biography.com/news/oj-simpson -kardashians-relationship.

Priscilla Presley told Robert Kardashian that she would not remarry until Elvis died, he resumed his romance with Kris. Heartbroken when Robert Kardashian dropped her, Kris took Robert back and resumed the relationship. This time, she promptly moved in with him in his Beverly Hills mansion. Robert Kardashian and Kris were married two years later, on July 8, 1978. Robert bought a bigger, 7,000 square-foot mansion in Beverly Hills, where he and Kris began a family. They had four children: Kourtney, Kim, Khloé, and Robert Jr.

Robert Kardashian was born to Armenian-American parents in Los Angeles. He attended USC (as did O. J.) as an undergraduate, where he earned a degree in business administration in 1966. Following that, he attended the University of San Diego's law school where he graduated and began earning his living as a lawyer. He changed directions when he purchased Radio & Records, and he stopped practicing law when the trade publication was sold at a substantial profit in 1979. Following that, Robert pursued various business opportunities, including starting Movie Tunes, an in-theater music and advertising company.

His marriage to Kris lasted until 1991, but published reports indicate their relationship had been on troubled waters for some time. The Kardashians had their fourth and last child, Robert Jr., in 1987. But reports began circulating that "Kris had become bored" as a mother and started to act "rebellious." She lost weight, got a new hairstyle and look, and allegedly began seeking men outside her marriage. In 1989, Kris allegedly had an affair with Todd Waterman, a pro soccer player ten years younger than her.[4]

Most people don't realize that O. J. Simpson got a divorce just a few months after Robert Kardashian got a divorce and Robert Kardashian became estranged from all three of them—from O. J., from Nicole, and from his former wife, Kris. Clearly, whatever happened between the Kardashians and the Simpsons and between Robert and Kris

---

4   The history of Robert Kardashian's relationship with Kris Houghton is drawn largely from the following source: Jaimie Lee, "The real story of Robert Kardashian, his career and family life," SportsRetriever.com, February 20, 2019, https://sportsretriever .com/stories/the-real-story-of-robert-kardashian-his-career-and-family-life/.

was so upsetting to both relationships that both couples got divorces within a few months of one another.

It was a parting of the ways that had tragic consequences. For years, whenever he was in Hollywood, O. J. used to stay with the Kardashians. When O. J. and Nicole married, they along with their kids used to vacation together with Kris and Robert, along with their kids. Photographs show the happy families together on vacation, along with some friends. Until that incident, in 1990.

Now, let's explain what allegedly happened in the Jacuzzi that night in 1990.

The Incident

(VIDEO STARTS)

O. J. is sitting in the passenger's seat of a parked car. It is night. Norm Pardo is standing outside the car, videotaping O. J. through the car's open window.

Norm: I hear you are hung like a horse. Is there any truth to that, Mr. Simpson?

O. J.: Well, this lady came up to me this one time, and she said I don't do anybody unless there's at least 10 inches. So, I told her that I was sorry, but I was going to have to pass because I ain't cutting off two inches for nobody.

Norm: So, it's true then. You are hung like a horse!

O. J. laughs knowingly.

(VIDEO OFF)

From what O. J. told me, everything was great in his relationship with Robert Kardashian up until a little fling O. J. and Kris allegedly had. There was an incident that forever changed their relationship as "best friends."

Again, from what O. J. told me, the moment was when they were on vacation and late that night at the hotel O. J. and Kris found themselves alone in the Jacuzzi. Robert and Nicole were tired and went to their rooms, leaving O. J. and Kris together alone in the Jacuzzi. And then something happened.

O. J. said he stood up, pulled his shorts down, and O. J. said Kris reacted. "Her eyes bugged out of her head," is exactly what O. J. told me.

O. J. said from there he fucked that bitch until he "broke her."

At two or three o'clock in the morning, I can't remember what O. J. said was the exact time, he said they had to take Kris to the hospital. She came to his room and said, "Will you take me to the hospital?" And, O. J. said, "No, have Rob do it."

So, in my opinion, if I was Robert Kardashian and that happened to my wife, that would be the end of our friendship. After that incident, things went wrong and the Kardashians and the Simpsons both got divorces.

This is what O. J. told me: In 1990, O. J. said he cheated, having sex with Kris, and the friendship between the Simpsons and the Kardashians dissolved. In March 1991, Robert and Kris ended their marriage. One month later, in April 1991, Kris Kardashian married Olympic Games gold medal decathlete Bruce Jenner (now Caitlyn Jenner).

Like I said above, for almost two decades, from 1973 to 1990, a total of some seventeen years, O. J. and Robert Kardashian were "best friends," but after the Jacuzzi incident in 1990, with O. J. allegedly having sex with Kris, all that ended. Robert Kardashian and O. J. cut ties, and while O. J. remained friends with both Kris and Nicole, Robert Kardashian became estranged from both women. While Robert Kardashian got himself re-admitted to the bar so he could represent O. J. in the murder trial, I believe he did so to make sure the lawyer-client relationship would prevent him from being called to the stand to testify. I have reason to believe Robert Kardashian knew things about the murders of Nicole Brown Simpson and Ron Goldman that Robert Kardashian was desperate to keep from being made public.

That O. J., Nicole, and Kris had reconciled became obvious in the months before Nicole's murder. Even after their divorce, O. J. and Nicole stayed friends, despite blowups like the famous 911 telephone call we discussed in Chapter 1. O. J. vacationed with Nicole and their children around Easter 1994, only weeks before Nicole's death on June 12. A photograph from that vacation shows not only were O. J. and Nicole together with their kids on that vacation, O. J. and Nicole were also with Kris Kardashian and her four children (all fathered by Robert Kardashian). As you can see in the family picture from that vacation (Exhibit #1), the mature man standing next to Kris Jenner is too old to be Robert Kardashian. That is the point of the picture. Kris Kardashian and Bruce Jenner are there with their children, O. J. and Nicole are there with their children, there are other families, and I really don't know who they were. But the only one missing from that photo is Robert Kardashian.

Accompanying Kris on this vacation was Bruce Jenner. The vacation occurred after Kris and Bruce Jenner married, so Kris is now legally Mrs. Bruce Jenner, not Mrs. Robert Kardashian. The only one missing from that happy families' vacation was Robert Kardashian. Besides, while O. J. and Nicole socialized amicably after their divorce, Robert Kardashian evidently remained estranged from his wife until his death at fifty-nine years old, on September 30, 2003, from esophageal cancer. A set of those vacation photographs from the 1994 family vacation, published by *Star Magazine* in 1996, show family groups with children, Bruce Jenner going off to golf, everybody smiling.[5] Following his relationship with Kris, Robert Kardashian allegedly struggled in the last dozen years of his life to enjoy a successful long-term relationship with another woman.

O. J., Nicole, and the Hollywood Party Scene

(VIDEO STARTS)

---

5   Mats Meyer, "Kardashians Vacationed with O. J. Simpson & Nicole Weeks Before Violent Murder," *Star Magazine*, February 1, 2016, https://starmagazine.com/photos/oj -simpson-kardashian-vacation-pics/. The article appears to assume Robert Kardashian is standing next to his former wife Kris (seen in the bikini bathing suit), although the gentleman standing next to Kris Jenner in the photograph is not specifically identified by the magazine.

O. J. is in the front passenger seat of the car, with Norm Pardo in the back seat behind the driver, videotaping O. J. They are passing through yet another town on the way to yet another gig. O. J. is wearing a coat. It's winter and cold outside.

O. J.: So, we're talking. And I just say, look, Norm is gay. Teasing. You know how we tease. They wrote that shit in the paper. He's a redneck and he's gay.

Norm: They wrote, O. J. admits to Drugs, and his redneck manager is gay . . .

O. J.: I'm not really a drug guy. That ain't me, so don't give me that image.

O. J. pauses. Norm keeps the video going.

O. J.: In 1992, my friends gave me a surprise party. One of the girls brought ecstasy. So, everybody at the party took an ecstasy pill. Boy, what a party that was!

O. J. has just done a radio interview with Wendy Williams. She asked O. J. if he has ever done drugs. O. J. refused to answer the question on air. Williams concluded on air that if O. J. refused to answer that question, it meant he had taken drugs but didn't want to admit it. O. J. was reacting to the interview.

O. J.: Like she's saying, "You miss the drugs." Like me and everybody else ain't done something, once or twice. Other than that, I ain't done an illegal drug since last night.

(VIDEO OFF)

I came to learn after spending all that time with O. J. just how complex his life really was. Like this story, for instance. O. J. told me that Wendy Williams asked him if he was friends with Bruce Jenner, and all these people—if they were really still his best friends, or not? O. J. responded to Wendy Williams that he never was best friends with Bruce Jenner. Evidently Kris Jenner called Nicole and asked if O. J. would golf with Bruce because Bruce Jenner had no friends. O. J. told me that he golfed with Bruce Jenner once or twice, but that was it.

You have to understand, I have dozens of videotapes of O. J. in the clubs. There are women all over O. J., rubbing their bodies against him, and they are all stoned, with O. J. puffing on a blunt all night long. Nicole was the same. At parties, O. J. would flirt with the women and Nicole would flirt with the men. They allegedly were swingers. O. J. would be happy to take home one of the women, and Nicole one of the men, and they would have sex together, all four of them.

But that was the thing about O. J.—he really didn't care about women, not really. He would have sex with them and forget about them. That's why when Kris Kardashian came to ask him to take her to the hospital at 2:00 or 3:00 a.m. after the Jacuzzi incident, O. J. refused. O. J. told me that he had "f*cked Kris until he broke her." But afterwards it wasn't O. J.'s problem. He went to bed and fell asleep. When Kris showed up hysterical, needing to see a doctor, O. J. told her to let her husband take her to the hospital. That had to be humiliating to Robert Kardashian, having to explain to all the medical personnel in the emergency room how Kris got in that condition.

You have to remember that Witness #1 said that when she met O. J. in New York for the first time, it was just a few months before the murders and Nicole was there, in New York, with O. J., at the party where Donald Trump showed up. O. J. was there, Nicole was there, and Faye Resnick was there. Witness #1 described O. J. and Nicole as "best friends." That's what impressed Witness #1 about O. J. and Nicole. They were "best friends" even after they were divorced, and they still hung out together. Remember too, Witness #1 described how O. J. left Nicole and was flirting with the women, while Nicole did the same, flirting with the men. Witness #1 saw Nicole and O. J. hitting on other people together. Nobody in the press seemed to want to write about what she knew, that in the months before Nicole was murdered, O. J. and Nicole were getting back together. They were even at Donald Trump's wedding to Marla Maples and O. J. gave a toast. This was on December 20, 1993, a few months before the murders.

Robert Kardashian was left isolated and alone. Kris was remarried to Bruce Jenner and she had the kids living with her and Jenner.

O. J. had access to his kids, who lived with Nicole. And then when O. J. and Nicole vacationed with Kris, all their kids were with them. Robert Kardashian was the only one who was on the outside, looking in. I noticed too that Kris Jenner did not bear any resentment against O. J. over that sex incident in the Jacuzzi.

I think Kris Jenner always wanted to be like O. J. and Nicole. She wanted the famous person to be her husband. But she ended up with Robert Kardashian and he wasn't famous for anything. He was an ex-attorney. He wasn't even an attorney anymore. He was just a businessman. But everywhere Nicole went, everybody wanted O. J.'s autograph. I think that's why Kris dumped Robert Kardashian and married Bruce Jenner because everybody would want his autograph when they went into places, just like Nicole. The way I see it. Kris wanted everything Nicole had. She tried to do it with O. J., but she got broken. Still, that was okay with Kris. It just meant she moved on with Bruce Jenner.

"O. J. is a Lover, Not a Hater"

That is what you have to understand about how the media created the narrative that O. J. killed Nicole and Ron Goldman in a wild fit of jealousy. O. J. and Nicole were not faithful to one another. Quite the contrary. O. J. got turned on when people were sexually attracted to Nicole. And Nicole liked sex, allegedly with women as well as with men. O. J. didn't care about Nicole, whether she was faithful to him or not, because he really didn't care about women. He was drawn to Nicole more because they were friends, not precisely because they were lovers. "I thought from the first time I met her that Nicole was beautiful," O. J. once told me. He said he was immediately attracted to any woman who had Nicole's looks. But the media pushed the O. J. "jealousy narrative" because that is what sold, that is what made money. A lot of money was made portraying O. J. as a killer, money that wouldn't have been made if the media had cared to tell the public the truth. O. J. made a lot of millionaires out of reporters and authors, media personalities, who made their careers off portraying O. J. as a killer.

I learned in working with O. J. that he wasn't mean spirited. He was actually more like a child. I've said that many times. O. J. was like a little kid. He would ask me, "Can I go to the store?" You know, "Can I do this or that?" He constantly wanted to know where we were, what we were going to do there, what he was supposed to say, or how he was supposed to act. He never got free of being handled. He always had somebody there to take care of things. Even when he was in the gangs growing up in San Francisco, O. J. was the leader of the gang, but the gang members were always the ones who did things for O. J.—that's always the way it's been for O. J. throughout his life, in college, in professional sports—he always had handlers. That's what I was. I handled O. J.'s appearances after he got demonized as the murderer who got acquitted of these horrific murders.

That's why O. J. never went into a Walmart. I remember him standing there, looking at this Walmart. "I've seen these," he told me, "but I've never been inside one. I'm told you can buy anything you want in there." He never ate at a McDonalds or other fast-food places. He always dined at fine restaurants, and everywhere he went, people bought him food. Even when I was with O. J., people would buy him things, "Do you want food"—"Do you want a drink?"—"Do you want cocaine?" That's what people were always asking him, and they would hand him everything. It was almost like O. J. never had to deal with any of the real things, the mundane things, in his life. At first, I thought being with O. J. would be difficult because the media made him look like a pariah. But people loved O. J. It was more like being with George Clooney or Barack Obama. People came up to O. J. and adoringly asked him for his autograph.

The day I signed the contract with O. J., we were at a restaurant in Miami, Florida. There was a guy sitting on the side over there, giving O. J. an evil look. And that's when I noticed how O. J. worked. O. J. said, "I have to go to the bathroom." On the way to the bathroom, O. J. stopped at the guy's table and said, "You've got one of the most beautiful women in the world on your arm. You must be something." Before you knew it, the guy liked O. J. and they were shaking hands. O. J. knew how to turn people around, and he did not like people not to like him. O. J. wanted to be loved. He wanted to be adored. O. J. is a lover. He isn't a hater.

CHAPTER 4

The Suicide Note

———

What constantly surprises me about the O. J. case is that every aspect of this story is surrounded by lies, and rather than search for the truth, the media just magnified the lies, provided the lies advanced the "O. J. is guilty" narrative. I spent some twenty years with O. J., and I am still just now beginning to figure it out.

Take for instance the famous O. J. suicide note. That story has so many twists and turns it makes me dizzy trying to get my head around what was really happening.

Let's begin this saga here . . .

On Friday, June 17, 1994, five days after Nicole Brown Simpson and Ron Goldman were murdered, Robert Shapiro, O. J.'s lead "dream team" criminal defense attorney, and Robert Kardashian, identified as O. J.'s "best friend" and personal attorney, held a news conference.

But remember, after that little Jacuzzi incident Robert Kardashian and O. J. had a huge falling out. Far from being "best friends," Kardashian and O. J. weren't speaking to one another. Yet, Nicole is murdered, and Kardashian is back center stage. What was that all about?

Were Shapiro and Kardashian really working for O. J.?

Next, Shapiro announced the Los Angeles Police Department (LAPD) had notified him that morning that O. J. was being charged with first degree murder in the two deaths and that the LAPD had requested O. J. to surrender voluntarily at 11:00 a.m. Pacific Time.

When I went back and watched the 1994 video of Kardashian at the press conference, I realized that the ABC news report that star anchor newscaster Peter Jennings was broadcasting was about to include a reading of O. J.'s "suicide note" live on national television while the Bronco crawl was going on. *Some best friend*, I thought.

Here O. J. is being framed as the murderer and the Bronco drama is being played on national television as O. J.'s get-away escape, maybe even to Mexico, with the rumored disguise and "outlaw cash" O. J. has stashed in a bag in the back of the Bronco.

Now, O. J.'s top attorney and his best friend show up on national television reading a "suicide note." If I had attorneys and best friends like this, I would be concluding they worked for the prosecutors in the District Attorney's office.

Where Was O. J.?

Obviously, if O. J. was riding around the Los Angeles freeways with Al Cowlings when this press conference was going on, then he didn't surrender to the LAPD at 11:00 a.m. Pacific Time as Shapiro had just told the world he prearranged it. So, were Shapiro and Kardashian in on the escape plan?

"I had arranged the following means of surrender for the Commander of the Los Angeles Police Department," Shapiro explained to the press conference. "I was going to come down with Mr. Simpson in my car being accompanied by the psychiatrist, Dr. Fierstein, and by his good friend, Robert Kardashian. Because we were concerned about the potential for suicide, we were being followed by A.C. Cowlings, his lifelong friend, and Doctor Rob Heizinger."

So, hearing this, I'm asking myself, what happened? I would have assumed Shapiro had been conferencing with his client, O. J., in person, making the arrangements to bring O. J. downtown to the LAPD offices to be arrested. How did Shapiro lose his client?

"It was at that time that Dr. Fierstein went into the room to alert him (O. J.) that we discovered for the first time that O. J. was not present," Shapiro continued, beginning his explanation of how he made a deal with the LAPD without first securing the presence and agreement of O. J. to stay around and do what Shapiro was promising to the police chief O. J. would do.

"At that time, all of the professionals, the doctors, myself, and Mr. Kardashian were upstairs in a rather large house. O. J. was downstairs, and at the time that I was getting the message from the Los Angeles Police Department, he was wailing. He was with Mr. Cowlings. I did not, nor did anyone else to my knowledge tell O. J. that the police were coming to take him into custody."

So, we are supposed to believe that Shapiro didn't get his client, O. J. to the LAPD to surrender at 11:00 a.m. Pacific Time as prearranged because he didn't know where his client was—at least until he turned on his television and saw the Bronco chase in progress.

We are supposed to believe this is what happened: O. J. had failed to surrender himself at 11:00 a.m. Pacific Time, so Shapiro waited until the police chief called him to declare O. J. was now a fugitive running from the law. In response to that, Shapiro tells the police chief to send over a squad car and Shapiro will go downstairs to get O. J. ready to be arrested.

Next, Shapiro and the other "professionals"—maybe lawyers, a psychiatrist, another doctor, and his best friend—all went downstairs, they found O. J. had slipped out with A.C. Cowlings, unseen by any of them.

But wait a minute, if O. J. had written a suicide note, and Shapiro had a psychiatrist and O. J.'s best friend there to make sure O. J. didn't put a gun to his head, why did they leave O. J. downstairs alone? We are supposed to believe A.C. Cowlings finally arrived and the two of them decided to make a run for it.

But why did Shapiro, the psychiatrist, and Robert Kardashian leave O. J. alone if he was sobbing and thinking about killing himself?

It doesn't make any sense, unless it's all a big fabrication.

O. J. Explains the Bronco Ride?

"What is amazing is what they thought were facts in my case weren't facts in my case," O. J. explained to me.

"Take the Bronco ride, for instance," O. J. continued. "I was in three trials and never once did the prosecutors or the attorneys for the Goldmans bring up the Bronco ever in a court of law. The media brought it up, but the prosecutors never brought it up. Why? Because the perception was better than the fact."

Good point, I thought, especially because at criminal law the fact that a suspect becomes a fugitive can be entered by the prosecution at trial as evidence of guilt. So, what was the truth of the Bronco ride? We know the perception and the reason the media showed the Bronco "chase" on national television because the perception was that the "get-away" was "proof" O. J. was the murderer.

"With that Bronco ride, the LAPD knew where I was going before A.C. and I got into the Bronco at my home to leave my home that Friday, June 17, 1994," O. J. stressed. "A.C. called the LAPD and told them where I was going. A.C. arranged the whole deal, including that the LAPD would pick me up to arrest me when we got back home."

"Yes, I was really depressed, and I wanted to go to Nicole's grave before I got arrested. That's what A.C. told the LAPD and the LAPD allowed us to take the Bronco and go over there," O. J. said. "You see, flight can be construed as guilt. You see, if you tried to get away, the prosecutors can say in court that you were trying to get away, and the judge will instruct the jury that trying to run away is a sign of guilt."

O. J. knew that and that's why O. J. told A.C. to get on the phone with the LAPD to make sure before they took off in the Bronco that the LAPD knew O. J. wanted to go to Nicole's gravesite before he was arrested and that he wasn't running away. That is exactly what O. J. told me.

"The prosecutors never brought the Bronco ride up in any of my trials," he repeated. "But the public perception through the media was that I was fleeing, but the perception was better than the fact. So, if they brought it up at court, then the police would have to explain to the public that they knew where we were."

The LAPD always knew where O. J. was, and they knew why he went on the Bronco ride. O. J. had A.C. call the LAPD to tell them he was going to Nicole's grave. The police were waiting for O. J. to arrive at the end of the Bronco ride because O. J. had A.C. tell the LAPD to have the police at his home so they could arrest him after he arrived. The LAPD squadron of police cars followed O. J. in what was truly a freeway crawl at two miles per hour that the LAPD could have stopped anytime they wanted to stop the Bronco.

O. J. and A.C. in the Bronco got to Nicole's grave, but they found the police had blocked off access. So, O. J. had A.C. turn around and they headed the Bronco back to O. J.'s home. The police followed the Bronco on the highways to make sure O. J. did what he promised and to make sure O. J. didn't decide to escape. The police on the scene also knew they had to stay with O. J. in large part to control the gawking scene that developed all along the L.A. freeways when the Bronco chase become a national television event.

"Today, when I am speaking to these schools, people are always amazed that things about my case they thought were established facts didn't happen that way at all," O. J. said, clearly perceiving how the media for a long time have been working to create what we today call "fake news."

The truth is that "fake news" sells much better than truth, especially when the "fake news" can mix interracial marriage with abundant drugs and a sexually wide-open lifestyle.

O. J. knew the truth, he perceived the reality of what was going on, including how the media twisted the facts to frame O. J. as a modern-day Othello mad with jealous rage who brutally murders his beautiful white Desdemona. O. J. knew exactly what he was going to face in the media circus that was sure to occur.

If O. J. was worried about anything it was that he felt like the only black man around in the hands of a racist white mob determined to have a lynching. He was pretty sure the trial would be a circus and it wouldn't matter if he committed the murders or not. The press had already convicted him of the crime and a Los Angeles jury was almost certain to do the same. O. J. just figured "I'm a black man and they're going to nail me."

Sex, drugs, and rock-and-roll. The formula is an old one, but a good one, provided you are the "news media" and you are more interested in profits than in the truth. I constantly shake my head realizing the O. J. case is hard to solve, largely because the news media allowed all these different players to make money spinning their lies. Shapiro wrote a book,[6] Johnny Cochran wrote a book,[7] even O. J. wrote a book,[8] explaining "hypothetically" how he might actually have happened to murder Nicole after all.

As a result of the Goldman family winning the civil case against O. J. on February 7, 1997, O. J. was liable for the deaths of Nicole Brown Simpson and Ron Goldman. As a result, the civil court awarded $33.5 million in damages to the victims' families in 1997. The problem was that O. J. at the time was nearly broke and the Goldman family had no way to collect on a judgment for damages.

The Book Controversy

Years later, a controversy over O. J. Simpson's mock-confessional book, *If I Did It, Here's How It Happened*, developed that allowed the Goldman family to collect some of the damages the civil court had awarded. The book was originally scheduled to be published by Judith Regan under her imprint Regan Books at Harper Collins. The book became controversial when Regan scheduled Simpson for a television interview on Fox news to promote the book. At that time, Fox owned Harper Collins, and hence Reagan Books, under the News Corporation umbrella. When Fox affiliates objected, Fox cancelled the O. J. television interview, canned the book and fired Judith Regan, although about 400 thousand copies of the books hit the bookstores anyway.[9]

---

6   Robert L. Shapiro, *The Search for Justice: A Defense Attorney's Brief on the O. J. Simpson Case* (New York: Grand Central Pub, 1996).

7   Johnnie L. Cochran Jr., *Journey to Justice* (New York: One World/Ballantine, 1996).

8   The Goldman Family, *If I Did It: Confessions of the Killer* (New York: Beaufort Books, 2007).

9   Edward Wyatt, "Judith Regan Is Fired after O. J. Simpson Book," *New York Times*, December 15, 2006, https://www.nytimes.com/2006/12/15/business/media/15cnd -regan.html.

In 2007, a Florida bankruptcy court awarded the rights to that book to Fred Goldman, father of Ron Goldman, as partial settlement against the unpaid civil judgment the family held against O. J. Simpson. The Goldman family then managed to get Beauford Books in New York, a publishing company owned by Eric Kampmann, the owner of Midpoint Trade Books, a book distributor also operating out of New York City. Beauford Books published their 2007 version of the O. J. manuscript under a new title, *If I Did It: Confessions of the Killer*, and the Goldman family listed as author.[10]

Why did O. J. write that book? "They paid me $600,000 not to dispute that I wrote the book. All I had to do was let them put my name on that book," O. J. explained to me. "That was a lot of money and I had two kids to put through school. I didn't write a word of that book. The publisher hired a ghost writer, and I didn't even read it until it went into print." At the time, I told O. J. not to accept the deal, but I couldn't talk him out of it. O. J. explained to me that his kids needed the money for college, etc., etc. I tried to keep an open mind regarding everything O. J. told me, even though deep down inside, it wasn't all about everybody else, it was always about only him.

After that, the Goldmans got a court judgment for the $33 million in damages, O. J. had an issue with the Goldman's wanting his money, and I think he was afraid that everyone was taking everything away from him. So, anytime he had an opportunity to take something, then he would, even if he knew it was wrong. Just like, *If I Did It*, he knew it was wrong. Fox News knew it was wrong. The publisher knew it was wrong. I told O. J. not to take the money or do the book. But they paid him, and they paid him in cash. But what people don't really understand is that you can't sue O. J. Simpson.

So, in order for him to get paid, he would have had to get the money before the book was written. O. J. would have wanted the cash up front. So, they gave O. J. $600,000 in cash in a briefcase before the book was ever written. And O. J. never wrote the book, somebody else did it—a ghost writer wrote that book. And people don't put

---

10   Mike Celzic, "Families Feud Over O. J.'s 'If I Did It Book," Today.com, August 15, 2007, https://www.today.com/news/victims-families-feud-over-o-j-s-if-i-did-1C9011454.

that together. All O. J. had to do was not dispute the book. Not that he got to keep the money; O. J. paid off his house and did a few other things, and then they came and took that away from him and gave it to the Goldmans.

The Suicide Note Pushed to Center Stage

Next in the press conference, Shapiro turned to Robert Kardashian. With Kardashian at center stage, we were finally getting to the main event of this press conference sham.

Shapiro explained to the press that Robert Kardashian was more than O. J.'s best friend. He was also O. J.'s personal attorney. Shapiro continued, elaborating that in his capacity as O. J.'s personal attorney, Kardashian had that day witnessed O. J. signing a codicil to his will and received from O. J. three letters that were placed in sealed envelopes.

"Now, I would like to introduce to you Mr. Robert Kardashian, who is one of Mr. Simpson's closest and dearest friends, who will read a letter that O. J. wrote in his handwriting today," Shapiro told the press conference, doing his best to look like he was telling the Gospel truth.[11]

Here's What the Suicide Note Said

Let's let the suicide note speak for itself. Here are the key excerpts from the O. J. Simpson "Suicide Note" that Robert Kardashian read in its entirety to the press conference.

> "First, everyone understand I had (sic) nothing to do with Nicole's murder. I loved her, always have and always will. If we had a problem, it's because I loved her so much. Recently we came to the understanding that for now, we weren't right for each other, at least for now. Despite our love, we were different and that's why we mutually agreed to go our separate ways. It was tough splitting for a second

11   Peter Jennings, "Simpson's Lawyer, Best Friend Speak to Press," ABC News, June 17, 1994.

time, but we both knew it was for the best. Inside I had no doubt that in the future, we would be close friends or more.

"Unlike what has been written in the press, Nicole + I had a great relationship for most of our lives together.

"I don't want to belabor knocking the press, but I can't believe what is being said. Most of it is totally made up. I know you have a job to do, but as a last wish, please, please, please leave my children in peace. Their lives will be tough enough."

O. J. then supposedly thanked his friends by name in the note. Whoever wrote that note ended it to make O. J. sound like he felt remorse and was wanting to be forgiven for all the pain he had caused by slitting the throats of his former wife and the waiter trying to do her a favor. As an exercise in self-pity, the writer of that note had mastered the art.

As you read this suicide note, ask yourself what Shapiro and Robert Kardashian were doing with this press conference, given in the middle of O. J.'s Bronco ride being shown moment-by-moment as a phalanx of police squad tied up the Los Angeles freeways with the slowest and most incompetent "escape" ever attempted. Was Shapiro as O. J.'s lawyer pleading his client was innocent? Or establishing in the public's mind that O. J. was a killer who was on the run, defying Shapiro's gentlemanly agreement with the L.A. police that O. J. would surrender and agree to be arrested for a crime Shapiro was confident O. J. did not commit.

What was "best friend" and "personal attorney" Robert Kardashian doing reading a suicide note? Letting the world know that in all their years in business together and socializing with their families in neighborly harmony, Kardashian knew O. J. could never murder the mother of his children, whom they both loved? Or, stabbing O. J. in the back, portraying his buddy as preferring suicide rather than facing justice for the grisly double murder? Was Kardashian finally seizing the opportunity to get even with O. J. for O. J.'s Jacuzzi sex with Kardashian's wife that ruined Kardashian's marriage to the mother of his four children, now separated from him after the divorce decree gave custody to Kris?

Here's how the famous "suicide note" ends:

"I think of my life and feel I've done most of the right things. So why do I end up like this? I can't go on. No matter what the outcome, people will look and point. I can't take that. I can't subject my children to that. This way they can move on and go on with their lives. Please, if I've done anything worthwhile in my life, let my kids live in peace from you, the press.

"I've had a good life. I'm proud of how I lived. My momma taught me to do unto others. I treated people the way I wanted to be treated. I've always tried to be up and helpful. So why is this happening?

"I'm sorry for the Goldman family.

"I know how much it hurts.

"Nicole and I had a good life together. All this press talk about a rocky relationship was no more than whatever (sic) long-term relationship experiences. All her friends will confirm that I've been totally loving and understanding of what she's been going through.

"At times, I have felt like a battered husband or boyfriend, but I loved her; make that clear to everyone. And I would take whatever it took to make it work.

"Don't feel sorry for me. I've had a great life made great friends. Please think of the real O. J. and not this lost person.

"Thanks for making my life special. I hope I help yours.

"Peace + Love, O. J.[12]

The O. J. "suicide note" was written out in long-hand with the words printed in capital letters predominantly. The note was dated June 15, 1995, two days before the press conference where the note was made public.

In the first sentence, the words "I had" are overwritten by scribbles and blacked out so they cannot be read. Psychologist Andrew G. Hodges, M.D. also wrote a book on O. J., claiming to present a psychological profile of O. J. that "proved" O. J. was the murderer.

---

12 "O. J.'s Suicide Note," CNN.com, no date, http://www.cnn.com/US/OJ/suspect /note/index.html.

Hodges argued O. J. committed subconscious "slips of the pen" in writing the suicide note. He claims O. J.'s "conscience jumps into denial from the get-go." Here is what Hodges considered "proof" of O. J.'s guilt:

> "In the first sentence, he (O. J.) writes ' . . . understand I had nothing to do with Nicole's murder,' but then he scratches out the 'I had.' Through his actions, he is saying, 'I can't say I had nothing to do with her murder." Isn't this the kind of slip we would expect from a man who isn't an experienced killer, a man running for his life, a man whose actions have totally puzzled and overwhelmed him, a man who has just killed the one woman he believes he truly loved?"[13]

But the key point is that the "O. J." signature included a smiley face drawn within the "O." That was the give-away that convinced me the suicide note was a fake.

A lot of this never made sense to me. Kardashian never practiced law after he sold that R & R publication that made him and the record industry millions. In those years, the record industry lived and died by their ranking on Kardashian's R & R song charts. By re-establishing his license to practice law, he knew he would make it impossible to call him to the stand to testify in the O. J. Simpson murder trial. Kardashian had a lot about his relationship with O. J. and Nicole that he knew that he to hide from public view—more than just the alleged Jacuzzi incident that destroyed his marriage.

From that press conference five days after Nicole's murder, Kardashian positioned himself as O. J.'s "personal attorney"—the one human being in the world O. J. trusted with his "suicide note" that was a virtual confession of guilt as the murderer. From that moment to the end of the trial, Kardashian positioned himself as the main adviser to O. J.'s legal "dream team." From that position, Kardashian

---

13   Andrew G. Hodges, M.D., "O. J. Simpson: Decoding the suicide note," Andrew
-GHodges.com, no date, https://www.andrewghodges.com/forensic-thoughtprints/o-j
-simpson-decoding-the-suicide-note.

could guide the legal Dream Team in confidence in any direction he wanted to take, and Kardashian certainly understood how the attorney-client privilege would keep his "advice" to Robert Shapiro and Dream Team lawyers Johnnie Cochran and F. Lee Bailey safe from any and all outside scrutiny.

This role as "main adviser" to the lawyer Dream Team tied Kardashian tightly to O. J.'s actual functioning legal defense team, and it really didn't matter whether Kardashian had reinstated his law license, or he just assumed he could begin practicing law once again because he went to law school and early in his professional career had a functioning California law practice. Robert Shapiro and Dream Team lawyers Johnnie Cochran and F. Lee Bailey would certainly have won their objection if the District Attorney had wanted to call Kardashian to the stand. Yet, Kardashian's *New York Times* obituary claimed that Kardashian "who received his law degree in 1967 from the University of San Diego, reactivated his dormant lawyer's license after Mr. Simpson's arrest." The obituary also states that Kardashian "asserted attorney-client privilege and was never called to testify."[14]

Was Kardashian from the beginning telling Shapiro and Cochran that their job was to get O. J. acquitted at the trial, even though Kardashian "knew" O. J. was the murderer? If Kardashian was flaming the "jealous rage" motive the mainstream media was salivating to promote, could Kardashian have been equally keen to mask his own revenge motive to get back at O. J. for what he perceived O. J. had done to him, wrecking Kardashian's marriage to Kris—the last long-term relationship Kardashian was able to form with a woman in his remaining lifetime?[15] Remember: Kardashian passed away on September 30, 2003, eight years after O. J.'s murder trial and

---

14   Associated Press, "Robert Kardashian, a Lawyer for O. J. Simpson, Dies at 59," New York Times, October 3, 2003, https://www.nytimes.com/2003/10/03/us/robert -kardashian-a-lawyer-for-o-j-simpson-dies-at-59.html.

15   Kylie McConville, "Why Did Robert Kardashian Stop Being A Lawyer? The Answer is Pretty Straightforward," Romper.com, February 1, 2016, https://www .romper.com/p/why-did-robert-kardashian-stop-being-a-lawyer-the-answer-is-pretty -straightforward-4864.

acquittal. No one truly defending O. J. would have put that suicide note out there in the public five days after the murders.

Norman Pardo Proves O. J. Simpson Did Not Write the Suicide Note

The suicide note, in my opinion and in the opinion of O. J. as well, was not written by O. J. Simpson. It didn't really dawn on me until I looked at the signature.

Then I remembered all the things O. J. signed, contracts, all these different deals to all these places. O. J. has a very distinctive signature and every one of the many samples I have the signature was different than on the suicide note. In my opinion, and the opinion of everyone I've shown it to, that is not O. J. Simpson's signature on the suicide note. So, whoever gave that to the police, in my opinion, probably made the suicide note up.

But if O. J. did not write the suicide note, who did? And why? What we know for certain is that the suicide note becomes a piece of the puzzle. The suicide note was one of the first and most important supposed pieces of "evidence" to appear in this case, and the appearance was timely, framing as it did the "Bronco crawl" as a get-away attempt. It was Robert Kardashian who reappeared from retirement obscurity to read that note to the press on Friday, June 17, 1994, five days after the murder. On that day, Kardashian was not well known, and the family was still years away from their reality-show fame.

Was Robert Kardashian the ghost writer, or did he have one of his children scribble the note, smiley face and all? If revenge was Robert Kardashian's goal in stepping forward to be an O. J. "defender" after Nicole's death, the timely production of the "suicide note" was sufficient for Shapiro and Cochran to invite him to sit in a privileged position at the Dream Team defense table in the murder trial.

As the press conference concluded, Kardashian allowed the press to take pictures of the suicide note, including the last part with O. J.'s signature, with special emphasis on the smiley face signature. Did Robert Kardashian fabricate the suicide note? We will let you decide. As to Kardashian's law license, Kardashian's obituary published in the *New York Times* claimed that Kardashian "who received his law degree in 1967 from the University of San Diego, reactivated his dormant lawyer's license after Mr. Simpson's arrest." The obituary also states that Kardashian "asserted attorney-client privilege and was never called to testify."[16]

It always impressed me that the way that note was written was very childish, with the sentiments expressed very immature. None of it sounded anything like the way O. J. talked or thought. I always suspected Kim Kardashian wrote the "suicide note," but then that's just me. You will have to make up your own mind who wrote that note. I can't prove Kim Kardashian wrote that note but the handwriting does not look like Robert Kardashian's handwriting or O. J.'s handwriting. It looked like a little kid wrote that note and even put a smiley face in it. O. J. always scoffed at the idea the note was authentic.

I also believe the note was meant to make O. J. look guilty. Why else would you put a suicide note out there if you didn't do anything? The suicide note was never introduced at O. J.'s murder trial because the prosecution would have been forced to prove the handwriting was O. J.'s handwriting. I compared the signatures and the smiley face in the "O" of O. J.'s suicide note signature was something O. J. never did.

Barbara Walters Interviews Kardashian in 1996

In 1996, less than a year after O. J.'s acquittal on October 3, 1995, Robert Kardashian was interviewed on national television by ABC reporter Barbara Walters.[17] The headline of the interview was that Barbara Walters had gotten "a startling confession" from one of O. J.'s "closest friends." While Robert Kardashian had always claimed publicly that he believed O. J. to be innocent, a year after the acquittal Kardashian admitted to Barbara Walters that he now "has doubts."

---

16 Associated Press, "Robert Kardashian, a Lawyer for O. J. Simpson, Dies at 59," *New York Times*, October 3, 2003, https://www.nytimes.com/2003/10/03/us/robert -kardashian-a-lawyer-for-o-j-simpson-dies-at-59.html.

17 "1996: Barbara Walters interviews Robert Kardashian, longtime friend of O. J. Simpson," ABC News, October 10, 1996, https://abcnews.go.com/2020/video/robert -kardashian-longtime-friend-oj-simpson-doubts-innocence-33841038.

ABC's Hugh Downs, in introducing the interview, referred to Robert Kardashian as "a member of Simpson's defense team and a long-time confidant."

Walters opened the interview with film footage showing Robert Kardashian bringing a Louis Vuitton garment bag to O. J. Simpson's home—the bag that O. J. had taken with him the on the flight to Chicago in the early morning hours the day after Nicole and Ron Goldman were murdered. Walters noted "it had been speculated this bag may have contained Simpson's bloody clothes and/or the murder weapon." Walters also commented that Kardashian had renewed his law license to serve as Simpson's personal attorney. She observed that throughout the O. J. Simpson trial, Robert Kardashian was O. J.'s "closest adviser, who stood in the shadows and kept the defense's secrets and his feelings to himself."

Walters interviewed Kardashian in his Encino home, the same home in which he claimed O. J. slept for four nights after returning from Chicago—O. J.'s "hideout" as Barbara Walters characterized it. Kardashian claimed he had gone to O. J.'s home just to support him and that he did not know O. J. had gone to Chicago. He said that O. J. pulled up in his car to come home when he was standing there, and he took the garment bag from Cathy Randa who was in the car with O. J. returning from the airport. Kardashian claimed he took the luggage to his Encino home when the policeman guarding O. J.'s home refused to admit anyone to enter the residence. Kardashian insisted he forgot he had the bag and it remained in the trunk of his car. He stated categorically that he did not open the garment bag and he had no idea what its contents were. Kardashian also claimed that model and would-be actress Paula Barbieri slept with O. J. in Kardashian's home.

On the day O. J. was arrested, that Friday, June 17, 1994, Kardashian told him Robert Shapiro had called him about 8:30 a.m. Pacific Time and explained to him that he had arranged for O. J. to surrender himself to the LAPD by 11:00 a.m. Pacific Time that morning. Then at approximately 9:30 a.m., according to Kardashian's account, Shapiro arrived at Kardashian's home where the two of them visited O. J. in the bedroom where O. J. and Barbieri slept together. He claimed O. J. had a blank stare when Shapiro told him the details of the arranged surrender procedures. Next, Kardashian claimed, he went back to O. J.'s room and O. J. was looking at pictures of Nicole and their two children. He said O. J. had a gun wrapped in a towel. "I was stunned," Kardashian explained emotionally. "I knelt on the floor in front of the chair where O. J. was sitting and I took his hand," Kardashian relayed, saying he prayed with O. J. at that moment. From there, Kardashian explained to Barbara Walters that O. J. told him that O. J. had decided to kill himself.

Kardashian claimed his home was filled with attorneys at that moment when A.C. Cowlings arrived. That's when Kardashian claimed O. J. made his get-away. He said O. J. wrote the suicide note at Kardashian's desk but Kardashian claimed he did not then know what the note said since O. J. handed it to him in a sealed envelope. Kardashian further claimed he talked to O. J. during the "Bronco chase" and that O. J. told him that he had put the gun to his head and pulled the trigger, but the gun did not go off. Kardashian also claimed there was an audio recording O. J. made in his home that morning. Barbara Walters played it on air. The voice claiming (or pretending) to be O. J. on the audio tape does not confess to being the murderer, but the self-pity expressed makes the audio recording sound like a farewell statement. Kardashian claimed he saved O. J.'s life by talking him down from suicide both at his home and on the car phone in the Bronco. Not coincidentally, Kardashian's interview was occasioned by the publication of a book in which Kardashian told his story, including the suicide story.[18]

Kardashian's Story Does Not Add Up

The whole Kardashian suicide story has sounded fishy to me from the get-go. I have never been able to get over Kardashian's face the moment the jury announced their verdict that O. J. was not guilty. O. J. is instantly relieved. You can see him relax and a smile develops on his face. Johnnie Cochran, standing behind O. J. when

---

18 Lawrence Schiller and James Willwerth, *American Tragedy: The Uncensored Story of the Simpson Defense* (New York: Random House, 1996).

O. J. and the lawyers rose to their feet to hear the jury foreman read the verdict, puts his hand on O. J.'s shoulder and is jubilant. But Robert Kardashian, standing immediately in front of O. J. is stunned. He looks like he can't believe it. There is no joy in Kardashian's face, no smile, no hint of celebration. Instead, Kardashian stares ahead vacantly with that "deer in the headlights" blank look. I can't get it out of my mind, was Kardashian certain the jury would find O. J. guilty, and was that exactly what Kardashian wanted to happen?

The whole suicide story doesn't make sense because O. J. Simpson is not the kind of guy to feel sorry for himself. O. J. to the world has become the ultimate "Godfather," just like the crime boss Mafia Don. He's not what he used to be—he's not the superstar, the football player, nobody even cares about that anymore. All anybody cares about is that O. J. kills people and he gets away with it—he's a thug, he'll rob you, he'll sell you ecstasy, because it's always in the news that he's doing the bad things. But he's like "Teflon Don." You figure, he does all that shit, but nobody busts O. J., man. He has attorneys, he can get out of it. That's what the black guys figure—a lot of black people can't get attorneys, but O. J. can.

Every nightclub we ever went to, somebody would be up there wanting to be O. J.'s protector. "Oh man, it's O. J., he's important, this is the Juice," that's what the black guys in the clubs would say. They would get down on their knees and want their picture taken with O. J., the celebrity. They get so excited precisely because he's always doing the bad guy thing. Remember, all O. J. ever cared about was himself. O. J. is the ultimate narcissist—he loves himself above all others. The only thing that made any difference to O. J. was O. J.

But Kardashian is different. Did O. J. ruin his life? Kardashian lost his wife and his children—did O. J. destroy Kardashian's family? Was Kardashian's state of mind telling him that if O. J. was convicted of murder, he would lose everything that meant something to O. J., and the only thing that meant something to O. J. was O. J. His image— you destroy O. J.'s image, you destroy O. J. So, I think Kardashian could have thought he would just set this up so it would look like O. J. did it, so even if O. J. gets off, he will look guilty and it would destroy his whole image. O. J. would lose everything—he'd lose his career, it would be tanked, just like Robert's was.

He'd lose his wife for sure because she would be dead. I think Kardashian just had a plan that he was going to destroy O. J.'s entire life. I can't prove it, but that's the way it looks to me.

O. J. Telephones Barbara Walters from Jail, 1994

"The first week after I was arrested, on the ABC News show *20/20*, investigative journalist Barbara Walters gave a report that they learned that my Hertz contract was up and Hertz was not renewing my contract," O. J. told me. "This was my biggest contract. She also reported my NBC contract was up and they weren't renewing. Barbara Walters also said ABC News learned I was paying $55,000 a month in child support and alimony. Then Hugh Downs turned to her and suggested that might put a lot of pressure on any individual to make them do some crazy things."

What O. J. concluded from this was that Barbara Walters was giving America a motive for O. J. to kill Nicole. The facts were that O. J. had just just received a raise from Hertz, and signed an extension with them two weeks earlier. Six months earlier, O. J. had also signed an extension and received a raise from NBC. He also was not paying any alimony because he had already bought out of his divorce by making a cash settlement with Nicole.

"Barbara Walters couldn't have been more wrong," O. J. insisted. "All they had to do was to call Hertz or NBC, but they didn't do that. Instead, ABC broadcast a complete, fabricated lie—and this was Barbara Walters. I tracked her down from jail. She went on about how it was at the end of the show and they put it on the teleprompter, so she just read without really checking it."

O. J. didn't buy this excuse for a minute.

From jail, O. J. tracked Barbara Walters down through Roone Arledge, who ran ABC News. In 1985, Roone Arledge gave O. J. his first job on television, hiring O. J. to be a sports commentator. Roone Arledge gave O. J. the telephone number where he could reach Barbara Walters.

From jail, the next time O. J. got access to a telephone, he telephoned Barbara Walters. O. J. explained how the conversation went: "I said to her, 'Barbara, you know, everybody admires you and it's your integrity that's on the line, not some unknown guy who's writing something on a teleprompter.'"

So, in 2016, when Robert Kardashian teamed up with Barbara Walters to resume framing O. J. as the murderer, O. J. had come to expect that—both from Robert Kardashian and from the news media. The suicide note became an established part of the O. J. murder mystery even though it was "fake news." So too, the myth that O. J. was pressed for cash at the time the murders occurred was also "fake news."

But the most important point to understand is that Robert Kardashian shared the media's game portraying O. J. as a murderer because for the media the "O. J. guilty" story sold. For Robert Kardashian, the "O. J. guilty" story kept everyone from investigating the real question: "Who Killed Nicole?" If O. J. was guilty, why look any further to find the real murderer. If the answer was not O. J., then Robert Kardashian knew he had a lot of reasons to be worried.

Chapter 5

The Hired Killer

―――――

O. J. is in the front seat on the passenger side, I'm in the back seat with my video camera running—the usual setup. This particular day O. J. was in a good mood. He had just gotten a newspaper reporter to publish a story that I was redneck, and I was also gay. Well, the redneck part may be accurate, but O. J. was just amused at how gullible the reporter was, especially given that he was writing for a New York newspaper that was supposed to be so sophisticated and always accurate.

(VIDEO STARTS)

O. J.: Norm is gay.

Norm: I keep appreciating that gay part!

O. J.: Norm was pissed off, they had him in the New York paper, "O. J.'s redneck, gay . . . "—we were talkin', ya know, teasing, you know how we tease, and they wrote that shit in the paper—that Norm is a redneck and he's gay.

Norm: Yeah, that O. J. admits to drugs, and his redneck manager is gay.

[Norm, O. J., Del, and the driver laugh]

O. J.: Yeah, I admit I said it (about the drugs), but I meant, in 1992, my friends gave me a surprise party, and one the girls brought ecstasy. This is the first I heard of ecstasy. So, everybody at the party took an ecstasy pill. Boy what a party that was! Then they print, "he admits to drugs." Like me and everybody else ain't done something once or twice. Other than that, I ain't done an illegal drug since last night. I always smoke my doobie.

> **[O. J. is admitting he smokes a marijuana**
> **joint at night to go to sleep.]**

Del: Once he smoke his doobie man, it's good night.

(VIDEO OFF)

Sometimes, unfortunately, crimes go unsolved. What you think you know and what you can prove are often two different things. You can have an investigation where you believe the person is guilty or that you know who did it. But you have to have facts. You have to have evidence.

I became the "go-to" guy for everything O. J. Simpson. Because of that, people with information knew who to find. So, people would send me stuff. If the media hadn't made me the "go-to" guy, I would never have been able to solve this mystery.

The Secrets: Witness #2
This guy came to me last week. And he had a story I had not heard that turned out to be an important piece of the puzzle. Again, I want to add that this is "allegedly." We know Nicole had many lovers, but this particular guy was new to me.

Witness #2—The Tradeoff
"I became friends with a guy named Joseph Perulli, a thirty-three-year-old male model. I read up quite a bit about the case and I know that Perulli testified at the murder trial, against O. J., saying O. J. had anger issues.

"One night at a gathering, Perulli said to me, 'Come here, I want to show you something.' He pulls out from under his bed this nickel-plated twelve-gauge shotgun. And he says to me, 'Take a look at this!'

"Yeah, so Marcus Allen, the pro football player, came in and said, 'Just hold this for me for a while.'"

I asked myself what Marcus Allen giving Joseph Perulli the shotgun was all about. Then I remembered Perulli was a witness at the O. J. murder trial. I began to wonder if giving Perulli that expensive shotgun to hold 'for a while' might have been a tradeoff.

Nicole's Address Book and the 911 Call Re-Examined

The reason for the 911 call on October 25, 1993, was that O. J. wanted Nicole's address book, not because he was a jealous lover. We know O. J. himself did drugs—a lot of them. O. J. had other women—a lot of them. He knew the same was true about Nicole, that she was doing a lot of drugs and had a lot of sex going on in her Brentwood home—including group sex and lesbian sex.

O. J. didn't care if Nicole was into sex and drugs. What O. J. cared about was himself and his kids. He did not want Nicole bringing the drugs and prostitutes into the house while his children were sleeping in their beds upstairs. He also cared about himself. If Nicole was not going to take care of his children responsibly, he would have to find another solution.

At the trial, the prosecutors tried to establish whether O. J. kicked in the door or knocked the door down. But that point is really irrelevant. The prosecutors were trying to prove O. J. went insanely jealous over Nicole, so much so that he became violent. O. J. was angry and he wanted to stop Nicole, but not for the drugs and the sex per se, it was about the children.

The reason O. J. was at Nicole's house was to get her address book. You have to keep things in a simple form. If you're going to solve this case, you are not going to do it by running around chasing rabbits down the rabbit hole. You have to get to the meat. The meat was that he wanted that book. You can clearly hear on the 911 tape O. J. saying, "I want that black book." O. J. wanted that black book because he was going to take Nicole's drug problem into his own hands, he was going to deal with it on his own. O. J. was not going to get the police involved in Nicole's drug problems because O. J. didn't want the police involved in his life. So, O. J. just went and dealt with Nicole's drug problem himself—and as we shall soon see, appears to be with Robert Kardashian's help as well.

But there is one more part to this story. O. J. repeatedly told me that he was clear from any alimony or child payments because he had bought Nicole out at the time of the divorce. But let's go back to 1989, the fact that Nicole Brown Simpson and O. J. Simpson got into a huge fight—a fight that never sat well with him. He was ashamed he did it. And there were photographs taken of that fight. Nicole put those photographs of her badly bruised face from the 1989 fight in a safe deposit box and she told O. J. that if anything ever happened to her, those photographs would be made public, and O. J. would be ruined forever. So, was Nicole blackmailing O. J.? Could he have been stuck paying her drug debts that got into tens of thousands of dollars every month? I have never heard of anyone else taking photos of themselves in a compromising position and hiding them in a safe deposit box.

Then we will move up to 1993 and the infamous 911 call, when everyone said Nicole was fearing for her life because he wanted her black book containing all the phone numbers to her drug dealers and prostitutes hanging around with his children. O. J. wanted to protect his children and he wanted to protect himself. O. J. was concerned not only that Nicole's drug and sex lifestyle was not appropriate with his children, but he had also come to the conclusion that Nicole had become a liability for him—for O. J.—someone who was into drugs and sex too. If O. J. had just taken that address book and you didn't hear about that book later, then I would say the book didn't have anything to do with the murder. But the book resurfaces with a guy named William Wasz, and when I investigated that, some of the threads of the story started to come together and make some sense to me.

For O. J., it was never about sex. "I wasn't a guy running around chasing a lot of girls," O. J. said to me. "But I was unfaithful to both my wives. It is what I regretted most about my life. I made a vow about ten years ago that I never would do it again." It wasn't that

Nicole was indulged in sex, but what O. J. did not want was for the drug dealers and the prostitutes to be hanging around his kids.

(VIDEO STARTS)

The usual: O. J. riding in the car with Del and Norm.
O. J.: There's some pretty ladies at this club.
Del: Oh. Yeah. Yeah, 'specially Saturday nights.
O. J.: Del, that's what I'm talkin' about.
Driver: All kinds of girls.
O. J.: Cause Del only likes white girls. I like Cubans.
      [O. J. laughs hard, mouth open, eyes roll to heaven]
Del: Talk for yo' self, bitch.
O. J.: I'm happier already motherfucker!
Driver: Katmandu is about two blocks away too if you wanna go
    check that out as well.
O. J.: What's Katmandu?
Driver: It's . . . it's more of a white girl area.
O. J.: Fuck white girls!
      [O. J. leans back, smiling]
O. J.: A LOT!
      [O. J. bangs on his knee and dashboard]
O. J.: Often!
Del: You are talkin' my language!
      [O. J. leans to whisper to driver, glances at camera]
O. J.: Not me . . . give me a sister any day of the week.
      [O. J. glances at camera, laughing facetiously]
O. J.: The cameras on!

(VIDEO OFF)

The Car Accident: Nicole's Address Book Surfaces

Nicole's address book resurfaced when this guy, William Wasz, ended up in a car accident in Paula Barbieri's car on January 31, 1996, a couple of years after Nicole's murder. You remember that Paula Barbieri was O. J.'s last girlfriend before the murder. What's more, the police found Nicole's address book in Paula Barbieri's car that Wasz was suspiciously driving when he had the car accident that led to his arrest.

Although Wasz was arrested on January 31, 1994, the story of his arrest did not get published in the newspapers until July 21, 1994, some six weeks after Nicole was murdered. When Wasz was arrested in January, the fact he had Nicole's address book in the vehicle he was driving at the time, Paula Barbieri's stolen Toyota 4-Runner, was curious but not viewed as important enough for the police to report or the news media to make public. But when the *Orange County Register* published the story on July 21, 1994, after the murder of Nicole and Ron Goldman, the fact Wasz had her address book with him became important, as did the fact that when he was arrested, Wasz was driving the 4-Runner that he had supposedly stolen from O. J. Simpson's girlfriend at that time.

"A notebook belonging to Nicole Brown Simpson was found inside a Toyota 4-Runner stolen from O. J. Simpson's friend Paula Barbieri," the story run in the *Orange County Register* began on July 21, 1994[19]. In the next sentence, the newspaper quoted Lt. John Dunkin of the LAPD. "We do have it, and it's being evaluated for its evidentiary value," the *Orange County Register* reported Lt. Dunkin as saying. The newspaper further reported that police were declining to comment on the contents of the address book.

In the article the *Orange County Register* reported on July 21, 1994, the newspaper admitted the Newport Beach police actually had found the notebook on January 31, 1994, six months earlier, when Newport Beach police Sgt. Andy Genis arrested William Wasz, age thirty-one of North Hollywood, after Wasz led the police on a stolen car pursuit. The newspaper reported Wasz had stolen Barbieri's 4-Runner seven days earlier, on January 24, 1994, from a Beverly Hills valet parking lot as Barbieri had her hair done at a nearby salon. The newspaper reported Barbieri was the registered owner of the car. Newport Beach patrol officer Mike Pule first spotted the 4-Runner going north on

---

19 "CRIME: Nicole Simpson Notebook found in O. J. Friend's Car," *Orange County Register*, July 21, 1994.

Newport Boulevard at 30th Street after reports the driver was possibly drunk. The *Orange County Register* continued. "During the pursuit, Wasz drove into traffic and eventually crashed into two cars.

After a foot chase, Officer Pule caught Wasz, arrested him, and discovered that Wasz had been shot in the leg. The newspaper concluded the report by noting Wasz was linked to four armed robberies in Orange and Los Angeles counties. Subsequent investigations found that in addition to Nicole Simpson's address book, Wasz had in the car at the time of the arrest a sizeable quantity of drugs, a crack pipe, and a 9mm pistol. On the floor of Barbieri's 4-Runner, the police also found several discarded hypodermic needles that had been used for drugs. Wasz's shot to the leg resulted from a gunshot exchange with the police as Wasz attempted to escape on foot after crashing the 4-Runner into two cars during the police chase.

A second story the *Orange County Register* published the next day, on July 22, 1994, said that John Stewart, age forty-two, an attorney practicing law in Orange County, had recently approached the Newport Beach police, claiming he was Wasz's attorney.[20] On July 12, 1994, the Newport Beach police handed over to Stewart his client's possessions, including Nicole Simpson's notebook. The newspaper noted a detective from the LAPD on July 13, 1994, seized Nicole Simpson's address book from Stewart after Stewart admitted the "notebook" did not belong to Wasz. The Orange County article published on July 22, 1994, reported Stewart had misrepresented himself as an attorney for William Wasz and was under investigation for attempting to sell the address book to various news-media organizations and that the address book is currently being evaluated by the LAPD for its "evidentiary value." The article published July 22, 1994, also noted an unidentified source at CNN said the address book had a first page titled "Nicole's schedule" that listed her whereabouts and who she saw over several months last winter.

After his arrest on January 31, 1994, Wasz was held by the Newport Beach police. The subsequent police investigation resulted in Wasz

---

20 "CRIME: Attorney's Notebook Role Is Investigated," *Orange County Register*, July 22, 1994.

being charged and convicted for a series of petty thefts around Los Angeles for which he was imprisoned. He was given a twenty-year prison sentence and served time in three different prisons, including in a high-security section of Calapatria State Prison for a robbery unrelated to his incident stealing Paula Barbieri's Toyota 4-Runner. Wasz's story was quashed until four years later, with Nicole's address book dropping totally out of the picture. Nicole's address book may be central to why she was murdered, but the address book did not enter into O. J.'s murder trial, resulting in an acquittal on October 3, 1995, or in the Goldmans' civil trial that ended on February 7, 1997, with a judgment that Simpson was liable for the deaths of Nicole Brown Simpson and Ron Goldman.

Wasz's theft of Paula Barbieri's Toyota 4-Runner and his possession of Nicole's address book did not surface again until March 16, 1996, when his attorney Lawrence Longo wrote a proffer letter on Wasz's behalf to attorney Curtis Hazell in the office of the Los Angeles County District Attorney.

The Proffer

A proffer is a voluntary meeting between a criminal defendant or suspect and the government. In a trial, to proffer is to offer evidence in support of an argument, or elements of an affirmative defense or offense. In general terms, a proffer is an offer made prior to negotiations, an offer for acceptance of information in return for acceptance of terms favorable to the party making the proffer. In this case, Wasz appears to have calculated that the information he made about what he was doing in possession of Nicole Brown Simpson's address book in 1994, while driving around L.A. in a Toyota 4-Runner of which he claimed Robert Kardashian told him to steal from Paula Barbieri, O. J. Simpson's girlfriend at the time, might be worth enough to law enforcement authorities to get him favorable terms, possibly even terms to release him from prison.

In his proffer letter of March 16, 1998, Mr. Longo offered that his client, William Wasz (then still in prison) was willing to volunteer information to the Los Angeles District Attorney that Wasz believed would be material to the Nicole Brown Simpson murder. With the murders of Nicole Brown Simpson and Ron Goldman officially unsolved in 1998, we should have been able to assume the Los Angeles District Attorney's office would accept Longo's offer enthusiastically.

What did Wasz have to say?

Attorney Longo stated in his proffer to the District Attorney that William Wasz did not kill Nicole. This should have been obvious because Wasz was arrested on January 31, 1994, before Nicole and Ron Goldman were murdered, and he had been in prison ever since. In March 1998, with the proffer, Wasz took the risk of admitting he had been an accessory in a plot to murder Nicole Brown Simpson, only because he believed he could implicate Robert Kardashian in planning the murder, and that O. J. Simpson had been involved in the plot. In other words, Wasz was willing to turn state's evidence even if the evidence implicated himself because he believed he could identify Robert Kardashian as planning Nicole's murder.

The letter from attorney Lawrence Longo to Curtis Hazell, a lawyer in the Los Angeles District Attorney's office, began as follows: "Pursuant to your request, I would like to make an attorney proffer for your consideration. It is my understanding based upon my conversation with you that you might be interested in information my client could provide in regard to a solicitation to commit murder of Nicole Brown Simpson by Robert Kardashian." In his proffer Wasz says that while he did not kill Nicole, he has information that can explain how he came to be in possession of Nicole's address book and why he stole Paula Barbieri's 4-Runner. In what should have been a bombshell disclosure, attorney Longo revealed in the proffer that Robert Kardashian had solicited William Wasz, offering him $15,000 to kill Nicole—something the LAPD may have known investigating the murder, if only they had bothered to investigate in 1994 why Wasz had in his possession the address book and the stolen 4-Runner—evidence that led back to O. J. Simpson as the common denominator.

What follows is Wasz's story as Longo details it in the proffer. The proffer begins in the third paragraph by disclosing that in the fall of 1993, Wasz met Robert Kardashian, O. J. Simpson, and Paula Barbieri at the Roxbury Club in West Hollywood.

> **Note: In my own investigations, I found out that the actual date of that meeting was December 26, 1993, right after Nicole's 911 call, which was approximately two months earlier.**

The proffer continues to disclose that just before New Year 1994, Robert Kardashian met with Wasz at his home in Encino and offered Wasz an assignment. The purpose of the assignment was to follow Nicole and take pictures of her with any man who she might meet romantically. Wasz's surveillance of Nicole took place on January 6th and 7th, 1994. Wasz was to record this information in a notebook that at the time of the proffer was in the possession of the LAPD. As identified by the *Orange County Register* this notebook was the address book that O. J. Simpson took from Nicole on October 25, 1993, the day of the 911 call. The proffer specified that three telephone numbers in the book belong to O. J. Simpson, Robert Kardashian, and Paula Barbieri.

> **Note: In my investigations, I uncovered six handwritten pages headed "Nicole's Schedule" for what appeared to be the first weekend in January 1994, beginning on Thursday, January 6. The notes track Nicole: 1:30 p.m. at Beauty Shop on Riverside Drive in Burbank; Home at 3:00 p.m.; 6:00 p.m. at the Trader Vic's restaurant in the Beverly Hilton Hotel; 103 Roxbury Drive in Beverly Hills.**

These handwritten scribbles match a lengthy description published anonymously in 2013 that give a detailed account of Wasz's activities. The author of these anonymous notes says that Kardashian offered Wasz $1,000 to conduct surveillance on Nicole over the first weekend of January. Typically, to complete this "easy money" job, Wasz stole a Minolta 35mm camera. Wasz complained that Nicole's driving habits in her Ferrari left him "lost in her dust."

He managed to take photos of one male companion Nicole met, who he later identified as pro football star Marcus Allen.[21]

The next major event, according to the proffer, occurred on January 14, 1994, when Robert Kardashian asked William Wasz to meet him alone in his Encino home to offer Wasz a bigger assignment. At this second meeting, Kardashian offered Wasz $15,000 if he would kill Nicole with a 25-caliber bullet to the head. Robert Kardashian also told Wasz he was to steal Paula Barbieri's car and use it in the murder. The murder was to take place at the Rockingham, not at Nicole Simpson's home on Gretna Green.

The proffer continued to relay that on January 24, 1994, at approximately 10:00 a.m. Pacific Time, Kardashian called Wasz at his room at the Saharan Motel on Sunset Boulevard in Hollywood. Kardashian told Wasz to steal Barbieri's car from a parking garage in Beverly Hills between 3:00 and 4:00 p.m. while she was getting her hair done. After Wasz stole Barbieri's car, he drove to a mall in West Valley where he met Kardashian. While at the mall, Wasz took an envelope containing $7,500, which was to be partial payment for the killing.

Sorting Out the Backstory

What we learned is that when the police arrested Wasz, they found in Paula Barbieri's car in addition to Nicole Simpson's address book, a 9mm pistol, and a crack pipe. In the notebook, the police also found detailed notes that Wasz had made of Nicole's whereabouts hour-by-hour from the two days that Wasz was following her. In my opinion, Wasz was following Nicole not to find out who her male lovers were but where she was getting drugs.

Here is what I think happened—and this is strictly my opinion. O. J. Simpson had to pay Nicole's drug bills. In the notes published in

---

21　Administrator, "O. J. Simpson Case: Bill Wasz's Story," Conspiracy Research, ConspiracyResearch.proboards.com, October 13, 2013, https://conspiracyresearch .proboards.com/thread/11/simpson-case-bill-waszs-story.

2013, the anonymous tipster said Kardashian told Wasz that Nicole's drug habits were costing O. J. $35,000 a month. I believe that when O. J. went over to Nicole's home to get her address book, he was going to deal with that issue. If O. J. Simpson did not pay those bills, certain pictures would have surfaced—the photos Nicole had locked away in a safe deposit box show how severely O. J. beat her in their 1998 argument. I believe Nicole told her sister that if anything happens to her, Nicole's sister should put those pictures out there. At the murder trial, the prosecutors introduced photos of Nicole beaten and badly bruised as evidence O. J.'s jealous rages had a violent streak to them—a violent streak the prosecutors wanted the jury to believe could throw a switch in O. J.'s brain, inducing him to brutally butcher his unfaithful wife.

But I found that understanding all this is complex. The last person in the world that O. J. wanted hurt was Nicole. He still loved her. Besides, if those photographs of Nicole beaten and bruised up ever came out into the public, his life would be destroyed. When was the last time you had anybody with pictures of themselves beaten up hid away in a safe deposit box? Never. So, those photographs were Nicole's security. That no matter what Nicole Simpson wanted, O. J. was going to give it to her. And, if he didn't give it to her, his career would be over. Again, remember, O. J. didn't have any alimony or anything like that. He paid out on that and he didn't owe Nicole anything. O. J. had no debt with Nicole. He paid out when he got his divorce. So, the only money she could look forward to is the money she could get from those photographs. That's my opinion.

That Kardashian had Nicole's address book to give to Wasz indicates that O. J. and Kardashian may have been in together on the first assignment for Wasz: namely, to follow Nicole and take photos of her activities early in January 1994. Wasz was known to sell drugs to the Los Angeles club scene, and both Kardashian and O. J. may have been customers. But I don't believe O. J. was involved in the assignment to pay Wasz $15,000 to kill Nicole. What doesn't make any sense to me is why O. J. would tell Wasz to use the car of someone close to him to kill Nicole. What makes more sense, is that Kardashian told Wasz to steal Paula Barbieri's Toyota 4-Runner, knowing that vehicle traced back to O. J. This may have been part of Kardashian's calculation to frame O. J. for the murder. The proffer makes it clear the offer to kill Nicole Simpson for $15,000 was made by Robert Kardashian alone.

According to the proffer, O. J. Simpson and Paula Barbieri were at the first meeting Kardashian had with Wasz. That may simply have been an encounter at a Los Angeles club to buy drugs. But O. J. and Paula Barbieri were not at the second meeting Kardashian had with Wasz, or at any of the meetings subsequent to that when he allegedly solicited Wasz to murder Nicole, instructing him to use Barbieri's 4-Runner when he did so. The weird thing about Wasz's story is why did Robert Kardashian offer to help O. J. in the first place?

Imagine this: Kardashian says to O.J, "I'm mad at you over that little incident with my wife in the Jacuzzi. Now, you want me to help you get rid of drug dealers. No problem." But what if Kardashian also wanted to get rid of the drug dealers? What is clear is that after Wasz crashed the 4-Runner and got arrested, a second killer apparently was hired. You could see where things moved simple. William Wasz got into an accident and couldn't finish the job. So, they hired somebody new. But, if Nicole and Ron Goldman were murdered by a second hired killer, who hired the second killer? Could it have been Robert Kardashian alone? Remember: Wasz stated Robert Kardashian was the guy who alone hired him for the assignment the first time? By the time Kardashian offers Wasz $15,000 to kill Nicole, O. J. appears to have dropped from the scene. If a second killer was hired, was O. J. involved behind the scenes, just as he had been involved with Wasz at the beginning?

Remember when O. J. was caught, Robert Kardashian went out and inserted himself immediately into the case. Then, Kardashian had his license reinstated. It appeared he did that so he would have had attorney/client privilege and he wouldn't have to testify. So, that bothered me. I kept asking myself why Robert Kardashian would need his law license reinstated? Robert Kardashian hadn't practiced law in some twenty years. All of a sudden, Robert Kardashian needs to renew his law license. If you look at the trial, Robert Kardashian wasn't the lead attorney. So, I think the only reason he got his license back was to make sure he didn't have to testify at O. J.'s murder trial.

If Kardashian didn't have to testify, he wouldn't have to say, "We hired William Wasz." Given that Kardashian had his law license reinstated, O. J. couldn't say anything against Kardashian, and Kardashian couldn't say anything against O. J.

(VIDEO STARTS)

> **O. J.:** I stopped goin' to South Beach, nightclubs in South Beach in Miami. I couldn't go to South Beach. I used to go to South Beach, maybe once a month or somethin'. You can't go to the bathrooms in the club without somebody sayin', "Juice you want a hit?" or "Hey Juice you want this, hey Juice you want that?"
>
> **O. J. (continues):** You always get people handin' you something. Basically, it might be a line of coke or somethin' with a phone number, or something like that, right. I don't wanna get in a confrontation! I wanna take a leak an' get out of the bathroom. Take it, pretend you got it, go an' flush it, an' get outta the bathroom.
>
> **O. J. (continues):** It was just pervasive, this, people talkin', you take it and put it in your pocket. you drive home. Next day I wake up and I look over next to my bed. I got some business cards, a couple of phone numbers. I must have had two things I can only assume were ecstasy pills, another couple of things I can only assume were cocaine, and one little package of pot, right? All of 'em had them little phone numbers on them, right.?
>
> **O. J. (continues):** All I can say to myself was, if I got stopped by the cops drivin' home . . . and I told them I didn't know that was there? I didn't know that was in my pocket! Who's gonna believe that? That is ridiculous, right? Only way I can avoid it is I don't go to South Beach anymore!

(VIDEO OFF)

The William Wasz Story Is Quashed, by Everyone

The file I developed regarding William Wasz is one a lot of people don't want to talk about, even today. Even in 1998, the L.A. District

Attorney and the LAPD ignored Wasz's story. Finally, the Longo proffer got leaked to investigative reporter David M. Bresnahan. In 1998,
Bresnahan wrote a series of articles on the internet in an attempt
to force some law enforcement authority to take Wasz's story seriously. In May 1998, Bresnahan wrote that Robert Kardashian and
O. J. Simpson were reported to have had a shouting match following
a Bresnahan article charging that Kardashian paid a hit man to kill
Nicole Brown Simpson. "Apparently Kardashian blamed Simpson for
the information being made public, and Kardashian is now reported
to be 'very spooked,' according to the source in a recent interview,"
Bresnahan wrote.[22]

Yet, Bresnahan noted, the Los Angeles County District Attorney's
office had covered up the evidence that a conspiracy had taken place,
and, in spite of the recent publicity, that office is still not moving
forward with the investigation. Bresnahan concluded that the L.A.
District Attorney had never wanted to investigate Wasz to determine why he had Nicole Simpson's address book and why he stole
Paula Barbieri's Toyota 4-Runner. Bresnahan noted the story of Wasz
had come out very early after the murder of Simpson, but Wasz was
quickly discredited by both the defense and the prosecution. On
July 23, 1994, the *Los Angeles Times* picked up the *Orange County
Register* story about Wasz,[23] but Wasz's story never gained any trac-
tion, despite the evidence of the address book and the 4-Runner he
was involved with O. J. Simpson prior to the murders.

The L.A. District Attorney and the media were only interested
in evidence that advanced the racial Othello narrative that branded
O. J. as a football star who had advanced into professional football
fame because he was a thug, that his gang days growing up in San
Francisco had taught him he was meaner and tougher than anybody
else on the football field. The media ignored what I knew, namely,
that O. J. was pigeon-toed as a kid, so nearly crippled that his mother

22 David M. Bresnahan, "Still no interview for O. J. witness," *World Net Daily*, WND
.com, May 12, 1998, https://www.wnd.com/1998/05/3233/.

23 Ken Ellingwood, "Notebook Lands Attorney in Hot Seat Probe: Newport Beach
police say he may have misled them when he retrieved item found in truck stolen from
O. J. Simpson's girlfriend," *Los Angeles Times*, July 23, 1994.

fashioned for him crude metal braces in an attempt to cure the condition. What international soccer legends Maradona and Messi knew
was that pigeon-toed players are often the most successful on the
field. Those who have studied the issue have observed that pigeon-
toed athletes contact the ground with less energy dissipation and as
a result are able to apply greater propulsive force to the ground in a
shorter period of time.[24] But this doesn't fit into the narrative that
O. J. has a violent streak that was triggered by his jealous rage over
Nicole's sexual excesses after they split.

O. J. didn't look at me any different from how I looked at him. We
both grew up in the same situation. I grew up a cripple, in the Scottish
Rites Children's' Hospital. I had a fake hip put in when I was really
young. O. J. grew up a cripple. He had rickets. His mom actually had
to build leg braces out of metal for him to straighten his legs out. She
did that on her own. Both our fathers left us at a really young age to
fend for ourselves. So, we had a lot of synergies going into working
together. We grew up in a bad time. I grew up in the heart of Alabama
in the middle of the KKK riots. He grew up in the same situation.

O. J. told me that when he would go to different sporting events
when he was in school, they had to pull the curtains on the trains
because he wasn't allowed to ride in them. So, we both grew up in different bad times, maybe on different sides, but the same. I wasn't part
of the KKK—I never believed in those people—so I took the brunt of
that because if you're not on their side, you're against them. He grew
up without being able to show his face. He couldn't eat or drink in
certain restaurants. The race thing was there—it's always been there.
He just never really saw it. He never really looked at people as their
color. He started looking at color after Nicole's death and he found
out that color really did matter. He was on trial in Las Vegas and he
knew. He was going to go on trial in front of the jury and he called
me, and he said, "Norm, for the first time in my life, I feel like a black
man in the 1940s with an all-white justice system. They're going to
lynch me." He knew it because the day before, when the jury saw him

---

24 Mike Young, "Why are so many gifted athletes pigeon-toed?" EliteTrack.com,
May 7, 2008, https://elitetrack.com/blogs-details-3820/.

leaving the room, they snickered at him. I told him he should have used the race card, but O. J. Simpson did not want to use the race card.

From the evidence, we can conclude that the LAPD joined with the Los Angeles County District Attorney to put their blinders on, blocking out any and all evidence that supported other theories regarding who killed Nicole. The media was happy to latch onto a compelling racial/sex narrative the corporations running the media knew would sell—sensationalism always sells big and racially-charged stories of sexual abuse sell sensationally. Evidence that Kardashian hated O. J. for destroying his marriage with Kris, or that he was triggered when he saw the published vacation pictures showing he was not there in the union of happy families—that pictures of Kris with her new husband, Bruce Jenner, joined by all four of Robert Kardashian's children, together with a smiling O. J. and Nicole and their children which may have been too much for Robert Kardashian to bear. The O. J. Simpson murder trial became about punishing the angry black man, not about the truth, not about getting to the bottom of it and figuring out who really killed Nicole Brown Simpson and Ron Goldman. That's why I went on my quest. I wanted to know what really happened that grim night in Brentwood, California.

But the factual record is very clear that nobody cared to hear what William Wasz had to say, despite the fact he had some very important clues to offer. After serving ten years of his twenty-year prison sentence, Wasz was released. He worked for a brief time in Beverly Hills before his attorney Lawrence Longo found his body in his West Los Angeles apartment under suspicious circumstances on March 16, 2005. The coroner's investigator, Kelli Blanchard, estimated that Wasz had been dead for three days when his body was found. West Los Angeles Homicide detectives never investigated his death, nor was his death ever reported in the media. His death was caused by shotgun wounds.[25] No law enforcement authority ever bothered to take Longo's proffer seriously.

---

25 "Who Killed William Benson Wasz?" posted on Wikipedia by Luke Ford, November 27, 2007.

Wasz, a Big-Time Loser

In the final analysis, William Wasz was a classic low-life loser. He had a history of drug addiction and drug dealing. He was a petty theft who had a long rap sheet with law enforcement and a history of incarceration.

It looks like after Kardashian gave him the last $7,500 to kill Nicole, Wasz blew the money—probably on drugs—and went on a crime spree—probably in need of more cash.

On January 31, 1994, the day Wasz crashed Pauli Barbieri's 4-Runner, fled, was shot by police in the leg, and arrested, he had spent Kardashian's money largely on drugs and went on a crime spree. At noon that day he pulled an armed robbery of a Blockbuster video store and came away with $100 in cash and two videos: *Goodfellas* and *Scarface*—both mob glorification movies. It appears Wasz watched both movies, then at 5:10 p.m., he committed armed robbery on a Music Plus store, netting $200 in cash and some sound equipment. At 8:00 p.m., Wasz committed his third armed robbery, this time on Pizza Hut. He got another $100 in cash, but no pizza. After leaving Pizza Hut, Wasz drove two miles to Beach Liquor, where he stole $400 and a 12-pack of beer (brand unknown). Wasz committed all four of his armed robberies that day in Orange County, resulting in an All Points Bulletin issued by police for the Toyota 4-Runner.

At 9:25 p.m., a Newport Beach patrol car spotted the 4-Runner and attempted to stop Wasz. He accelerated to escape, thinking he could get away by running on the wrong side of the road. He collided with a 1989 Pontiac but continued driving the wrong way down the West Coast Highway for a quarter of a mile, where he collided with a 1993 Infinity. At this point he decided to take off by foot but evidently ended up either shooting himself in the leg, or more likely shot by the police. The charges against Wasz multiplied when the Newport Beach Police Department realized Wasz was driving a stolen vehicle. Inside the truck, the police found a handgun, drug paraphernalia, the sound equipment stolen from Music Plus, and $500 in cash. When Paula Barbieri recovered her stolen vehicle, she found Wasz had totaled the front end. The truck was filled with hypodermic needles, pornographic magazines, and bullet holes (probably resulting from the police chase). Also found were some 8 x 10 black-and-white photos Wasz, an out-of-work "actor," had to promote his make-believe acting career.

It also turned out that in January 1994, Paula Barbieri and O. J. Simpson were not a couple. Paula and O. J. broke up between May 1993 and May 1994. In January 1994, O. J. was attempting to reconcile with Nicole—explaining the vacation photographs early in 1994 when O. J. and Nicole joined Kris and Bruce Jenner and their two families of children, without Robert Kardashian being invited. In May 1994, O. J. and Paula resumed their romantic relationship, after O. J.'s attempt to reconcile with Nicole had failed. The next month, on June 12, 1994, Nicole Simpson was murdered.[26]

How Exactly Does William Wasz Fit into the Puzzle?

In prison and frustrated that nobody was taking the Longo proffer and his story seriously, Wasz attempted to write several books that would tell the world about his experience with Robert Kardashian hiring him as a hit man to kill Nicole. To this day, Wasz has been discredited as "debunked" nonsense, the attempt of a two-bit drug addict and petty theft to write himself into the sensational O. J. Simpson story. Wasz did not live to see any of his books in print.

When you deal with the Kardashians, they have a billion dollars after their reality television success, and everything goes away— except the truth. But I can't help asking what a legitimate attorney like Lawrence Longo would be doing by writing a proffer for Wasz to an attorney in the Los Angeles District Attorney's office without first checking out for himself whether Wasz's story was true? Longo's proffer makes clear that he is writing at the request of attorney Curtis Hazell, who worked in that DA's office. Clearly, in their initial conversations, Longo had managed to capture Hazell's interest in learning more about what Wasz had to say.

But the facts remain the facts.

---

26 This paragraph and the preceding two paragraphs are drawn from this source: Brian Hess, "What's Wasz Got to Do With It?" OJSimpson.co, May 3, 2018, https ://ojsimpson.co/fact-check-bill-wasz-oj-simpson/.

Robert Kardashian, O. J. Simpson, and Paula Barbieri first met William Wasz at the fashionable Roxbury Club on December 26, 1993, during the time O. J. Simpson was trying to reconcile with Nicole. Given the setting in which they met, the most likely assumption is that Kardashian, O. J., and Paula hooked up with Wasz to buy drugs from him. It appears a bouncer at the Roxbury Club introduced Wasz to Kardashian because the young women they were with that night wanted cocaine. Wasz was known in the Los Angeles club scene to have a thriving cocaine business. Evidently, Kardashian gave Wasz his phone number, and subsequently the allegations were both Robert Kardashian and O. J. bought cocaine from Wasz. Kardashian himself was evidently not a drug user, but Kardashian evidently bought drugs for various business clients who Wasz claimed were involved in organized crime activities that included money laundering, prostitution, pornography, sports betting and point shaving.

Wasz evidently further claimed that he, Robert Kardashian, and O. J. were involved in what turned out to be a drug business for several months, with Wasz buying the cocaine for $60 to $70 and sold to Kardashian and O. J. for their personal use and the use of their clients/friends/business associates. Wasz reportedly claimed he met Kardashian at a McDonald's restaurant on Ventura in Encino, not far from Kardashian's home there. Wasz also claimed O. J., and sometimes Nicole making purchases for herself and O. J., would meet Wasz outside O. J.'s Rockingham home.[27]

If Wasz was lying, what was he doing with Nicole Simpson's address book, driving around in a Toyota 4-Runner that had been stolen from Paula Barbieri? O. J. got possession of Nicole's address book/notebook during the 911 call on October 25, 1993. By New Year's 1994, when Robert Kardashian offered Wasz $1,000 to conduct surveillance on Nicole, Kardashian had possession of the address book. O. J. had to have given the address book to Kardashian and my guess is that Kardashian told O. J. that he needed the address book because he was going to give it to Wasz. This makes credible Wasz's story he was paid

---

27 Administrator, "O. J. Simpson Case: Bill Wasz's Story," *Conspiracy Research*, op.cit.

$7,500 to kill Nicole, something Wasz did not accomplish because he blew Kardashian's money—most likely on drugs—and went on a crime spree before being arrested on January 31, 1994.

Wasz's story also had to be suppressed because it made both Robert Kardashian and O. J. look bad. If the prosecutors pushed Wasz's story, then O. J. didn't kill Nicole because maybe he (and Kardashian) hired someone to kill her. That would mess up the prosecutors' story that O. J. went into a jealous rage and killed both Nicole and Ron Goldman. I think there may have been an agreement between the prosecutors and Johnnie Cochran to suppress Wasz's story. With Robert Kardashian now a lawyer on O. J. Simpson's Dream Team, the prosecutors and defense attorneys may just have agreed that William Wasz would not be brought into the O. J. murder trial. There was no blood from either Nicole or Ron Goldman ever tied to O. J.'s person, or his shoes, or anything. So, if William Wasz was excluded from O. J.'s murder trial, there was nothing to tie O. J. to the murders.

But to me, assuming William Wasz's story is true, this is the main point of the Wasz story: With Wasz getting himself arrested and thrown in prison, Robert Kardashian (and maybe Kardashian together with O. J.) was left without a hit man to finish the job. What makes sense next is that Kardashian (and possibly O. J.) did not give up the idea of killing Nicole after Wasz was imprisoned. What if Kardashian (and possibly O. J.) needed to find another hit man?

CHAPTER 6

Glen Rogers, Serial Killer
(a.k.a. James Peters)

———

N ow, we move over to the next subject, Mr. James Edward Peters. This has baffled people for a long time because all the relevant receipts in the case are under the name Mr. James Peters.

For instance, we have here two receipts from California in 1994 under the name James Peters:

- One receipt acknowledges that $405.00 was paid by James Peters on April 1, 1994, to rent until April 30, 1994, apartment #2 at 11448 Cumpston Street in North Hollywood, a few blocks away from Nicole's home.
- The second receipt acknowledges that on July 1, 1994, James Peters paid $425.00 to rent the same apartment until July 31, 1994.

These receipts document that James Peters lived at 11448 Cumpston Street, Apartment 2, in April 1994, two months before Nicole was murdered and in July 1994, the month after Nicole was murdered.

But the most important theory was that Glen Edward Rogers was operating in California under an alias, calling himself James Edward Peters.

We had to unravel this mystery to get to the heart of the case. It took me nearly twenty years, but I finally got to the bottom of this.

Let me explain how I did it and what I found to be the truth, despite how strange the truth turned out to be . . .

Clue #1: James Peters was in California in June 1994

I began by searching out documentary evidence of who James Peters was and I had some help from others looking into this who were willing to share with me the documents they found.

We found a letter from the William J. Galvin Custom Painting Co., located in Canoga Park, California—a neighborhood located northwest of Los Angeles between Thousand Oaks and Burbank, dated June 15, 1994, three days after Nicole was murdered that reads as follows:

> "This letter is to inform you that on June 14, 1994, Mr. James Peters was absent from work, due to the fact that some of the ceiling in his apartment fell on him and he was unable to work that day. There-fore, losing wages for that day.
>
> "Any questions please contact Bill Galvin."

At the bottom of the letter was the following notation in handwriting: 8.75 hr. x 8 = TOTAL $70.00. That notation appears to document that James Peters lost 8.75 hours work on Tuesday, June 14, 1994, two days after Nicole was killed, on Sunday, June 12, 1994.

What this letter proved was that James Peters did work in the Los Angeles area as a custom painter in June 1994. It also proves that an injury, here assumed to be a falling ceiling in what would appear to be Apartment 2 at 11448 Cumpston Street, occurring most probably on Monday, June 13, 1994, injured Mr. Peters, causing him to lose that day's work and pay.

Clue #2: Mark Peters was killed in Ohio in 1993

We also found proof-positive documentation that a Mr. Mark Peters had been murdered after he disappeared in 1993, and that his body had been found by police in January 1994. As we investigated how

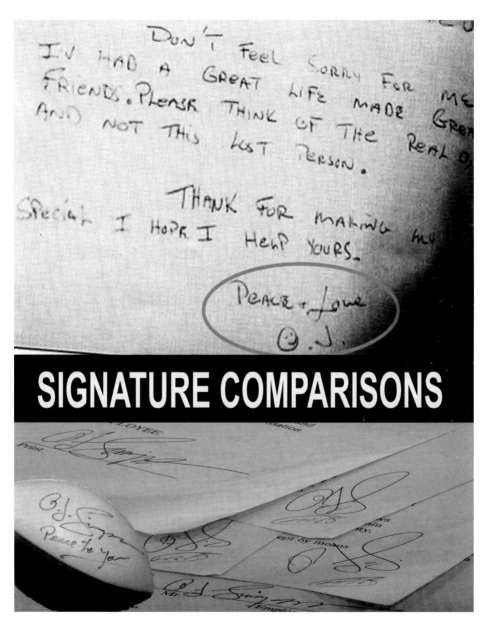

Exhibit 1: O. J.'s Forged Signature on "Suicide Note" Compared to O. J.'s
Autograph Signatures

LAW OFFICES OF LAWRENCE M. LONGO

7871 W. Manchester Ave.
Suite E
Playa del Rey, CA 90293
(310) 457-3911
Fax: (310) 457-0146

March 16, 1998
Mr. Curtis A. Hazell
District Attorney Office
210 West Temple Street
Los Angeles, Ca 90012

Re: Attorney Proffer of William Benson Wasz

Dear Curtis:

Pursuant to your request I would like to make an attorney proffer for your consideration. It is my understanding based upon my conversation with you that you might be interested in information my client could provide in regards to a solicitation to commit murder of Nicole Brown Simpson by Robert Kardashian.

I have spoken to my client and I believe that he would cooperate with the District Attorneys Office in connection with this investigation.

In the fall of 1993, Bill Wasz came into contact with Paula Barbieri, Robert Kardashian and O.J. Simpson. The contact with these individuals was made at the Roxbury [Club] in West Hollywood.

Just before the New Year, Robert Kardashian met with Wasz in his home in Encino and offered him an assignment. The purpose was to follow Nicole and take pictures of her with any man whom she might meet with romantically. The surveillance of Nicole took place on January 6th and 7th, 1994. This information was documented in a Notebook – the notebook is currently in the custody of the LAPD. The three phone numbers in the book belong to O.J., Kardashian and Barbieri.

On about January 14 Bill Wasz met Robert Kardashian again in his Encino home. At this meeting Kardashian offered Wasz $15,000 if he would kill Nicole with a 25 caliber bullet to the head.

Robert Kardashian also told Wasz he was to steal Paula Barbieri's car and use it during the murder. The murder was to take place at the Rockingham and not at Nicole Simpson's home on Gretna Green.

On January 24 at approximately 10am, Kardashian called Wasz at his room at the Saharan Motel on Sunset Blvd. in Hollywood. Kardashian told Wasz to steal Barbieri's car from a parking garage in Beverly Hills between 3 and 4 o'clock while she was having her hair done.

After Wasz stole Barbieri's car he drove to a mall in West Valley where he met Kardashian.

While at the mall Wasz took an envelope containing $7,500, which was to be partial payment for the killing.

If you desire to interview my client in regards to the above information please contact me as soon as possible.

If you have further questions, please do not hesitate to call me.

Very truly yours,

LAW OFFICES OF LAWRENCE M. LONGO

Exhibit 2: William Wasz Proffer Letter, Professing Innocence

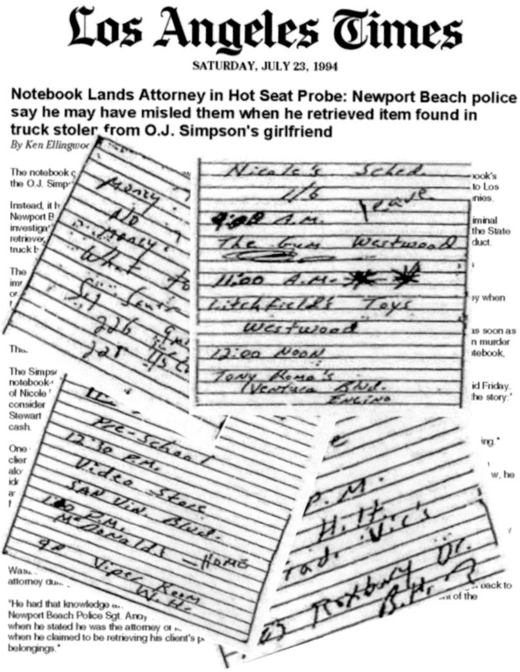

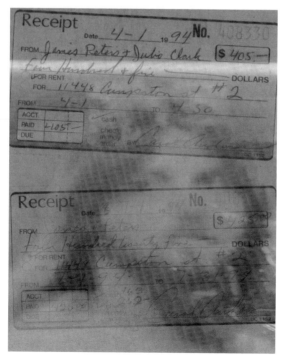

Los Angeles Times

SATURDAY, JULY 23, 1994

Notebook Lands Attorney in Hot Seat Probe: Newport Beach police say he may have misled them when he retrieved item found in truck stolen from O.J. Simpson's girlfriend

By Ken Ellingwood

Exhibit 3: William Wasz Notebook Entries Tracking Nicole

Exhibit 4: Glen Rogers (aka James Peters) rent receipts

Exhibit 5: Newspaper Report of Mark Peters murder

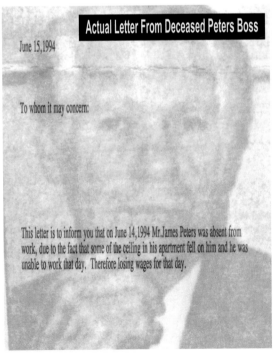

Exhibit 6: Letter Documenting Glen Rogers's (aka James Peters) Missed Work

5-13-2013

Dear Mr. Pardo

hi my name is Glen Rogers, i am at this time on death Raw in florida.

please tell OJS, that im very sorry for the death of his wife, i do hope his court hearing gets a ruling in his favor, seems to me hes being punished not for the crime convicted of. But the crime they think he got away with, that he didn't even do, But ttak our Justice system, i would like to speak to you & your lawyer, about certain things relative to your case and mine here. i understand craig Brandt here in florida may be able to help, i am out of gas on appeal, only because of lawyers getting me time Bared, with a real lawyer i can get my full appeal heard, i do beleave you need to hear me out, you wont have to take my word, a full taped statement in your case was made in 1995, i would need a court order to releau it to you. also with lawyer present i made a phone plea deal with a CA, D,A, now has been removed from office scense that day, i hope to be working with you soon, befor they get rid of me,

thank you for your help.

Glen Rogers #124400

Exhibit 7: Glen Rogers's First Letter from Prison to Norm Pardo

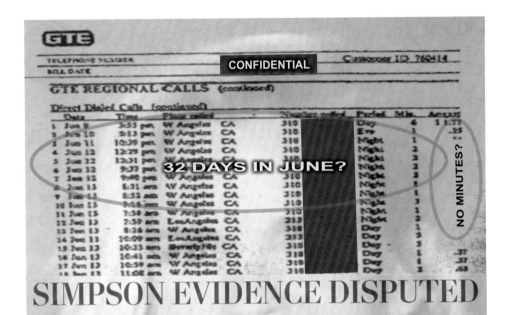

SIMPSON EVIDENCE DISPUTED

By **Christine Spolar**
June 28, 1994

LOS ANGELES, JUNE 27 -- A coroner's report today provided information that O.J. Simpson's attorneys said could help buttress the former football superstar's alibi for the night his ex-wife and a male friend were killed. But Nicole Brown Simpson's father questioned the accuracy of the coroner's report.

The report states that Nicole Simpson was "last known to be alive at about 2300 hours {11 p.m.} speaking to her mother on the telephone."

https://www.washingtonpost.com/archive/politics/1994/06/28/simpson evidence

Exhibit 8: Nicole Brown Simpson's Altered Phone Records from the Night of Her Murder

Facsimile Transmission

Los Angeles County Sheriff's Department

From: Name: Larry Bryant
            Fax Number: 323 415 3519
            Voice Phone: 562 484 4001

To:

PRIVATE

FAX NOTES:

* Sgt. Larry Bryant called ▮▮▮▮▮▮▮ To inform
  ▮▮▮▮▮ that ▮▮▮ Request for Ron Goldman's
  arrest photographs were denied.

* Bryant acknowledged That each arrest
  under case file 91C00362, People v. Ronald Lyle
  D.O.B. 7/02/68   Goldman
  has separate arrest photograph, believed To be
                                            four.
* Bryant stated That Goldman's arrest
  Photos protected from public access by Cal. law.

* Bryant would not reduce his remarks To writing
  These Notes were made by ▮▮▮▮▮▮ after
  receiving Sgt. Bryant's call.

Exhibit 9: Ron Goldman's LAPD-Sealed Arrest Records

LIFE IS A TRIAL FOR GOLDMAN MOM

Turns out that one member of Ron Goldman's family had some experience with the criminal-justice system *before* the O.J. case: **Patti Goldman**, Fred Goldman's current wife and Ron's stepmother, was previously married to the notorious Marvin Glass, who died last week. Once a high-flying Chicago lawyer, Glass was accused in the mid-eighties of being in cahoots with his drug-dealer clients, acting as a middleman for a $100-million marijuana-and-cocaine-smuggling ring and then racking up huge legal fees when his cronies got busted. Charged with racketeering in Chicago, he was prosecuted by novelist-cum-lawyer **Scott Turow**, who denounced Glass in 1986 as a "one-man crime wave" and called a witness who testified that Glass paid him $2,500 to shoot an ex-partner. Hit by a truck on a Florida highway the year before, Glass was confined to a wheelchair throughout the proceedings, which Patti attended loyally every day, a spooky precursor of her role in the O.J. trials a decade later. Glass, who evidently contracted HIV while recovering from his Florida accident, died of pneumonia in Chicago on May 16. He had three children with Patti, who divorced him after the trial and married Fred.

Exhibit 10: Newspapers Document Goldman Family Ties to Marvin Glass, Organized Crime in the U.S., and the Colombian Drug Cartels

Chicago Tribune

Lawyer Charged In Theft From Relative

May 07, 1985 By Bonita Brodt and Douglas Frantz.

Chicago lawyer Marvin Jay Glass has been arrested and charged with felony theft after $8,000 allegedly was stolen from his vacationing mother-in-law's safe deposit box, police said Monday.

His arrest comes amid a wide-ranging federal investigation into his financial affairs and spending habits. Glass is a former Cook County state's attorney whose lucrative legal career has been shadowed by scrapes with the law.

Glass was arrested Thursday morning after he walked out of the Deerbrook State Bank in Deerfield, according to Tom Sheahan, a detective with the Deerfield Police Department.
In a briefcase that Glass had carried into the vault with him, police recovered $8,000 believed to have been taken from his mother-in-law's safe deposit box, Sheahan said.

Police contacted Glass' **mother-in-law, Elaine Goldman,** vacationing in Palm Springs, Calif.

``She said that she did not give him permission, that he had no right to go into the box,'' Sheahan said.

Exhibit 11: Marvin Glass Arrested After Allegedly Stealing $8,000 from the Bank Safe Deposit Account of his Mother-in-Law, Elaine Goldman

1   GIL GARCETTI
2   DISTRICT ATTORNEY
     Patrick Dixon
3   Deputy District Attorney
     State Bar No. 068130
4   Major Crimes Division
     210 West Temple Street
5   Los Angeles, California   90012
     (213) 974-3920
6
     Attorneys for Plaintiff
7

COUNTY OF
LOS ANGELES

1997 NOV 10 PM 2: 11

STATE SERVICE
COMMISSION

FILED

NOV 10 1997

JOHN A. CLARKE

S. Kadohata

BY S. KADOHATA, DEPUTY

8   SUPERIOR COURT OF THE STATE OF CALIFORNIA

9   FOR THE COUNTY OF LOS ANGELES

10

11	PEOPLE OF THE STATE OF CALIFORNIA,	)	NO. BA 109525
12	Plaintiff,	)	ORDER SEALING
13	vs.	)	RECORDS PURSUANT TO CLAIM OF
14		)	OFFICIAL INFORMATION
15	GLEN ROGERS,	)	PRIVILEGE, EVIDENCE CODE
16	Defendant.	)	SECTION 1040

17

18   GOOD CAUSE HAVING BEEN SHOWN, IT IS HEREBY

19   ORDERED THAT:

20   All records In the matter of Lea P. D'Agostino, case

21   number 97-222, now before the Civil Service Commission of Los

22   Angeles County, are sealed pursuant to the District Attorney's

23   claim of Official Information Privilege in the above entitled

24   matter. Specifically, the District Attorney's claim of official

25   privilege, pursuant to Evidence Code section 1040, is sustained

26   as to all records, papers and documents filed or to be filed or

27   created by the Commission during its proceedings, including, but

28   not limited to, all sound recordings and/or transcripts of

1   proceeding conducted by the Commission in case number 97-222.

2   Each of these records is hereby ordered sealed and not disclosed

3   to the public or to anyone unless authorized by the District

4   Attorney, until further order of this Court.

5   Order of the Court.

6   IT IS SO ORDERED.

7

8   DATED: NOV 10, 1997

9

10   JOHN H. REID
                 JUDGE OF THE SUPERIOR COURT

11

12

13

14

15

Exhibit 12: L.A. District Attorney Gil Garcetti Seals Glen Rogers Criminal Records

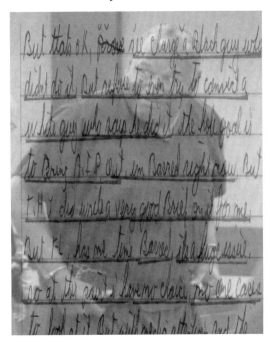

2-14-2013

Glen Edward Rogers now on florida
Row, make the following statement: —
simpson and myself did not contract
one another to do anything to his wife. —

Glen Edward Rogers

❋ 124400

U.C.I. death Row.

Exhibit 13: Glen Rogers Letter from Prison to Investigators, Claiming He Did Not Contract with O. J. to Kill Nicole

But thats ok i'll charge a black guy who
didn't do it. but refuse to even try to convict a
white guy who says he did it. the hole goal is
to Bring R.I.P out. im Barred right now. But
R.H. did write a very good Brief out for me.
But R.H. has no time Barred, its a huge issue.
so at this point i have no choice, no one cares
to look at it. But with media attention, and the

Exhibit 14: Glen Rogers Letter Claiming the LAPD Framed a "Black Guy" (O. J.) as Nicole's killer, But Let Go the "White Guy" Who Actually Committed the Crime (Namely Himself)

Exhibit 15: First Bloody Glove Found Near Ron Goldman's Body

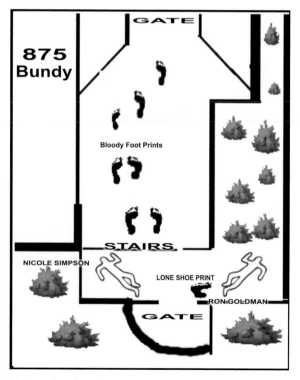

Exhibit 16: Bloody Footprints Found at 875 Bundy

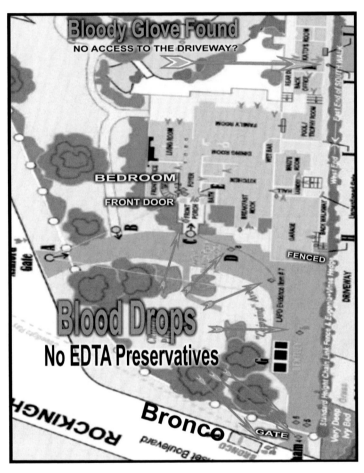

Exhibit 17: Blood Drops at O. J.'s Mansion; Second Bloody Glove Found

Lopez: "El Bronco' at Simpson's house around time of murders

LOS ANGELES (AP) - Speaking Spanish before a video camera and an empty jury box, a maid who lived next door to O.J. Simpson offered crucial alibi testimony Monday. She said she saw his white Bronco parked outside his estate at the hour prosecutors contend he was two miles away killing his ex-wife and her friend.

Rosa Lopez took the stand after two days of legal wrangling that intensified over a Lopez statement that prosecutors contend the defense purposely hid. Infuriated prosecutors say the report on the undisclosed interview has Lopez making no mention of the Bronco.

Under questioning by defense attorney Johnnie Cochran Jr., Lopez gave a meticulously detailed scenario of her activities the night of June 12.

Her employers were in Europe, she said, and her main task was to walk their golden retriever periodically. She took the dog out about 8:15, she said, and saw a white Bronco parked in the street "a little bit crooked."

About 9 p.m., she said she saw a black car, apparently Simpson's Bentley, leave his estate next door and head toward Sunset Boulevard with a blond-haired person in the passenger seat.

Simpson's houseguest Brian "Kato" Kaelin has said he accompanied Simpson to McDonald's at about that time.

About 9:30, Lopez said she heard footsteps coming from Simpson's property and became frightened. She said she "ducked down" in her bedroom but a short time later heard Simpson's voice.

"I felt safer when I felt that he came back," she said through an interpreter.

When she took the dog out just after 10 p.m., she said the Bronco was still parked in the same position.

Lopez said she wasn't wearing a watch but checked a clock each time she left her room. Prosecutors were expected to seize upon that point along with the fact that Lopez was unable to see a TV screen in the courtroom without borrowing eye glasses from her attorney.

Prosecutors contend Simpson drove the Bronco to Nicole Brown Simpson's home, where he allegedly killed her and her friend Ron Goldman about 10:15. With no witnesses to the fatal slashings, they have framed the time of murder by the howl of Ms. Simpson's white Akita.

Later that evening, about 11 p.m., Lopez heard a voice she recognized as Simpson's, she said. Testimony at his preliminary hearing indicated Simpson was in his driveway about that time, waiting as a driver loaded bags into a limousine for a trip to the airport.

An hour later, Lopez testified, she heard voices coming from Simpson's house and the barking of Simpson's dog, a black Akita. By then, Simpson had already left for Chicago.

Lopez said she saw no one because she was afraid to look. But the dog, which she recognized as Simpson's dog, was noisy for a long time.

"It barked and it cried, sir," she said.

Lopez, who on Friday appeared tired, looked refreshed. Friday's warmup suit was replaced by a deep blue dress with a beaded collar, dark stockings and high heels. The Salingers, the Brentwood couple she worked for, were in court for part of the day.

The morning after the murders, Lopez testified, she was awakened about 8 a.m. by the gardener's leaf blower. Later, she answered the doorbell and found a man identifying himself as Detective Mark Fuhrman, she said.

Lopez testified she told Fuhrman about the voices. She said he didn't take notes and no police came to follow up as he had promised.

"I'm still waiting for them," she said.

Exhibit 18: Eyewitness Testimony of Housekeeper Rosa Lopez on Seeing O. J.'s Bronco Parked Outside His Mansion

TESTIMONY OF MR. BODZIAK

MR. GOLDBERG: Sir, what is your occupation and assignment?

MR. BODZIAK: I'm a special agent of the Federal Bureau of Investigation. I'm currently assigned in the FBI laboratory as an examiner of questioned documents, footwear and tire tread evidence.

*****

MR. GOLDBERG: And starting with the Bronco carpet, did you have occasion to see the Bronco carpet, LAPD item no. 33 for identification?

MR. BODZIAK: Yes, I did.

MR. GOLDBERG: And where was it that you saw that?

MR. BODZIAK: I saw that at the Los Angeles Police Department laboratory.

MR. GOLDBERG: On what date?

MR. BODZIAK: I believe it was September 1st, 1994.

MR. GOLDBERG: Was anyone present when you saw it?

MR. BODZIAK: Yes. Present initially were Greg Matheson of the Los Angeles Police Department. There was two representatives from my laboratory to assist in the photography. Do you want the names of everyone?

MR. GOLDBERG: No, that is okay.

MR. BODZIAK: Okay. There were two representatives of the Defense that were present and there were two other observers from the Los Angeles Police Department laboratory who stood in the background just to observe the procedure.

MR. GOLDBERG: And did you see Mr. Matheson take any cuttings or samples from that item in your presence?

MR. BODZIAK: Yes, I did.

*****

MR. GOLDBERG: [Are the shoe prints on the Bronco carpet consistent with the Bruno Magli Silga soles?]

MR. BODZIAK: No. I think that these--these in here, (Indicating), probably show it as well as any, and actually there is--there isn't enough clarity throughout this whole thing to really point to it and say positively that is what it represents, but rather you are seeing a change of direction and that is what you would expect if there was some blood here and the carpet tuffed up. But there is also the phenomena of when you get into a Bronco that is up rather high and you step up into it with your shoe, there is going to be some movement in getting into a vehicle, and because of the thick nature of this carpeting, I wouldn't expect to see, necessarily, a clear rendition of--at that point of the shoe.

MR. GOLDBERG: Okay.

MR. BODZIAK: So I couldn't eliminate and I couldn't positively associate it with the Silga sole.

*****

Exhibit 19: Testimony of FBI Special Agent William Bodziak that Bloody Footprints Were Not O. J. Simpson's Bruno Magli Shoes

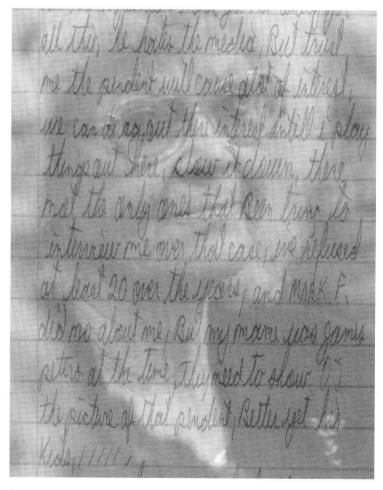

all this, He hates the media, But trust me the pendent will cause alot of interest, we can drag out there interest untill i play things out here, slow it down, there not the only ones that Been tring to interview me over that case, ive refused at least 20 over the years, and MICK F. did me about me, But my mom was James peters at the time, They need to show O.J the picture of that pendent, Better yet his kids, / / / / ,

Exhibit 20: Mother of Glen Rogers Photographed Wearing Nicole Brown Simpson's Angel Pin; Glen Rogers Letter on the Angel Pin's Importance as Evidence He Murdered Nicole

```
 1  GIL GARCETTI
    District Attorney of Los Angeles County
 2  BY: WILLIAM W. HODGMAN,
    Deputy District Attorney
 3  State Bar No.: 81916
    18000 Criminal Courts Building
 4  210 West Temple Street, Room 18-205
    Los Angeles, California 90012
 5  (213) 974-3881

 6  Attorney(s) for Plaintiff

 7

 8              SUPERIOR COURT OF THE STATE OF CALIFORNIA

 9                 FOR THE COUNTY OF LOS ANGELES

10
    PEOPLE OF THE STATE OF CALIFORNIA,    )    CASE NO.:  BA097211
11                                        )
                        Plaintiff,        )    APPLICATION, DECLARATION
12                                        )    AND ORDER FOR PERMANENT
                    v.                    )    RELEASE OF EXHIBITS IN
13                                        )    CUSTODY OF SUPERIOR COURT
    ORENTHAL JAMES SIMPSON                )
14  a k a  O.J. SIMPSON,      •           )    DEPARTMENT 100
                                          )
15                      Defendant.        )
                                          )
16

17          TO:  COURT EXHIBIT CUSTODIANS OF THE SUPERIOR COURT.

18          GOOD CAUSE HAVING BEEN FOUND, IT IS HEREBY ORDERED that all

19  prosecution exhibits in your custody for the above-entitled case be permanently

20  released to the Los Angeles County District Attorney's Office through Deputy

21  District Attorney William W. Hodgman and his agents or designates.

22  DATED:  4-24-98

23                                             THE HONORABLE JOHN H. REID
24                                             Judge of the Superior Court
25

26

27
```

Exhibit 21: L.A. District Attorney Gil Garcetti Seals O. J. Trial Records

Mark Peters was murdered, we found the culprit turned out to be a famous serial criminal, Glen Edward Rogers, who is now in prison on death row awaiting execution.

Our investigation became serious when we uncovered a newspaper article published in the *Journal-News* in Hamilton, Ohio, a small town north of Cincinnati, on December 7, 1993.[28] The article stated that Mr. Peters, seventy-two years old, was a longtime resident of Hamilton, Ohio, who had served in World War II and was discharged in 1945. Mark Peters had been missing ever since October 22, 1993.

[The actual names in this section below have been altered]

But the son of the deceased, Mark Peters, insisted that his father disappeared in August 1993, a month or two after the elder Peters, a retired electrician, felt sorry for Glen Rogers and took him into his home as a favor to Glen's mother, a friend of Mark Peters. "Dad was trying to help him out and find a job," his son said. "Dad didn't realize the guy was like that." Glen Rogers never did get a job, but he helped himself to Mark Peter's beer and cigarettes. His son said his father never said much about his "roommate," but he figured Mark got fed up with Glen and was about to throw him out shortly before his father disappeared. "He told me he wanted me to come home for some reason or another," his son said. "He wouldn't tell me why. I never saw him again."[29]

Police find Body of Mark Peters

On January 10, 1994, police had found a body presumed to be that of Mark Peters that the police reported as tied to a chair and murdered in a cabin of the Rogers family in Lee County, Kentucky, owned by Glen Rogers. But for some reason, reports of Mark Peter's murder did not begin making the newspapers again until 1996.

On January 26, 1996, the newspapers began picking up an Associated Press report that Kentucky Governor Paul Paton had signed an order to extradite suspected serial killer Glen Edward Rogers

---

28 John Niehaus, "Daughter frets: Where's my Dad?" *Journal-News*, Hamilton, Ohio, December 7, 1993.

29 Associated Press, "Police in Rogers Case Converge on Kentucky," *Los Angeles Times*, Thursday, Valley Edition, November 16, 1995.

to Florida.[30] In return, Florida Governor Lawton Chiles agreed to let
other states try Rogers for murder if he managed to escape a death
penalty in Florida. These reports were among the first to note that
Rogers was also suspected of murdering his former roommate, Mark
Peters, who was found in January 1994 in the Rogers family cabin in
Lee County, Kentucky. But the case for which Glen Rogers was being
extradited involved the murder in Florida of a woman, not the murder of Mark Peters in Hamilton, Ohio.

Rogers had been arrested on November 13, 1995 by Kentucky
State Police and was charged with wanton endangerment and criminal mischief after the police chase. At the time he was being extradited to Florida, in late January 1996, Rogers had not yet been charged
with the murder of Mark Peters. Florida had charged Rogers with the
stabbing death of Tina Marie Cribbs in Florida in a motel bathtub in
early November 1995. When Kentucky State Police arrested Rogers,
he was driving a car owned by Cribbs. Newspapers in January 1996,
keying off Associated Press bulletins, began characterizing Rogers as
"a drifter who crisscrossed the country," employed here as a carnival
worker, and there as a printer's assistant, or a painter, committing
murders wherever he went.[31]

Then on March 13, 1996, the Associated Press finally began turning their attention more seriously to the Mark Peters murder, report-
ing that two bone fragments had been discovered at the Rogers family
farm in Kentucky that was owned by suspected cross-country serial
killer Glen Rogers.[32] The bone fragments were discovered near the
spot in the cabin where police found the decomposed body of Rogers's
former roommate, Mark Peters, seventy-three years old, of Hamilton,
Ohio. Kentucky National Guard, along with Kentucky State Police
and the FBI, began combing the forty-acre Lee County farm following the finding of the bone fragments. The AP also reported that

30 "Kentucky to Send Suspected Killer to Florida," *The Stuart News/Port St. Lucie
News*, in Stuart, Florida, January 26, 1996.

31 See, for example: "Suspect Gets Week to Fight; Florida Wants Him," *Dayton Daily
News*, Ohio, Saturday, City Edition, January 27, 1996.

32 See, for example: "Rogers investigation focuses on family farm," The *Commercial
Appeal*, Memphis, Tennessee, Wednesday, Final Edition, March 13, 1996.

Rogers had told police he was responsible for the deaths of more than seventy people. The AP also noted that body of Mark Peters was found in January 1994 tied to a chair in the cabin on the farm. The AP commented that Rogers had lived with Peters in Hamilton, Ohio, Rogers's hometown.

On Thursday, March 14, 1996, Glen Rogers's brother, Clay Rogers, in an interview with WLEX-TV in Lexington, Kentucky, said authorities who searched the family farm that week should look harder because the property was a cemetery for other victims of unsolved murders.[33] Clay Rogers further said he believed authorities would find buried on the farm bodies from unsolved homicides going back twenty-five years. On Saturday, March 16, 1996, the AP reported Glen Rogers had refuted his brother's claims. "I've never talked to anyone about killing anyone or anything of that nature," Glen Rogers told WTVQ-TV in Lexington, Kentucky. "I don't know why (Clay) is saying this. Maybe he needs the attention on national TV."[34]

On March 22, 1996, newspapers reported preliminary tests indicated bones found on the Rogers family farm were from Mark Peters whose body was found tied to a chair in the cabin on the farm. Kentucky Forensic Anthropologist Emily Craig told reporters the size, location, and weathering of the bone fragments indicated they were from the body presumed to be Mark Peters.[35]

On May 3, 1996, Phillip Baker, one of O. J. Simpson's civil attorneys, contacted Glen Rogers's attorney to inquire about a photo taken of Glen Rogers and Nicole Simpson together at the House of Blues in North Hollywood the day before her murder. I have reason to believe the photograph does exist and that it was confiscated by the FBI. I actually saw the photo online before it was taken down, and why would Simpson's attorneys contact Glen regarding a photo if they did not personally see it?

---

33 See, for example: "Murder suspect's brother says more bodies possible," *The Tampa Tribune*, Friday, Florida Edition, March 15, 1996.

34 See, for example: "Suspect in multiple killings denies brother's TV Claims," *The Advocate*, Baton Rouge, Louisiana, Saturday, Metro Edition, March 16, 1996.

35 "Tests Indicate Bones on Farm Are from Body Found in 1994," *Herald Leader*, Lexington, Kentucky, March 22, 1996.

On May 7, 1997, in Tampa, Florida, in the trial for the murder of Tina Cribbs, Glen Rogers was found guilty. On July 11, 1997, Florida sentenced Glen to the death penalty, specifically the electric chair. Rogers was also indicted in Kentucky for the murder of Mark Peters.

[The Informant's name below was replaced to protect their identity.]

That's where I uncovered the interview transcript where Redd, another anonymous informant who became our Witness #2, explained that Glen Rogers did not kill Mark Peters. The story Redd told was that Glen kidnapped Mark Peters and kept him alive in the trunk of his car. Glen kept him there to sign checks.

In that interview, Redd said the following: "Glen was running around taking checks out, having them sign checks and cashing them all over the place. He took his ATM card. He was going to different machines . . . " Redd claimed the family of Mark Peters had no idea what happened to their father. But Redd claimed Mark Peters died of a heart attack he had while Glen kept him locked inside the car's trunk. Glen then disposed of the body.

On January 10, 1994, Redd discovered the body in the back room of the cabin but claimed at the time he didn't know who it was. "He looked like the crypt keeper," Redd said.

Redd claimed Mark Peters took Glen Rogers into his home because he was courting Rogers's mother at the time, giving her cash, buying her gifts and jewelry, and made her insurance payments. "Mark Peters had plenty of money," Redd claimed. "So, Glen was going to take away from Peters the thing he thought his mom was attracted to, which was the money." Redd claimed that when Peters died of a heart attack in the trunk of the car, Glen went to Peters's home and loaded up on furniture. Redd says that Glen drove the body to the cabin on the family farm in Kentucky. "When Glen stuck the body in the back room, he had every intention to put it somewhere else," Redd said. "But there was a nosey woman up the street, so Glen had to stick the body some place real quick."

Redd said Glen tried to stuff the body in the floorboards of the house, that Glen thought about lighting the cabin on fire to incinerate the body. "So, he stuck the body in that corner, and he threw all the furniture on top of the guy in the back room," Redd continued. "That's why when the police found the body they said Glen had tied Mark Peters to a chair."

Glen Rogers, under the alias James Edward Peters, was in California from January 1994 through June 1994

The answer to this question is "Yes." After the murder of Mark Peters, most likely in December 1993 or January 1994, Glen Rogers fled Florida to take up residence in Los Angeles, California. After the murder of Nicole Simpson, Glen Rogers gave his mother various handwritten notes that he asked his mother to keep in a safe-deposit box, showing them to nobody. I managed to get ahold of these notes in the process of my investigation. One of the informants who came to me gave me a lot of documents, including the documents Glen Rogers gave to his mother for safekeeping. One of these documents provided my first clue that Glen Rogers began using the identity of Mark Peters in California, starting January 1994.

Among the papers was a handwritten note that read as follows:

James Edward Peters
SSN 282-XX-XXXX
6-30-61

Glen Rogers was born on July 15, 1962. Presumably he changed "Mark" to "James" and added his own middle name, "Edward," to create the alias. Also, Glen Rogers appears to have assumed the Social Security Number (SSN) of Mark Peters after Glen murdered him. A birth date of June 30, 1961, while not Glen Rogers's actual birth date, would be a lot closer than the actual birth date of Mark Peters, a veteran of World War II, close enough to Rogers's actual birth date to pass without being seriously questioned. It appears Glen Rogers assumed the identity of Mark Peters, using a legitimate SSN that would allow him to be employed and pay taxes, with a bogus birthdate that would never be questioned so long as Glen Rogers did not apply for a U.S. passport under the assumed identity.

Remember: Glen Rogers's middle name was "Edward." Peters is the last name of Mark Peters, the man Rogers murdered, leaving the body tied to a chair in the cabin on his family farm. Consider the following evidence I found over the years, showing that Glen Rogers was in Los Angeles in January 1994, living at 11448 Cumpston Street in North Hollywood, in an apartment rented by James Peters (according to the rent receipts discussed above). The evidence also supports that James Edward Peters in Los Angeles was not using his own Social Security Number.

I verified independently that Glen Rogers's Social Security number was 291-XX-XXXX in 1993, when he was living at 1176 Hunt Avenue in Hamilton, Ohio, and working for Ascot, Inc. in Hobart, Ohio, and separately, for Olsten–Cincinnati, Inc. in Fairfield, Ohio. I also verified through pay receipts that William J. Gavin Painting paid James Peters income under the assumed SSN 291-XX-XXXX on February 2, 1994; March 2, 1994; March 16, 1994; March 30, 1994; April 13, 1994; May 11, 1994; May 25, 1994; and June 8, 1994.

Just as I was not able to find any rent receipts for Glen Rogers in Los Angeles after July 1994, I was unable to find any work records or pay receipts for Rogers after June 8, 1994.

I found a Western Union Fax Transmittal form that was used by Glen Rogers to send a résumé to "Al" on January 25, 1994, evidence Glen Rogers was in California that month. The letter that was faxed by Glen Rogers was dated January 25, 1994 and was addressed to "Al" in Pasadena, California. The letter read in part as follows:

> Imagine my surprise to find you now operating in Utah after all these years. I am faxing you a copy of my resume as you requested and am anxious to discuss the possibilities of working with you and your firm.
>
> I will be in Utah this coming weekend and will call on you Saturday. I would enjoy seeing you again if possible while I am here.

The above documentation from William J. Gavin Painting in Canoga Park, California, makes it clear Glen Rogers did not land a job with

"Al" in Utah. Instead, he stayed in Los Angeles where he worked as a custom painter.

I found a certified letter dated May 11, 1994, sent by attorneys Cordell & Casey in Houston, Texas, to Glen Rogers, at 11448 Cumpston Street in North Hollywood (the address of the apartment rented by James Peters, according to the receipt referenced above). That letter concerned a custody issue regarding Glen Rogers's two children in the 314 Judicial District Court of Harris County, Texas. From the contents of the letter, it appears the two boys were going to continue in foster care with Glen Rogers granted telephone visitation rights.

The envelope of a certified letter sent by Katherine Tyra of the Harris County District Court was postmarked March 26, 1994, addressed to Glen Rogers at 11448 Cumpston Street #2 in North Hollywood, California. A "Family Service Plan" sent by the Texas Department of Protective and Regulatory Services, mailed to Glen Rogers on May 6, 1994, indicated that his sons were to be placed with relatives. The form from the Texas agency noted: "Discussed plan with Father on phone as he is living in California."

From this evidence, it is clear Glen Rogers had assumed the identity of Mark Peters while he was using the alias James Peters. It is also clear that Glen Rogers was living in Los Angeles under this assumed name from January 1994 until at least Wednesday, June 8, 1994, the date of his last pay receipt from William J. Gavin Painting—4 days before Nicole was killed that Sunday, June 12, 1994.

California Convicts Glen Rogers for 1995 Murder of Sandra Gallagher

On Tuesday, June 22, 1999, a Los Angeles jury convicted Glen Rogers and sentenced him to death for first-degree murder for killing Sandra Gallagher in September 1995. Rogers met Gallagher, a thirty-three-year-old mother of three, in a bar on September 28, 1995, as she was having a drink celebrating a $1,250 win in a California Lottery game. Glen offered her a ride home. Several hours after she left McRed's Cocktail Lounge with Rogers, in the early morning hours of September 29, 1995, her body was found inside a burning truck on Victory Boulevard in Van Nuys, California. Cause of death in Gallagher's case was determined to be neck strangulation.[36]

June 1999 was five years to the month since Nicole Brown Simpson was murdered. What is clear from Glen Rogers being convicted in 1999 for the murder of Sandra Gallagher that he committed in Los Angeles in September 1995, was that Rogers did not completely leave Los Angeles in 1994 after Nicole was murdered. On Friday, July 16, 1999, Los Angeles Superior Court Judge Jacqueline Connor gave Glen Rogers his second death penalty sentence, this time in California, for the murder of Sandra Gallagher.[37]

In 1999, at the time of his conviction in Los Angeles for the murder of Gallagher, Glen Rogers was already on Death Row in Florida where in 1997, he had been found guilty of murdering Tina Marie Cribbs. As this book is being written, Glen Rogers is in a Florida State Prison, also known as Raiford Prison, in unincorporated Bradford County, awaiting execution for the murder of Tina Marie Cribbs.

But Glen Rogers seemed to be in constant trouble in Los Angeles. In August 1994, Rogers showed up in a Los Angeles jail on arson charges. Then in June 1995, Rogers was back in a California jail, on charges that he attacked two men with a knife, trapping one of them in an elevator as he held a blade to his throat. Glen pleaded no contest to assault with a deadly weapon and was given six months in jail and three years' probation by Hollywood Municipal Judge Michael Mink. But the Sheriff's Department that runs the jail released Rogers after just forty-two days because the overcrowded jail needed his bed for more dangerous criminals.[38]

Then, in September 1995, Rogers was in a California courtroom again, this time in Van Nuys, after being arrested on a spousal abuse

---

36 Associated Press, "Jury convicts Florida Death Row inmate Glen Rogers in L.A. murder," *Associated Press State and Local Wire*, Tuesday, AM cycle, June 22, 1999.

37 Associated Press, "'Cross-Country Killer is Given Death Sentence; Glen Rogers Was Sentenced in Los Angeles for a 1995 Slaying. He Is Already on Florida's Death Row," *Orlando Sentinel*, Florida, Saturday, July 17, 1999, Metro Edition.

38 Michael Fleeman, "Man Suspected in at Least 5 Slayings Fell Through the Cracks," *Associated Press*, November 16, 1995, https://apnews.com/article /a6e8bdddae84cb1e302009e6919b6861.

complaint filed by a woman he lived with. Because he was on probation over the June 1995 conviction, he could have been sentenced to as long as two and a half years in jail. Instead, Municipal Court Commissioner Rebecca Omens sentenced Rogers to two days in jail, a $100 fine, and participation in a domestic violence program, the standard sentence in misdemeanor spousal assault cases. How Rogers slipped through a lenient justice system to continue murdering defied reporters and investigators even at that time.[39]

I was not able to find any rent receipts for Glen Rogers in Los Angeles after the receipt for the apartment at 11448 Cumpston Street in North Hollywood for July 1994. Given the number of murders in different states where Glen Rogers was the suspect, the evidence suggests that the "cross-country" serial killer was not stationary in Los Angeles but moved freely around the country. Newspapers at the time reported that after the murder of Sandra Gallagher, Rogers disappeared, only to reappear in Jackson, Mississippi, where police suspected Rogers in the murder of Linda Price, thirty-four, found dead in her bathtub.[40] That arrest occurred in Kentucky on November 13, 1995, when Rogers was arrested for the murder of Tina Marie Cribbs, who was also found dead, having been stabbed to death in her bathtub. At that time, he was wanted for the murder of Sandra Gallagher and was accused of murders in three additional states.

The Sordid Rogers Family History

The Rogers family in backwoods Kentucky had a history of making and selling moonshine. Claude Rogers Sr., Glen's father, was born in 1924 and was drafted into World War II and served in the Pacific. In the fighting in Guam, it was alleged that Claude Rogers was found mutilating Japanese. Their mother Edna was born in 1931, and they had seven children. In the 1950s, Claude Sr. had a history as a womanizing drunkard. He was known to be violent, frequently beating his wife and children.

---

39 "Another One Slips Through the Cracks," *Los Angeles Times*, Thursday, Home Edition, November 16, 1995.

40 Nicholas Riccardi and Julie Tamaki, "Valley Murder Suspect Linked to More Deaths," *Los Angeles Times*, Wednesday, Valley Edition, November 8, 1995.

In 1962, the family moved to Hamilton, Ohio, where Glen was born on July 15 that year. In 1964, Edna ran away with the kids, sleeping in the station wagon for a few days. In 1965, Glen's siblings claim to have found the remains of an infant brother, and watched his father bury a neighbor whom Claude Sr. had murdered. The next year, in 1966, Claude Jr. tortured his brothers by burying them alive. In another incident, Claude Sr. held Glen underwater until he nearly drowned. That was the year Claude Sr. discovered that Glen's pastime was torturing insects and impaling them as trophies. Family lore was that Claude Sr. had murdered some one hundred persons.

In 1974, Glen was sent to a juvenile detention youth camp, where he was sexually abused. By 1978, Glen quit high school at the age of sixteen. Two years later, Glen married his fourteen-year-old girlfriend after she got pregnant by another man. Glen had a second son in 1981, but the marriage failed as the family descended into marijuana, crimes including larceny, and domestic abuse, leading up to a divorce in 1983, alleging domestic abuse.[41]

Glen's years as a young adult are filled with repeated episodes of being sent to juvenile detention and/or jail, being involved in petty crimes, and living in a dysfunctional family with equally troubled siblings. In 1986, Glen was treated for acute alcoholism. On September 8, 1986, he wrote a suicide note. In 1987, Glen told Ohio taxi driver Wayne Brockman that he killed his father. On November 9, 1987, Glen was sentenced to two years in prison for breaking and entering, as well as for forgery. The next year, on July 5, 1988, Glen is reputed to have killed his first woman, launching his career as the "cross-country serial killer."

From April 10, 1990, to October 12, 1993, Glen had totaled a history of fifty-two arrests from all over the country. After Clay told police on January 3, 1994, that he had found the body of Mark Peters in the family cabin in Kentucky, Glen went on the run to California, assumed the alias identity, and rented an apartment in North Hollywood adjoining Los Angeles. On January 10, 1994,

---

41 Henry Chu, "Contradictions Fill Suspect's Past," *Los Angeles Times*, November 12, 1995.

police found the remains of Mark Peters exactly where Clay told them to look.

What appears to be the case is that Glen Rogers never completely left Los Angeles, given his continued legal problems there through 1995 when he was arrested for the murder of Sandra Gallagher. Since 1995, Rogers has never gotten out of prison. Given that he has bragged of killing seventy people and is known as the "cross-country" serial killer, it is likely Rogers was active killing people in and outside California after Nicole Simpson was murdered on June 12, 1994.

Glen Meets Nicole Brown Simpson

On January 31, 1996, the *Journal-News* in Hamilton, Ohio, reported that Hamilton attorney James Cooney claimed his client Glen Rogers met Nicole Simpson in a Los Angeles bar. At this time, Rogers was being extradited to Florida to face criminal charges for the murder of Tina Marie Cribbs. "He did tell me that he did meet Nicole Brown Simpson—he did know her," Cooney said. "He described a scene that would be believable to me. But he denies all wrongdoing."[42]

[The names in this section were altered to protect their identities.]

One of the investigators working on the Nicole Simpson murder sent me a taped interview with Redd. In that interview, Redd said Glen sent the picture of Glen and Nicole to their mother, and their mother showed the photograph to Redd. I've searched hard, but after the FBI confiscated that photograph, as I said, all copies seem to have disappeared. At any rate, Redd insisted he and Glen's mother both knew Glen "was dating" Nicole, who Redd commented was "a very beautiful woman"—a comment that seemed to suggest Redd and Glen's mother thought Nicole was prettier than the other women victims Glen had picked to kill.

Redd also said that right after his mother got that picture of Glen and Nicole from Glen, before Nicole was killed, the FBI accompanied by U.S. Marshalls came with a warrant in a raid to their mother's

---

42 Denis Nichols, "Rogers Tells Attorney He Knew Nicole Brown Simpson," *Journal-News*, Hamilton, Ohio, January 31, 1996.

home, and they took everything pertaining to Glen at that time, including letters, tapes, and photographs. "They even took photos from Mom's picture album," Redd said. "They also took the picture of Glen and Nicole, and we never got any of that stuff back." Redd said he believed the FBI conducted the raid because they were investigating the murder of Mark Peters.

I also want to make sure you go back to what Witness #1 told me about she and two of her girlfriends meeting with Dodi Fayed and Nicole at that famous nightclub, The Gate, on La Cienega in Los Angeles. You will recall that in Chapter 2, we heard from Witness #1 that there was a quiet guy sitting between Dodi and Nicole, a guy with sandy blonde hair. That description matches Glen Rogers and fits with Redd's insistence Glen had met Nicole and was dating her.

One more point from Witness #1 is important. Witness #1 also said the quiet guy with sandy blonde hair was wearing pointed shoes that caught her attention. She also noticed that Dodi Fayed had small hands and he was wearing gloves. Witness #1 also said that when she and her father were watching the O. J. murder trial on television, the bloody gloves were established to have been bought at Harrods department store in London. That is correct. As a preview, we will also be able to establish in later chapters that the shoes Glen was wearing were Bruno Magli shoes that also came from Harrods.

I said in Chapter 2 that I would say more about Glen Rogers. Now, reading this chapter, you are getting a sense of what I meant. Glen Rogers was a dangerous serial killer, and when Witness #1 saw the sandy blonde quiet guy that night, there were a lot of women living that soon would be dead, including Nicole. That Glen's shoes were Bruno Magli shoes bought at Harrods also turns out to be a very important clue that you should not miss. Witness #1 later told me the two henchmen who grabbed her friend and her may also have been wearing the same brand gloves Dodi was wearing. Witness #1 thought Dodi may have bought a pair of those gloves for all the guys working with him closely, possibly including Glen Rogers, as well as the two henchmen.

The Case Takes a Strange Twist: Glen Starts Writing Letters from Prison

After I put out word that I wanted to communicate with Glen Rogers, I got a letter Glen sent from the prison in Raiford, Florida, on May 13, 2013.

Note: In this printed version of Glen's letter, I have corrected the capitalization, spelling, and punctuation. I have divided it into paragraphs to make it easier to read. I have added notes to clarify some of the points Glen is making.

The letter read as follows:

5-13-2013
Dear Mr. Pardo,

Hi, my name is Glen Rogers, I am at this time on death row in Florida.

Please tell OJS [O. J. Simpson] that I'm very sorry for the death of his wife. I do hope his court hearing gets a ruling in his favor.

[Note: In May 2013, O. J. Simpson got a court hearing on his request to a new trial in the armed robbery case regarding his personal memorabilia, including sports memorabilia.[43]]

Seems to me he's being pursued not for the crime [he was] convicted of, but the crime they think he got away with that he didn't ever do [i.e., murder of Nicole Brown Simpson and Ron Goldman].

But that's our justice system.

I would like to speak to you and your lawyer about certain things relative to your case [i.e., murder of Nicole Brown Simpson and Ron Goldman] and mine here [murder of Tina Marie Cribbs]. I understand [attorney] Craig Brandt here in Florida may be able to help. I am out of gas on appeal, only because of lawyers getting me time bared [time behind bars]. With a real lawyer, I can get my full appeal heard.

---

43 Associated Press, "O. J. to get court hearing," ESPN.com, May 10, 2013, https://www.espn.com/nfl/story/_/id/9261160/oj-simpson-get-vegas-court-hearing-bid-new-trial.

I do believe you need to hear me out. You won't have to take my
word. A full taped statement in your case [i.e., murder of Nicole
Brown Simpson and Ron Goldman] was made in 1995. I would
need a court order to release it to you. Also, with a lawyer present, I made a phone plea deal with a CA DA [California District
Attorney] CA DA [who] now has been removed from office since
that day.

I hope to be working with you soon, before they get rid of me.

Thank you for your help.

Glen Rogers

There were several shocking aspects of this letter. First, that Glen
Rogers made a full taped statement to the police in California
concerning the Nicole Brown Simpson and Ron Goldman murders. Second, that a California district attorney, very possibly Los
Angeles' Gil Garcetti, may have made a plea deal with Glen Rogers
over the telephone. Garcetti served as Los Angeles County District
Attorney two terms, from 1992 until November 7, 2000. That
fits Glen's description of a district attorney who was not in office
in 2013.

Why would Glen Rogers make a taped statement to police unless
he was involved in the case? Why would Glen Rogers make a plea
deal with a prosecutor if he did not have criminal liability in the case?
I interpreted what Glen Rogers was saying as an admission that he
had participated in the killing of Nicole Brown Simpson and Ron
Goldman, that he had made a full confession on tape to the police
about his involvement, and that he gave state's evidence, informing
on some other party or parties who was/were also involved in the killing. So, I began to contemplate that Glen Rogers may have murdered
Nicole Brown Simpson. After all, he murdered a lot of women with
a knife, so why not Nicole? That Ron Goldman showed up and got
murdered could just have been bad timing.

What further surprised me was that after a confession and a plea
deal, the police just released Glen Rogers. The jury in the O. J. murder trial was sworn-in on November 9, 1994. O. J. Simpson's "not
guilty" verdict was announced by the jury on October 3, 1995.

Glen Rogers killed Sandra Gallagher on September 28, 1995, fled California, and was arrested in Kentucky by state police on November 13, 1995. Glen Rogers was not in police custody until November 13, 1995, and the first legal issue he faced involved extradition orders by Florida and several other states. I viewed it as extremely unlikely Glen Rogers said anything of material value until after he was extradited and convicted of first-degree murder in Florida. The most likely time Glen Rogers was in custody in 1995, when he could have given a statement to police, was in June 1995, when he was charged with aggravated assault with a deadly weapon for attacking two men with a knife. As we noted earlier in this chapter, Glen Rogers was released from jail after only forty-two days in prison.

If Glen Rogers told police about his role in the Nicole Simpson Brown murder case, why was he released from prison? Certainly, when prisoners were released because of overcrowding, any criminal who had involvement in the high-profile murders involving O. J. Simpson would not have been released to make room for "more dangerous criminal offenders." But equally puzzling was why Glen Rogers was never mentioned by either the prosecution or the defense in the O. J. Simpson murder trial.

Glen Rogers letter made clear that he gave a taped statement and entered a plea deal "in your case," meaning my case, a case Glen Rogers correctly assumed involved investigating who killed Nicole. So, California police in 1995 knew Glen Rogers was not James Peters. Statements by LAPD Detective Mark Fuhrman, the detective most responsible for collecting evidence at the Nicole Simpson murder scene, appear disingenuous when Fuhrman excused himself, saying after the fact that he did not investigate Glen Rogers at the time of the Nicole Simpson and Ron Goldman murders because he didn't realize that James Peters was Glen Rogers.

After that first letter, Glen and I exchanged several letters. I also came into possession of letter correspondence between Glen and Redd. The Nicole Simpson murder was a topic Glen discussed in those letters and he revealed a lot about how he claimed to be involved. He was angling, throwing tempting teases about what he might reveal while suggesting how I could help him by getting better lawyers to keep him alive longer on Death Row, or possibly even to win an appeal. I came to conclude that Glen knew too much about the case to be lying.

But more about that later. Witness #1 was right when her friends with sons or daughters in the FBI or in the CIA told her there were "too many strings" to the Nicole Brown Simpson murder case, and that I should consider there was another party there at Nicole's Brentwood home that was kept hidden from the public—someone the FBI actually thought was the person who killed both Nicole and Ron Goldman.

But more about that later. At this point in the story, you are only starting to realize how complicated the Nicole Brown Simpson case really is—and how hard the LAPD, the FBI, and the L.A. District Attorney's office worked to make sure the truth that they knew never became public knowledge.

How Glen Rogers Became an Expert at Gaming the Justice System

In Hamilton, Ohio, Glen, Redd, and Claude Sr. were allegedly involved in any number of major crimes, ranging from killing neighbors, committing robberies, growing and selling marijuana, having sex as pre-teens with underage teenage girls—a long litany of crimes. But to stay off criminal charges, he agreed to work with Hamilton police officer Thomas Kilmore, who had known Glen for sixteen or seventeen years, and the family for twenty-five years. Glen agreed to work as a confidential informant for the Hamilton Police Department. Working with undercover narcotics officers, Glen would identify drug dealers in bars and local hangouts, make drug buys in sting operations, whatever was needed to get evidence of criminal drug activity. Eventually, Glen turned this into a lucrative business, agreeing to work with narcotics units for pay.

Glen and Redd learned forensic tricks. "We learned a little bit about forensic pathology," Redd bragged to an interviewer. "When Glen went to do something, he was worried about it, he'd stop at a car wash. Get in the garbage can and remove cigarette butts, always wearing gloves to avoid leaving fingerprints. He would get hair from the vacuum at the car wash. The goal was to plant trace evidence as false leads." The two had learned to buy clothes at the Salvation Army that had somebody else's DNA, particles of someone else's skin. Then they would take a shower, coating themselves afterwards with Vaseline, to create a barrier so they would not lose hair or skin cells when pulling off a crime—no body evidence, that was the goal. If apprehended by the police, the brothers would exchange evidence or inform on others, all in return for immunity from prosecution. The two lived a low-life underworld existence in which they learned to read marks by their clothes and their mannerisms. They mastered how to break burglar alarms and set up front operations with phony legitimate businesses designed to mask criminal activity. They learned how to kill . . . and not get caught.

With the Nicole Simpson case, Glen Rogers may even have mastered how to get caught committing the crime yet manage himself so that he came away with a plea deal that let him off with immunity from criminal prosecution.

1997: The L.A. District Attorney Seals All Records on Glen Rogers

One of the most remarkable documents I came across in my twenty-year quest to find the truth was a 1997 document from the California Superior Court for the County of Los Angeles that sealed all records pertaining to Glen Rogers. The date stamped on the court order was November 10, 1997, and the case was *People of the State of California, Plaintiff vs. Glen Rogers, Defendant*. The court order referred to the "matter of Lea P. D'Agostino." Who was Lea D'Agostino? She was a prosecutor in the office of Los Angeles District Attorney Gil Garcetti—the Los Angeles District Attorney under whose jurisdiction Glen Rogers was given a plea deal in 1995 and O. J. Simpson was tried and acquitted for the murders of Nicole Simpson and Ron Goldman.

Lea D'Agostino, it turns out, was the prosecutor in Garcetti's office who supervised the prosecution of Glen Rogers, then known nationally as the "Cross-Country Killer" for the murder of Sandra Gallagher, the last murder Glen Rogers committed in California.[44] D'Agostino had been assigned the case days after the Gallagher killing, when Rogers fled and was apprehended in Kentucky for the murder in Florida of Tina Marie Cribbs.

But D'Agostino had fallen into disfavor with Garcetti. She persuaded then-Los Angeles Attorney James Hahn to challenge Garcetti in the 1996 election. Garcetti found out. She shared a table with Garcetti at a dinner on March 16, 1997. Confronted by Garcetti, D'Agostino admitted the rumor was true. She was working politically to unseat Garcetti. D'Agostino had managed to get Rogers extradited to California in October 1998, and, we noted earlier, on June 23, 1999, Rogers was convicted of murdering Sandra Gallagher, and on July 16, 1999, the state of California sentenced Rogers to death.

D'Agostino had ambitions to run for District Attorney in the next few years. What possibly was in the criminal files California held on Glen Rogers that was so explosive that Garcetti petitioned Los Angeles Superior Court Judge John Reid to seal those records forever? Glen Rogers was not extradited to California to face trial for murdering Sandra Gallagher until October 1998. Why didn't Garcetti wait to seal all Glen Rogers files until after Glen Rogers was extradited? Glen Rogers knew how important those sealed records were—important enough that Glen Rogers made asking me to get a lawyer to unseal those records the pivotal focus of the introductory letter he wrote me from the Florida prison Death Row on May 13, 2013. Something in the files California had on Glen Rogers was so explosive that Garcetti wanted them sealed in November 1997. This would suggest the explosive material in files California held on Glen Rogers were not considered to be material either to get Rogers extradited or to put him on trial for his life in the Sandra Gallagher case.

D'Agostino also must have thought the Glen Rogers records had some value to her, so much so that her use of the records was a threat

---

44 The paragraphs on Lea D'Agostino are drawn from the following source: Roger M. Grace, "'Dragon Lady' Breathes Fire at DA Garcetti for Depriving Her of Case She Nurtured," *Metropolitan News-Enterprise*, Wednesday, September 1, 2010, http://www .metnews.com/articles/2010/perspectives090110.htm.

to Garcetti in 1997. Perhaps Garcetti was planning to run again to remain Los Angeles County District Attorney in 2000 and beyond, or to pursue some other elected political office. D'Agostino may have seen value in holding on to those records even if there was nothing in those files that pertained to the Sandra Gallagher murder. Perhaps in D'Agostino's mind, the Glen Rogers files continued to have a political value to D'Agostino in her strategy to run for political life itself. Running against Garcetti's record in the Glen Rogers case might be just the ticket to get herself elected Los Angeles County District Attorney. This would especially be the case if Rogers had admitted to prosecutors in his 1995 recorded statement, or in his plea deal, something material about the role Glen Rogers played in the deaths of Nicole Brown Simpson and Ron Goldman. How would Garcetti explain to voters that he had released a serial killer and suppressed material information Glen Rogers had given prosecutors in 1995— information considered sufficiently valuable to prosecutors that Glen Rogers induced the Los Angeles District Attorney to give him a plea deal and let him go.

Glen Rogers knew exactly what was in the sealed files, and he knew those files included his 1995 statement made to the Los Angeles prosecutors and the plea deal he accepted from those same prosecutors. Over time, Glen Rogers let it be known what he was thinking. "The L.A. Police Department don't want it to come out that they had James Peters in the jail for an aggravated assault with a knife, released him for work release, and he had no job, and he went on to kill other people," Redd told me that Glen Rogers must have been thinking something like this: "If I was a police officer or a district attorney and I just released America's most wanted criminal under the wrong name without even checking out the story, that's something that's going to embarrass a lot of police and I'm sure nobody would want that to come out."

Redd was right. But what tantalized me was more than that. What if the Los Angeles Police Department and the Los Angeles County District Attorney released Glen Rogers in 1995, knowing that he was Glen Rogers, not James Peters, and that he played a role in the murders of Nicole Brown Simpson and Ron Goldman—knowing maybe

even that Glen Rogers was the murderer. My mind boggled thinking that might be true. But then, I couldn't get out of my head that
first letter Glen Rogers wrote me from Death Row. Why was Glen so
determined to get those records unsealed?

There's a lot more to cover here, but—as I said—Glen wrote
more letters, and I'm fixing to look at those right here, pretty soon.

CHAPTER 7

The Goldman Family Saga

If you thought what you have read so far was surprising, especially given what you heard before about O. J. Simpson and the Nicole Brown Simpson case was surprising, and probably pretty weird, I guarantee you that you haven't heard anything yet. At least, not until you read this chapter.

The question we are going to ask in this chapter is this: Who exactly was Ron Goldman?

Now, you probably think that's a silly question. Everybody knows who Ron Goldman was. He was the victim, the obliging young waiter from the Mezzaluna restaurant who got viciously killed because he brought Nicole Simpson the eyeglasses her mother left on the table after Nicole ate her last meal with her children.

In the mainstream narrative, Ron Goldman has become the poster-boy victim of all time—a handsome, vibrant, young man cut down in the prime of life by O. J. Simpson, a black man whose jealousy over his white, ex-wife drove him to virtually sever Goldman's head from his neck by wielding a stiletto knife in anger. Nobody in history, the mainstream narrative goes, ever paid a greater price for doing a favor. How unfortunate that all Ron Goldman wanted to do was to satisfy a valued customer in a restaurant establishment he did not even own. In the mainstream narrative, we need look no farther than Ron Goldman for proof no good deed goes unpunished. Speak no ill of victims we are told, lest you disgrace yourself.

That was the version of the Ron Goldman story that I thought was true, until I started investigating. Let's start here, with the story about the Mezzaluna restaurant and the eyeglasses grandma left behind after a beautiful dinner out with her daughter and her grandchildren. What really happened?

How Grandma Lost Her Prescription Eyeglasses in the Gutter Outside the Restaurant That Fateful Night

On Tuesday, February 7, 1995, Day 2 of the O. J. Simpson murder trial, Karen Crawford was sworn in to testify. Under direct questioning by prosecutor Marcia Clark, Crawford explained she worked at the Mezzaluna restaurant in Brentwood, California, on San Vicente Boulevard. For the past year and a half, she was the manager at the Mezzaluna on Sunday nights, and she bartended. On the night Nicole was murdered, June 12, 1994, Karen Crawford was the manager. She testified that she knew Nicole as a regular customer, and she had known Ron Goldman since he started working at the Mezzaluna as a waiter early in 1994, about 4 months before June 12.

Crawford recalled that on Sunday, June 12, 1994, Nicole Simpson came to the Mezzaluna with a large party that included several adults and some children. She recalled that Nicole that evening wore a black halter dress that hung above the knee, and that Nicole and her party were seated at the large table that was usually set up across the front of the restaurant in front of the bar area, placed there to accommodate large groups. She confirmed the accuracy of a restaurant receipt that confirmed Tia, not Ron Goldman, was the server. Nicole's total bill for dinner that night was $179.95, plus a gratuity of an additional $34.00, for a total of $213.85. The receipt showed that the time from when Nicole and her party were seated was one hour and fourteen minutes. Crawford testified she remembered Nicole and her party leaving the Mezzaluna between 8:30 and 9:00 p.m. Pacific Time.

Next, Crawford affirmed a phone record that showed she received a phone call at the restaurant at 9:37 p.m. from Mrs. Brown, Nicole's mother. Mrs. Brown said she had lost her eyeglasses and she asked Crawford if Crawford could look for them. Crawford found the eyeglasses in the street by the gutter. She put the glasses in a white business envelope that she sealed and placed behind the bar in the restaurant's "lost and found" area. She wrote on the envelope, "Prescription Glasses, Nicole Simpson Will Pick Up Monday." Mrs. Brown, in the earlier call, had told Crawford that she lived too far away to come and pick the eyeglasses up, if Crawford managed to find them, but that Nicole would come by the Mezzaluna and pick them up.

Then at 9:45 p.m., Crawford received a second call, this time from Nicole who asked Crawford if she could speak with Ron Goldman. By this time Goldman had taken off his vest and tie because he was finished working that night, but he was still wearing the black pants and white dress shirt that were part of his waiter's uniform. When Goldman hung up, he asked Crawford for the eyeglasses, saying he was going to drop off the eyeglasses at Nicole's. Ron explained to Crawford that he was on his way that evening to meet a couple of guys from work at the Baha Cantina in Marina Del Ray. Crawford saw Goldman leave the restaurant by the front door approximately 10 minutes before 10:00 p.m.. Goldman's timecard for June 12, 1994, showed he came in to work at 4:30 p.m. and he clocked out at 9:33 p.m..

Ron Goldman, Nicole Simpson, and the Ferrari

Under cross-examination by defense attorney Robert Shapiro, Crawford testified she remembered seeing Nicole greet Ron Goldman when she entered the restaurant, and Crawford further testified that when Nicole entered the restaurant, she and Ron may have hugged, but she could not remember if they kissed.

Shapiro's questions seemed out of place given the mainstream narrative, but that the mainstream media may not exactly be the truth shouldn't surprise any reader by now. On June 15, 1994, three days after Ron Goldman was murdered, the *Los Angeles Times* published an article looking into who Ron Goldman really was.[45] The article portrayed Ronald Lyle Goldman as living "a nonstop merry-go-round of working out at a trendy gym, serving dinner at a trendy restaurant and dancing at trendy nightclubs." The article noted that Goldman "had model good looks, a body sculpted by daily weightlifting sessions and tennis, and a magnetic personality that friends said made them want to hang around him, just to see what he would be up to next."

The *Los Angeles Times* reported Goldman, twenty-five "had an extremely close" relationship with thirty-five-year-old Nicole Brown Simpson, with whom he exercised, accompanied to dance clubs, and often met for coffee and dinner during the previous month and a half. "He told others that he was just friends with Simpson," the *Los Angeles Times* continued. "But he boasted of her stunning good looks and talked about the special kick it gave him to see heads turn when the two of them pulled up in her white Ferrari in front of The Gate, a fashionable West Hollywood dance club, with him behind the wheel."

The newspaper article commented that "Goldman, an aspiring model, often dated beautiful women who were drawn to his dark good looks." The *Times* explained that Goldman had moved from Chicago in 1987 and quickly became enamored with the California lifestyle, becoming an avid surfer, volleyball player, and nightclub hopper." He appeared on the Fox television dating show *Studs*. He had once arrived to have lunch with one of his male friends at Café Montana in Santa Monica driving Nicole's Ferrari, with its recognizable L84AD8 license plate, but Nicole was not with him.

Three days after Nicole's murder was too early for the mainstream media to complete Ron Goldman's victimhood apotheosis, but already the *Times* rushed to insist that Ron and Nicole were "just friends," and that their relationship was "innocent, platonic.' *Sure, I thought to myself, that's what all thirty-five-year-old hot babes claim for the twenty-five-year-old hunks they allow to drive their red Ferraris on*

---

45 Matthew Mosk and Carla Hall, "Victim Thrived on Life in Fast Lanes, His Friends Recall," *Los Angeles Times*, June 15, 1994, https://www.latimes.com/nation/la-oj-anniv -goldman-story.html.

the L.A. freeways. But the mainstream narrative was already starting to kick in, as the *Times* was quick to reassure readers that Goldman did not drink or take drugs, and that he stuck religiously to a low-fat diet. The hype was very much sexy Jewish guy from Chicago makes it big with the beautiful people in fashionable Beverly Hills club/beach scene. The spin was building strong, acknowledging only one hiccup. "A neighbor who lived nearby on Gorham Avenue in Brentwood said Goldman was struggling to make the rent until he got a new job this year as a waiter at Mezzaluna, an upscale restaurant," the article reported in passing.

Somehow, I couldn't help myself from seeing it through my jaded eyes as a story of Kosher boy from Chicago gets his break to land big in LA after landing waiter gig in trendy Brentwood eatery. "Sure, Ms. Simpson, just let me run those eyeglasses your mom left behind over to you right away, now that the kids are asleep," I could almost hear Ron Goldman say when Nicole, not the mother, called the Mezzaluna at 9:45 p.m. and asked to speak with Ron, please. As manager of the Mezzaluna that night, Crawford was happy to hand over the eyeglasses to Goldman—one more item out of "lost and found" that Crawford could now forget about. Crawford didn't give it a second thought when she saw Goldman bounce out the front door at approximately 9:50 p.m., confident the eyeglass mission would be accomplished, and it would be on her watch when a restaurant waiter volunteered to go out of his way to do a good deed for a valued customer.

Clocks at the Mezzaluna Told Wrong Time

In her testimony, Karen Crawford said there were errors on the time-card that Ron Goldman used to clock into and out of work.

For instance, one day had a time punched "in," but no time punched "out." "Wednesday?" Crawford said looking at the timecard when on the stand. "There is a stamp 'in' and I don't know exactly whether he (Ron Goldman) worked that day. Maybe someone accidentally punched 'in' on his timecard and realized that it was not their card. That is a possibility. Maybe he punched 'in' and they didn't need him, and he just left, and he didn't punch 'out.' Maybe he was there for just a few minutes. I can't tell you for sure what that is. He may have worked and forgotten to punch 'out."

On February 7, 1995, at the O. J. Simpson murder trial, under cross-examination by Shapiro, Tina Gavin, a waitress at the Mezzaluna who had worked with Ron Goldman since Goldman began there as a waiter in January 1994, testified that the employee timeclock at the restaurant told the wrong time because the clock in the mechanism that stamped the timecards was off one hour because it had not been changed for Daylight Savings Time. Tina Gavin was the waitress who served Nicole's party at the Mezzaluna that fateful night. The clock device on the ordering devices the waiters used to order food and the clock in the cash register that should have matched the credit card processing times were also both inaccurate.

This would mean that the time Goldman actually punched "out" on June 12, 1944 was 10:33 p.m. Pacific Daylight Savings time, not the 9:33 p.m. Pacific Standard Time that the timeclock "out" stamp for Ron Goldman that night indicated. The question of getting accurately the time different events occurred that night at the Mezzaluna was critical. Crawford stated that Nicole's party left the restaurant between 8:30 and 9:00 p.m., and that she received the phone call from Mrs. Brown looking for her lost eyeglasses at 9:37 p.m.. Mrs. Brown told Crawford on the phone after Crawford found the glasses that it was too far to drive for her to return that night to retrieve the eyeglasses. The drive that night was estimated to have taken approximately two hours to get from the restaurant in Brentwood to Mrs. Brown's home in Dana Point, Orange County, California. We know this thanks to the careful detective work done by author T. H. Johnson. In his 2010 book *Pursuit of Exhibit 35*,[46] Johnson determined travel was slowed down because of an ongoing five-year highway construction project to build the HOV lane system. Johnson found the California Department of Transportation recorded enormous traffic volume that evening because of the reduced number of automobile

---

46   T. H. Johnson, *Pursuit of Exhibit 35 in the O. J. Simpson Murder Trial and its Hidden Secrets* (CreateSpace Independent Publishing Platform, Large Print Edition, October 22, 2010). Updated as *Serpent Rising*, November 22, 2012.

lanes operating given the ongoing HOV lane construction. But if Nicole's party left the Mezzaluna at approximately 8:30 p.m., how did Mrs. Brown make the phone call from her home to the Mezzaluna looking for her glasses only one hour after they left the restaurant?

A restaurant in which all the critical time devices used to run the business were not telling the precisely correct time is another oddity in the legal case against O. J. Simpson. Shapiro exploited these oddities effectively in a cross-examination to deconstruct the prosecutor's case and raise serious, largely unanswered questions about the government's narrative that was increasingly parroted by the mainstream media as the trial progressed.

Prescription Eyeglasses Missing One Lens?

Here is how the eyeglasses story was portrayed at the trial and by the mainstream media: "Absent-minded grandma loses her prescription eyeglasses that restaurant manager finds on the street outside in a gutter." So, I guess that prescription was not very strong, or why else wouldn't grandma be wearing those eyeglasses when she left the restaurant so she could see properly walking around outside on the street? We are led to assume the glasses were prescribed primarily for reading and that Mrs. Brown had the eyeglasses with her when she arrived at the restaurant and sat through dinner. After all, I assume she read the menu before ordering food for herself and very possibly helping with the children.

When the eyeglasses were recovered from the murder crime scene, Andrea Mazzola, the criminalist working with the police who recovered most of the blood evidence from the crime scene, testified that she saw nothing unusual about the eyeglasses when she found them. On the stand at the O. J. Simpson trial on August 23, 1994, Mazzola couldn't explain why she hadn't noticed the prescription eyeglasses entered into evidence at the trial were missing one lens.[47]

Even worse, at the end of four days of often tedious testimony, Mazzola dropped another bombshell, admitting she did not put her

---

47 "Criminalist admits altering testimony in Simpson case," *Tampa Bay Times*, October 3, 2005.

initials on envelopes used to identify evidence at the crime scene. The magnitude of this failure was huge in that without her initials, no chain of custody could be established for any of the key evidence found at the crime scene. Without proper documentation, it would have been easy for anyone to tamper with the evidence, including the eyeglasses. So, the truth is, there was no proof the eyeglasses found at the crime scene were Grandma's, or even worse—no proof any eyeglasses belonging to Grandma or anyone else were ever found by anyone.

But no prosecutor working for District Attorney Garcetti ever let a massive procedural error like this derail a really good mainstream narrative that was selling strong with a public who fell for the Othello story as hard in 1994 as did the public in Shakespeare's time. So, what if the defense caught Mazzola in this little lie? So, what if properly tagging the evidence found at the crime scene jeopardized a judge not playing for the camera throwing the prosecutor's case out on procedural grounds? A criminalist who altered her testimony under oath was sure to be forgiven and forgotten as the juggernaut of the O. J. Simpson case proceeded on a track Garcetti and his prosecutors would be certain to find the football superstar guilty of murder in the first-degree.

But that wasn't what bothered me the most about the Mezzaluna story. In Italian, *mezzaluna* means "half moon," and that was a good name for the Nicole's "Last Supper" dinner because everything about this double murder story was turning out to be half-looney; that is, if judged by the standard of truth. Everybody just accepted the eyeglass story.

But what bothered me was that the entire scenario painted by the prosecutors to explain why Goldman was murdered depended upon Grandma losing her glasses at the restaurant. We are to assume that if Grandma had not lost her eyeglasses, Ron Goldman might never have been killed. If Goldman were at Nicole's Brentwood home only to return the glasses, the prosecutors want us to assume O. J. Simpson's plan that night was to kill Nicole. Given the way the prosecutors presented the case, we are supposed to assume the only reason Goldman got killed was he was returning to Nicole her mother's eyeglasses and his timing was unfortunately bad. That is part of the "no good deed goes unpunished" narrative that is essential to seeing Ron Goldman as the unfortunate victim.

But what I couldn't get out of my head was that portraying Ron Goldman as a victim killed because of bad timing depended upon us seeing him as the innocent waiter just going out of his way, beyond the call of duty as a good employee eager to please a regular customer. But what if the truth was different—that Ron Goldman was living the southern California Hollywood Beverly Hills life of a gigolo? What if Ron Goldman were not just a waiter, but was instead a player in the chic Beverly Hills party scene, replete with drugs, sex, and rock-and-roll? Why was Karen Crawford unsure when Shapiro asked her if she saw Nicole hug or kiss Ron Goldman when she came into the Mezzaluna that night?

There was another thing that puzzled me about the Ron Goldman narrative of that Mezzaluna night, and again it involved how screwy the timelines the prosecutors constructed that night were, especially given the distances and travel times involved with getting around Los Angeles. Anyone who has ever been there will know immediately what I'm talking about.

How Did Ron Goldman Get to Nicole's Home in Brentwood?

I kept asking myself how Ron Goldman got there that night? Everybody in the case just assumed Ron walked to Nicole's house.

But from the beginning, that puzzled me. From the Mezzaluna restaurant to the Baha Cantina in Marina Del Ray where Ron was going that night is twenty-eight minutes by car. If you are walking, it takes two hours and thirty-one minutes. And if there was no car, how was Ron going to get from Nicole's residence to the Marina?

But do you really think he walked? Ron had to get to Nicole's house first, to drop off the eyeglasses, before he headed out to the Baha Cantina in Marina Del Ray, where he was going to meet "some guys" and party until who knows what hour in the early morning of the next day, Monday, June 13, 1994.

At approximately ten o'clock that night, the time Karen Crawford alleges she saw Goldman leave the Mezzaluna through the front door, do you really think Ron Goldman was going to walk two and a half hours to get to the Marina Del Ray for his meeting? I guess the prosecutors just assumed that because the Mezzaluna was in Brentwood and Nicole lived in Brentwood, the Mezzaluna and Nicole's house were just around the corner and he could have just walked the half mile to her condo, but the prosecution failed to take into consideration he was actually en route to the Marina which was over two and a half hours by foot.

Ron Goldman did walk daily from his apartment to the Mezzaluna, going to and from work. And he could have walked to Nicole's. But that night, Ron was planning to go to Marina Del Ray after bringing back to Nicole her mother's eyeglasses. But Ron, who was experienced walking around Brentwood and would know that Nicole's place is directly on the way to the Marina del Ray, would still need a ride to avoid the long walk after dropping off the eyeglasses to get to his final destination that night and meet up with the guys waiting for him at Marina del Ray.

So, I started looking for evidence that Ron Goldman drove that night, but I couldn't find any. I couldn't even find any evidence that Ron Goldman ever owned a car in Los Angeles. In his deposition given on February 9, 1996, Fred Goldman, Ron Goldman's father testified that Ron did not have a driver's license at the time of his death. Parenthetically, this suggests Ron Goldman was driving without a license when driving around in Nicole's Ferrari in the weeks before they were both murdered.

The police searched the neighborhood all around Nicole's house, and they couldn't find a car. So, now everybody knows that at Nicole's Brentwood residence, when Ron Goldman was murdered and Nicole Simpson was murdered, a car belonging to Ron Goldman was not there. Uncritically, everybody assumes Ron just walked from the restaurant over to Nicole's place.

What makes sense to me is that Ron Goldman had to get a ride to Nicole's, a ride he expected to wait for him so they could drive to Marina Del Rey to meet with some guys. The Marina Del Rey closes early on Sundays, which raises another question. Why was Ron going all the way to Marina Del Ray to meet some guys who were at a restaurant that would be closing maybe even before he got there? At best, Ron could have expected to get to the Baha Cantina in time for last call on drinks. On Sunday, the Baha Cantina closes after the last person leaves, but generally they stay open only to 11:00 p.m., especially on Sundays. What was the meeting at the Marina Del Ray all about? That's a question I knew I would have to get around to answering, but whatever the meeting was about at the Marina Del Ray was not immediately apparent to me.

So, if Ron did get a ride, then the guy who drove him over to Nicole's house, had to wait for him to drop off the eyeglasses. I imagine Ron would have said to that driver guy something like this: "I'm going to take these eyeglasses in there. I'll be right back."

But that person who drove Ron Goldman to Nicole's place would have waited, and by waiting, that person would have seen or certainly heard the murder. Right?

Yes, that person would have seen the murder, unless that person was part of the murder.

If that were the case, the person who drove Ron to Nicole's house and participated in the murder could have just gotten back in their car, and driven away after murdering Ron, finding Nicole, and murdering her too. That would explain why no car having anything to do with Ron Goldman was found parked around Nicole's house after the murder. Now, the missing car finally makes sense, but only if the person driving that car was involved in murdering Ron Goldman.

Realizing this, I knew I had uncovered a very important clue. Whoever drove Ron Goldman from the Mezzaluna restaurant to Nicole's place that night probably participated in Ron Goldman's murder. I couldn't prove that yet, but I was on the trail to find out.

What I next needed to find were the evidence files the prosecutors had on Ron Goldman. Clearly the Los Angeles County District Attorney Gil Garcetti had to have asked the same questions I was asking, and Garcetti would have expected the prosecutors handling the O. J. Simpson murder case would have found answers consistent with the case the government presented at trial. Clearly, the prosecutors had to have figured out how Ron Goldman moved around Los Angeles that night.

You will never guess what I found . . .

More Sealed Files

Evidently, Ron Goldman had a criminal record. A letter from the Municipal Court in Malibu, California, referenced a criminal file identified as follows: Case File 91C00362, *The People of the State of California v. Ronald Lyle Goldman*. The letter was written on December 15, 2000, to deny access to the file because it included "judge's notes and police records." These files were not officially "sealed," but the judge had to give permission for anyone to examine those files, and the judge was not about to give permission.

We determined that the file originally had been six inches thick. But when we finally got the file unclamped and handed over, the file consisted only of three pages that contained nothing more than the docketing history of the defendant's arraignments. Officials at the Malibu Municipal Court told us the three pages were all that was left because the rest of the file had been destroyed. I had an uncomfortable feeling of *déjà vu* realizing the same had happened with the records of the statement and the plea deal Glen Rogers had done with Garcetti in 1995, before he was released back into society. Rogers readily admitted the California DA gave him the unique opportunity to resume his life as a killer. While we don't have the exact day of Glen's deposition or of his plea deal, I was able to determine Garcetti's office interviewed Glen in 1995 by Garcetti's office during the O. J. Simpson trial that started on September 26, 1994 and ended October 3, 1995.

All attempts to get ahold of Ron Goldman's criminal records were being blocked. On Friday, September 7, 2001, the Los Angeles County Sheriff's Department affirmed that Goldman's case file, 91COO362, documented multiple arrests, possibly as many as four different arrest incidents, and each separate arrest had its own arrest photograph. But the Sheriff's Department was protecting Goldman's arrest files from public access under some unspecified requirement of California law.

On November 27, 2001, an official letter on letterhead referencing both office of James Hahn, then Mayor of Los Angeles, and Bernard Parks, then Chief, claimed that under the California Public Records Act, the Los Angeles Police Department considered all files related to the LAPD investigation into the 1994 murders of Nicole Brown Simpson and Ron Goldman to be exempt from public disclosure. All requests to obtain such records, including the arrest photos or files from Ron Goldman's various arrests, were therefore being denied. Clearly, those files contained information officials in the state of California and the city of Los Angeles wanted no one to see, not now, not ever.

In his deposition on February 9, 1996, Fred Goldman acknowledged that Ron Goldman had been arrested by police, but he suggested there were only two arrests, and both were for traffic accidents. If Ron Goldman's criminal arrest record involved only him driving without a license, why would California suppress the records?

It is alleged that Ron Goldman dealt cocaine openly in L.A. at the Cheviot Hills Tennis Court parking lot, says investigator and author T. H. Johnson, who was largely responsible for the detective work that got Los Angeles officials to admit Ron Goldman had multiple criminal records. Johnson claims California was able to hide Ron Goldman's criminal file for the same reason Los Angeles County DA Garcetti sealed serial killer Glen Rogers 1995 recorded statement and plea deal. It appeared that both of them most likely got away with committing crimes because when caught by police, both Glen Rogers and Ron Goldman probably became informants and Government Code Section 6254 of California state law allows authorities to seal the criminal records of informants who give authorities material information valuable in prosecuting other, more serious criminals.[48] That was basically the same trick Marvin Glass used in the FBI Operation Greylord to avoid a 210-year prison sentence.

---

48 T. H. Johnson, "Fred Goldman You Lied So You and Daughter, Kim, Need to Sit Down," on his blog "maddoggbutkickingbrown's real truth!" August 24, 2018, and September 30, 2018.

Glen resumed his killing spree in Los Angeles after he was released, and his first victim was Sandra Gallagher, who he strangled and set afire in her truck the evening of Thursday, September 28, 1995 into the early morning hours of Friday, September 29, 1995. The jury was scheduled to begin deliberations in O. J. Simpson's murder trial that Monday, October 2, 1995. This strongly suggests the trigger for Glen Rogers to resume his killing spree by murdering Sandra Gallagher was the start at the beginning of the next week of the jury deliberations. Like many serial killers, there is bizarre desire to leave clues as to their identity in the pattern of the people they kill. Glen Rogers killed Sandra Gallagher very possibly because he wanted to leave District Attorney Garcetti a signal that the serial killer who most probably confessed to involvement in Nicole Brown Simpson and Ron Goldman murders was back on the loose, resuming his killing ways. The question remains who Glen Rogers informed on as the real force behind the Nicole and Ron Goldman murders as a precondition of getting Garcetti to release him under the plea deal.

Marvin Glass and the Colombian Drug Cartels

The mainstream narrative portrays Fred Goldman, the father of Ron Goldman, to have been a dedicated father who was inconsolably bereaved by the brutal death of his son. Most people remember the photographs of Fred Goldman, with his ample brown hair, distinctive mustache, and 1970s large frame tinted eyeglasses, sitting stoically in the courtroom through the O. J. Simpson murder trial ordeal. On one side holding one of Fred's hands was his daughter Kim, Ron's sister. On the other side holding Fred's other hand was his loving wife, Patti, Ron's stepmother. When the jury announced O. J. Simpson's acquittal, Kim began sobbing loudly and uncontrollably. Patti looked shocked as she hung her head down to her legs in disbelief. Fred just sat there, shaking his head "No," and through his disbelief looking desolate but angry. The Goldman's "fight for justice" had just begun. Fred dogged O. J. Simpson every way he could, determined to get revenge against O. J. for killing his son.

In February 1997, the Goldmans won their civil suit against O. J. Simpson, predicated on the presumption O. J. was the murderer.

The court awarded the Goldman's $8.5 million in compensatory damages, with another $25 million to be split with the family of Nicole Brown Simpson. O. J. was forced to sell his Heisman Trophy, netting the Goldmans a mere $250,000.[49] After that, the Goldmans had a hard time collecting, since O. J.'s financial condition following the trial left him judgment proof. Fred Goldman considered the civil verdict a vindication, but it was not yet justice.

Then, on October 3, 2008, the Goldmans finally felt they got the justice they sought when the Las Vegas jury found O. J. Simpson was guilty on twelve criminal counts in the high-profile kidnapping/robbery case involving his sports memorabilia. The judge and jury in that case had bought into the mainstream media's narrative that O. J. had murdered Nicole and Ron Goldman, and this was the sweet moment when the Goldmans and much of the American public could get what they viewed was justice. The judge in that case, Jackie Glass, delayed the sentencing to October 3, 2008, the anniversary of the day thirteen years earlier when the Los Angeles jury acquitted O. J. of murder, October 3, 1995. The television audience listening to the final verdict in the O. J. murder trial was estimated at a record 140 million. As we noted earlier, O. J. was sentenced to thirty-three years in prison, but he was released on parole in 2008 after serving nine years.[50] As I said, it was in 1999 that I started my twenty-year association with O. J. Simpson. By the way, after putting off scheduling O. J.'s sentencing so dramatically, Judge Jackie Glass went on to become a reality television star in her own right, as the host of *Swift Justice with Jackie Glass* on the Headline News (HLN), an affiliate of CNN. A close witness claims she started filming her reality show during the O. J. Simpson kidnapping/robbery trial in Las Vegas, proving the outcome of that trial was predetermined.

---

49 "Fred Goldman Biography," Biography.com, updated March 27, 2020, https://www .biography.com/crime-figure/fred-goldman.

50 Ethan Alter, Senior Writer, Yahoo Entertainment, "Here's what happened when the O. J. Simpson verdict was announced 25 years ago," Yahoo.com, October 2, 2020, https://www.yahoo.com/lifestyle/oj-simpson-verdict-announced-25-years-ago -002310638.html.

Okay, that's the mainstream narrative of the O. J. Simpson we all know.

But who are Fred Goldman and Patti Goldman, really? I decided to investigate. What I discovered surprised me, but then it also didn't surprise me. Everywhere I looked, the murders of Nicole Brown Simpson and Ron Goldman kept coming back to the same theme— illegal drugs, and a lot of them.

The Patti Goldman Drug Underworld Backstory

Fred's wife at the time of the O. J. Simpson murder trial was Patti Glass Goldman. Before Fred Goldman, Patti was married to Marvin Glass, a notorious but famous drug criminal. In 1986, when Patti was married to him, Chicago attorney Marvin Jay Glass was sentenced to eight years in federal prison after pleading guilty to his involvement in a $100 million drug importation ring tied to the Columbian drug cartels.[51] Glass had begun his career as a District Attorney who became the prosecutor in Cook County, Illinois, the county that includes Chicago. Unable to earn enough money there to satisfy him, Glass graduated to working with Columbian drug smugglers who financed Glass's millionaire lifestyle by paying him a percentage of all the cocaine and marijuana entering the Chicago market. His job was to introduce the Columbian drug cartels to drug dealers in Chicago who would sell the cocaine and marijuana to users.

He was arrested in 1985 for money laundering and charged with enough federal criminal counts to have served a potential sentence of 210 years if convicted of everything. But having once worked as a prosecutor, Glass knew the tricks of the trade, so he cut a plea deal that was the equal of the plea deal that serial killer Glen Rogers cut with Los Angeles County District Attorney Gil Garcetti in 1995 that got Rogers a "get-out-of-jail-free" card to continue his murder spree. Glass agreed to wear a wire in Operation Greylord, one of the FBI's most successful sting operations ever investigating public corruption

---

51 Maurice Possley, "Sentencing Shoots a High-Roller Down," *Chicago Tribune*, July 17, 1986, https://www.chicagotribune.com/news/ct-xpm-1986-07-17-8602200640 -story.html.

in the United States. On March 15, 1984, a federal jury in Chicago found Harold Conn guilty on all four counts of accepting bribes to be passed on to Illinois judges in Cook County. FBI undercover operations ended up with 92 Cook County officials indicted, including seventeen judges, forty-eight lawyers, eight policemen, ten deputy sheriffs, eight court officials, and one state legislator.[52]

Glass's case also involved famous lawyer and author Scott Turow, who is perhaps best known for writing *One L* while he was a student at Harvard Law School, the book that led to the long-running television show about law school, *Paper Chase*. In his career as a federal prosecutor, Turow led the probe in Chicago against Marvin Glass in Operation Greylord. It was Turow who convinced Glass to wear a wire—a secret recording device—to record conversations Glass had with Ronald Ofshe, a drug dealer arrested in Miramar, Florida, for possession with intent to distribute four and a half pounds of cocaine. Ofshe hired Marvin Glass to represent him as co-counsel. While representing Ofshe, Glass had learned that federal prosecutors planned to involve him in Operation Greylord for his role bribing Illinois judges. To get the plea deal, Glass convinced Turow that by wearing a wire on Ofshe, Glass's legal client, Glass could provide Turow with a conspiracy to smuggle two thousand pounds of marijuana as well as to launder money.[53] Before Turow was done with Marvin Glass, he managed to call a hit man who testified that Glass had paid him $2,500 to shoot and kill Michael Pritzker, an ex-partner, over a gambling debt.[54]

Throughout Glass's 1986 trial, his "faithful and loving wife" Patti sat in the courtroom every day just to stand by her man— her drug-dealing criminal husband, Marvin. Six months later, the same "faithful and loving wife" left Marvin Glass, taking with her

---

52   "Operation Greylord," FBI.gov, no date, https://www.fbi.gov/history/famous-cases/operation-greylord.

53   William B. Crawford Jr., "Attorney Panel Probes Lawyer, Author Turow," *Chicago Tribune*, August 5, 1987, https://www.chicagotribune.com/news/ct-xpm-1987-08-05-8702270133-story.html.

54   Michael Lacey, "Stranger than Fiction," *Phoenix New Times*, June 7, 1989, https://www.phoenixnewtimes.com/news/stranger-than-fiction-6412676.

their three children. Patti divorced Marvin Glass in order to marry
Fred Goldman. One commentator on this melodrama asked what I
thought was a very important question: "Is it a coincidence that the
son of Fred Goldman, the man who stole Marvin Glass's wife, was
viciously murdered sometime later?" If Marvin Glass harbored ven-
geance toward Fred Goldman for stealing his wife and taking away
his children, Marvin Glass may have felt justice would be served by
making sure Fred Goldman's family was destroyed when he lost his
only biological son, namely Ron Goldman.

Seems Marvin Glass paid for his sins. In 1985, when he was still
under investigation and on the run from law enforcement, he was
hit by a truck on a Florida highway and confined to a wheelchair.
Although he was sentenced to twenty-seven years in prison for his
crimes, Marvin Glass got out of prison early, with one commentator
claiming Marvin Glass was released in Fort Worth, Texas, after serving only two years. Marvin Glass was a free man as of October 20,
1989. After he was released from prison, Marvin Glass moved to Los
Angeles, where he reconnected with Fred Goldman and his ex-wife
Patti Glass, who was now Mrs. Patti Goldman. Finally, Marvin Glass
died of AIDS in Chicago on May 15, 1997.[55]

That same commentator noted the following about the Marvin
Glass psychodrama with his ex-wife Patti and her new husband Fred
Goldman:

> Knowing, and understanding the full powerbase of her ex-husband,
> Patti Glass and Fred Goldman relocate to California as soon after
> their wedding as circumstances will permit. For nearly eight years
> they live quietly with Fred's children, safely beyond the reach of
> Marvin Glass—hoping AIDS will claim him before he is free.[56]

---

55 "Obits," Poz.com, November 1, 1997, https://www.poz.com/article/Obituaries
-November-1997-15991-7714.
56 Johannes Scmidt, "Psychoceramics: O. J. and the Columbian Cartel," Dev.Null.org,
December 16, 1997, http://dev.null.org/psychoceramics/archives/1997.12/msg00071
.html.

That same commentator had an astute observation about the role Ron Goldman played in this psychodrama. Consider the following:

> In 1994, Ronald Lyle Goldman has proven himself to be a failure. He is a Hollywood wannabe Actor, without a SAG; a wannabe model, without an agent; unable to pay his parking tickets, his driver's license was revoked—yet, in blatant disregard for the law, he drove borrowed cars; living beyond his visible means, he filed bankruptcy—yet he had access to hundreds of thousands of dollars necessary to build an upscale restaurant.
>
> When a vengeful man (Marvin Glass) knows he's dying of an incurable disease, and wishes to reap vengeance over the loss of a loved one, would he kill that person—thus quickly sending them on ahead—or would he want them too to suffer the loss of someone near to them?[57]

Looks like Marvin Glass was not the only one in the O. J. Simpson drama to appreciate the sweet taste of revenge. Glass believed he got HIV from a blood transfusion in the medical work done after the accident. He died on May 16, 1997, in Chicago, of pneumonia.[58]

But if you think this chapter has been unexpected so far, it is just about to get a whole lot weirder . . .

Fred Goldman, Mystery Man

Fred Goldman was born in Chicago on December 6, 1940—just a year and a day before the Japanese attacked the U.S. Navy at Pearl Harbor. Fred did not become a public figure until his son, Ron, was murdered. He also had a daughter, named Kim. Fred Goldman had three marriages. His first was to Sharon Rufo, from 1967 to 1974, the

---

57 Ibid.

58 "Life Is a Trial for Goldman Mom," *New York Magazine*, June 2, 1997, p. 10, https ://books.google.com/books?id=OugCAAAAMBAJ&pg=PA10&lpg=PA10&dq =marvin+glass+drug+dealer+obituary+1997&source=bl&ots=Cz6kgB3278 &sig=ACfU3U00E0BQYOXGMMyDwOIAgczgtNSteA&hl=en&sa=X&ved =2ahUKEwjOxb2zktjuAhXwQd8KHR7rCyIQ6AEwEnoECAoQAg#v =onepage&q=marvin%20glass%20drug%20dealer%20obituary%201997&f=false

mother of Ron and Kim. His second marriage was to Joan Goldman, from 1977-1978. As we noted earlier, he married Patti Glass in 1987. Fred and Patti Glass live today in Phoenix, Arizona, and he lists his profession simply as "businessman." Goldman's net worth in 2021 was estimated at $3 million. Most biographies of Fred Goldman correctly note that not much is known about Fred Goldman's parents, his early life, and his educational background.[59] Today, at over eighty years old, Fred Goldman has gained weight, and his abundant hair along with his distinctive mustache have turned grey, but from recent photographs he appears to be wearing eyeglasses very similar in style to those he wore during the O. J. Simpson murder trial, now some twenty-five years ago.

As you probably suspect, I had a lot of questions about Fred Goldman that I was unable to answer, despite the twenty years I spent investigating and researching this case. I wanted to know what Fred Goldman did in Chicago to earn a living. How did he meet Marvin Glass? Was Fred in business with Marvin Glass? What was his relationship to Patti Glass while she was married to Marvin? How did Fred and Patti meet? Why were they married so quickly, only six months after Marvin Glass was convicted in 1986? I wondered if Fred Goldman worked for Marvin Glass in the drug business. Maybe that was why Fred Goldman kept what he did in Chicago so secret. Why did Fred and Patti Goldman move to Los Angeles after they married? I could not find any employment for Fred in L.A., nor any business he claimed to own. Goldman claimed in 2021 that O. J. had paid him only $132,000 in the wrongful death suit.[60] So, what's the source of Fred's $3 million net worth today? I simply could not find out, no matter how hard I looked.

It was mind-boggling, totally mind-boggling, especially for me. Remember, I'm "Spiderboy." I created one of the first search engines

59   Becca Bleznak, "Fred Goldman Net Worth 2021: Age, Height, Weight, Wife, Kids, Bio-Wiki," WealthyPersons.com, January 1, 2021, https://www.wealthypersons.com /fred-goldman-net-worth-2020-2021/.

60   "O. J.'s Only Paid $132K in Wrongful Death Suit . . . Owes Millions," TMZ.com, February 3, 2021, https://www.tmz.com/2021/02/03/oj-simpson-fred-goldman-132k -wrongful-death-ron-goldman-nicole-brown-simpson/.

on the internet back in 1995. I could find everything about everybody, anytime, anywhere. My search engine was called "Spiderboy," and my theme was "Spiderboy Rules the Web." When Marvel Comics sued me for $1 billion because I held the trademark to "Spiderboy," I found out enough about them to shut them down. Yet, I couldn't break Fred Goldman to find out any answers to these questions that I still have. Marvel Comics had some two hundred attorneys that were coming at me at all different directions while I was fighting them with my company.

Finally, from what I discovered, my one attorney called the state's attorney's office, and I was going to have the president of Marvel Comics arrested over this information I found on the internet. With that, Marvel Comics shut down coming after me, and they decided they didn't want to talk about "Spiderboy" anymore. They called off their two hundred attorneys and asked me if I would leave it alone. My attorney said, "Once Norman goes into the trenches, it's hard to get him out." They kept me in court for two years, strangling my company, Spiderboy International. Every time I would go for an investor, they would say, "I can't invest in your company because you have a billion-dollar lawsuit from Marvel and we're not going to mess with that. If we give you a million dollars, Marvel Comics will just take it."

Marvel Comics had Spiderman, Spider Girl, and Spider Woman, and they felt it was only right they should have that name, Spiderboy, too. They felt Spiderboy ought to be in their family, not mine. Marvel Comics said my relationship with O. J. was damaging their image. But with what I found on the web, I shut them down, so I go by the Spiderboy nickname even today. I won in that I kept the "Spiderboy" nickname, but I lost because it was the end of the dot com boom. I had to rename my company, and it merged into a telecom company that grew into a public entity with stock valued at $100 million.

Yet I couldn't find anything out about Fred Goldman. He's a dark hole—information goes in, but nothing comes out. I came to the conclusion there are some things that can't be found out because whoever is hiding the information worked hard to make sure nothing could be found out. Fred Goldman falls into that category—it's obvious Fred Goldman wants to keep most everything about his life a secret. That just ends up intriguing somebody like me—what can be so dangerous for us to know that Fred Goldman has determined nobody can find records that prove anything for sure about who Fred Goldman is or what Fred Goldman does.

Investigator T. H. Johnson largely agrees that there was more to the Fred Goldman story than the public knew at the time of the O. J. Simpson trial, or even now. Johnson pointed out that Fred Goldman said in his book about his son, *His Name Was Ron*, Marvin Glass was in close proximity to Goldman and Goldman's family when Glass was in Los Angeles after his release from prison. Patti Glass kept custody of her three children after she divorced Marvin Glass. But while living with Fred Goldman, all three children—Brian, Michael, and Lauren—still carried the surname of their father, Marvin Glass. Johnson reported Fred Goldman was an abusive stepfather who allegedly abused both Brian and Michael. Johnson also reports that in Chicago, Goldman allegedly beat Marvin Glass with his own cane in his wheelchair at a Jewish Social Center in a northern suburb. Johnson claimed Fred Goldman was abusive even to his own son, Ron, who allegedly engaged in fisticuffs with Fred more than once.

Johnson noted that on an interview on ABC's *20/20* Kim Goldman was asked what Fred did for a living and she said she didn't know what work he did.[61] We would be speculating, but a good reason to assume Fred Goldman was close to Marvin Glass would very likely be that they worked together, possibly even when Marvin Glass was fronting for the Colombian drug cartels. People who allegedly engage in the drug business have a reputation for finding that it is a hard business to get out of, both because of the money and out of fear over quitting.

"Fred Goldman and his daughter, Kim, have simply acted like two grifters still trying to extort money from the case where the police and the L.A. DA placed the blame for their son's death on O. J. Simpson,"

---

61 T.H. Johnson, "Fred Goldman You Lied So You and Daughter, Kim, Need to Sit Down," op.cit.

Johnson wrote.[62] O. J. would agree. In 2018, O. J. begged Fred Goldman to stop dragging him to court on every "unconfirmed rumor" he was making money.[63]

But a key point to remember here is that Fred Goldman only won his civil lawsuit against O. J. for wrongful death because the mainstream narrative portrayed Ron Goldman as the innocent victim murdered viciously by O. J. only because Ron wanted to do a favor for Nicole Brown Simpson and her mother, Judith Brown, and his timing was unfortunate. Had Ron Goldman's criminal record been made available to the public on June 13, 1994, Fred Goldman might today have no judgment to collect the more than $33 million that he still argues publicly that O. J. Simpson owes him. Few understand even today that after Fred Goldman married Patti Glass, and possibly even before, Ron Goldman lived with a family whose backstory was the Chicago criminal underworld and the Columbian cocaine trade.

Let's face reality about the Hollywood glitterati club crowd—that group more properly characterized is the poster case for the sex, drugs, and rock-and-roll lifestyle that make famous the rich and glamorous Beverly Hills "tinsel town" socialites driving around L.A. in their Ferrari and Lamborghini sports cars. Faye Resnick, who at that time was staying with Nicole Simpson in her Brentwood home and is reputed to have had a romantic relationship with Nicole,[64] was actually checked into a drug rehabilitation center in Marina del Ray the day Nicole and Ron Goldman were killed. Five years earlier, Resnick was introduced to Nicole by Kris Jenner, who was then locked in divorce proceedings with Robert Kardashian.[65] Nicole herself was known to be a "party animal"

---

62   Ibid.

63   Cheyenne Roundtree and Hannah Parry, "O. J. Begs the Family of Ron Goldman," DailyMail.com, January 22, 2018, https://www.dailymail.co.uk/news/article-5299831 /OJ-Simpson-responds-Fred-Goldmans-suit.html.

64   "Nicole Led 'Dangerous Life,' Family Friend Testifies," *Desert News*, April 2, 1996, https://www.deseret.com/platform/amp/1996/4/2/19234355/nicole-led-dangerous -life-family-friend-testifies.

65   Ralph Frammolino and Shawn Hubler, " 'Diary' Opens a New, Lurid Chapter," *Los Angeles Times*, October 20, 1994, https://www.latimes.com/archives/la-xpm-1994-10 -20-me-52588-story.html.

who was into cocaine and good-looking guys[66]—facts that Ron Goldman surely must have appreciated. Other reports indicated that on one occasion Faye Resnick and Nicole had allegedly freebased cocaine while driving through Los Angeles, and that Nicole's cocaine abuse, like Resnick's cocaine abuse, was becoming "reckless and dangerous."[67]

So, I hate to tell you, but with that much said, the story still gets even weirder . . . in fact, a lot weirder . . .

Did Fred Goldman Marry His Sister?

In one of the many genealogical searches that I did over the years on Fred Goldman, I kept running across a listing that said Fred Goldman's mother was Elaine Goldman.

Then I ran across an article published in 1985 in the *Chicago Tribune* that said Chicago attorney Marvin Glass had been arrested with felony theft after $8,000 allegedly was stolen from his vacationing mother-in-law's safe deposit box.[68] The newspaper reported that Marvin Glass was arrested after he walked out of the Deerbrook State Bank in Deerfield, Illinois. The article also reported Deerbrook police had contacted Glass's mother-in-law, Elaine Goldman, who was vacationing in Palm Springs, California. Of course, Marvin Glass's wife at that time was Patti Glass, who later married Fred Goldman.

The first thing that struck me was that I had been looking for a connection between the Goldman family and Marvin Glass. Well, here it was . . . Marvin Glass was married to a woman whose mother was Elaine Goldman. But if Patti Glass's mother was Elaine Goldman

---

66 "Nicole Brown Simpson Was Involved in Drug-Fueled Parties & Steamy Affairs Before Death," RadarOnLine.com, June 3, 2016, https://radaronline.com /exclusives/2016/06/oj-simpson-nicole-brown-murder-party-sex-affairs/.

67 "Framed in America," theunredacted.com, February 21, 2018, https://theunredacted .com/oj-simpson-framed-in-america/.

68 Bonita Brodt and Douglas Frantz, "Lawyer Charged in Theft from Relative," *Chicago Tribune*, May 7, 1985, https://www.chicagotribune.com/news/ct-xpm-1985-05 -07-8501280277-story.html.

and Fred Goldman's mother was Elaine Goldman, does that mean Fred Goldman married his sister?

So, an investigator contacted Marvin Glass's son, Brian Glass, and asked Brian if he could explain this. He did so. Brian said that Elaine Jacobs was married to Edgar Jacobs. They were the parents of Patti Glass. But Elaine and Edgar Jacobs divorced, and subsequently Elaine married Morey Goldman. So, Elaine Jacobs, i.e., Elaine Goldman, was the mother of Patti Jacobs, i.e., Patty Glass, i.e., Patty Goldman (fathered by Edgar Jacobs), and Elaine Goldman was also the mother of Fred Goldman (fathered by Morey Goldman).

The investigator had emailed Brian Glass to ask if Elaine and Morey Goldman were related to Fred Goldman, just to make sure. "Of course, they are related," Brian Glass emailed in response.

Ron Goldman's Waiter Friend Shot and Killed

Some fifteen months after Ron Goldman was murdered, Michael Nigg, 26 years old, a friend of Ron Goldman, was also murdered. Nigg was a waiter at Sanctuary in Beverly Hills, another trendy restaurant like the Mezzaluna, and an aspiring actor, and a L.A. hanger-on like Ron Goldman. Both were getting-old, twenty-some year old guys waiting for their "big break" in Hollywood. Also, like Ron Goldman who had appeared on *Studs.* on January 20, 1992, Michael Nigg appeared on the Fox network late-night game show *Liars*. If these connections were not enough, Kim Goldman had dated Michael Nigg in San Francisco in 1992.[69]

Nigg was murdered when he was going to dinner with his girlfriend, Julie Long, in the Fairfax District of Los Angeles. At approximately 10:30 p.m., Michael Nigg pulled his car into a lot in the 300 block of North Poinsettia Place. After getting out of his car and getting $40 from an ATM machine, Nigg was approached by two armed men who demanded he give them the cash. When Nigg refused, he was shot in the head. The robbers then fled in a car driven by a third suspect. The

---

69 Brian Heiss, "World Exclusive: Kim Goldman Dated Michael Nigg in 1992," OJSimpson.com, May 3, 2018, https://ojsimpson.co/kim-goldman-dated-michael-nigg-in-1992/.

robbers neglected to take with them either Nigg's wallet or the $40 cash he had just gotten out of the ATM machine, another strange tidbit.

Before working at Sanctuary, Nigg had worked as a waiter at Mezzaluna, where he befriended Ron Goldman. Nigg quit working at Mezzaluna in May 1994, a month before Ron Goldman was killed.[70] Nigg appeared to live beyond his means, driving a Mercedes while working as a waiter. While there is no proof Nigg's murder was tied to drug trafficking, the unsolved crime involved the second waiter at that time who was killed in Los Angeles, with connections with Ron Goldman that are impossible to dismiss.

---

70 "Friend of Ronald Goldman Fatally Shot by Thieves." Associated Press, September 12, 1995, https://apnews.com/article/3df5f7cce88a1a904ec4afca879e80ad.

CHAPTER 8

Glen Rogers Talks

———

That press release I issued wanting to speak to Glen Rogers was more effective than I anticipated. After that first letter that Glen wrote me from prison, Glen started sending letters to my home address from prison.

Even more surprising, Glen Rogers started communicating to me and others regarding all the details he knew surrounding the murders of Nicole Brown Simpson and Ron Goldman. I promise you this chapter may be a rough ride but I believe the twists, turns, and surprises will be worth it—provided you want to know the truth.

Not in my wildest imagination could I have ever expected what Glen Rogers revealed in those letters. What's more, everything he said turned out to be true. How did I know that? First, what Glen said about the murders made sense. Second, to my great surprise, I was able to track down and verify every detail of the story Glen Rogers gave me.

Did Glen Rogers Do It?

There is a theory out there that Glen Rogers did the killing. You can easily find it on the internet. At first, I didn't think too much of Glen

Rogers. But the more I found out about Glen, the more I kept digging, the more interesting Glen Rogers became.

That first letter was an eye-opener, as we have already discussed. But I kept wanting to know if Glen Rogers was the murderer. If O. J. wasn't the murderer, I had to know if O. J. Simpson had hired Glen Rogers to kill Nicole.

Then, on February 13, 2013, Glen wrote this short note. It read as follows:

> I Glen Edward Rogers, now on Florida Death Row, make the following statement—O. J. Simpson and myself did not contract with one another to do anything to his wife.
>
> Glen Edward Rogers
> Death Row
> Raiford, Florida

What struck me right away was that Glen Rogers specified that he did not contract with O. J., but he said it in a way that sounded to me like he was leaving something open that was implied but not said directly. Was Rogers saying he didn't contract with O. J., but he did contract with somebody else to kill Nicole?

And then I noticed he specified O. J. had not contracted with him to "do anything" to Nicole. Glen did not use the word "kill." That seemed important. Was the incident on June 12, 1994 not planned to be a murder, but an attempt to "harm" Nicole? Or maybe just to "scare" Nicole.

What I also noticed was that Glen Rogers did not mention Ron Goldman. In saying outright that he had not contracted with O. J. to do anything to Nicole, Glen was not ruling out that O. J. or someone else other than O. J. might have hired Glen Rogers to harm or to scare Ron Goldman. Was Ron Goldman the target that night, not Nicole?

Glen was a serial killer. He clearly didn't mind killing people, yet this denial was very carefully written, and it said nothing about murder. I began to wonder if the murders of Nicole Brown Simpson and Ron Goldman happened because something that night went terribly wrong.

The more I thought about it, the weirder this part started getting too. I began to conclude that everybody in this Nicole saga was whacked with some kind of a mental problem or other. The whole story was messed up and the more I unraveled, the more messed up it became.

In the first letter, Glen had stressed that he believed I needed to hear him out. But he also pointed out that I would not have to take his word that what he had to say was true because he had made "a full taped statement in my case" in 1995. In mentioning "my case," Glen was saying that "my case" was the murders of Nicole Brown Simpson and Ron Goldman.

I concluded from this that Glen was telling me his 1995 deposition to Garcetti's office must have disclosed why and possibly even how the Nicole Brown Simpson and Ron Goldman killings happened. To be believable to the prosecutors in 1995, Glen's deposition had to have disclosed information about himself, very likely information that implicated Glen himself in the killings.

But a confession would have demanded Garcetti would have to stop the O. J. murder trial, because the prosecutors had predicated O. J. prosecution on the theory O. J. was the murderer. But there was more to what Glen was saying in this short note. He got a plea deal after he gave his deposition. But to get a plea deal, Glen would have had to say more than how he was involved in the Nicole Brown Simpson and Ron Goldman murders. He would have had to inform on someone else.

Glen gave his deposition to Garcetti in 1995, while the O. J. trial was going on. If what Glen said in that deposition solved the case such that O. J. was not guilty, why did Garcetti let the trial continue? If Garcetti let the jury proceed to deliberation and if the jury had found O. J. Simpson guilty, Garcetti would not have been able to intervene, even if Glen Rogers had proved to Garcetti that O. J. did not commit the murders. I began to conclude that Garcetti and the LAPD wanted O. J. to be found guilty and very possibly the prosecutors did not care whether in truth O. J. was the murderer, or not.

I recalled that Glen had closed his earlier, first letter by commenting that he hoped to be working with me soon. Now, with his second, short note Glen Rogers sounded like he was getting ready to tell me what he knew. By saying he had not contracted with O. J. to "harm" Nicole, Glen was hinting he knew the truth, and it sounded to me like he was getting ready to tell me the whole story of what happened that night, including how he was involved.

What kept going through my mind was Glen's second statement in that short note, when he commented the additional point that "O. J. Simpson and myself did not contract with one another to do anything to his wife." If the encounter at Nicole's condo in Brentwood did not have anything to do with Nicole, what was going on?

Glen ended the first letter underscoring that he wanted to start working with me with some urgency, denoted by his adding " . . . before they get rid of me." Glen knew he was on Death Row and he was preparing to face death. But before he did that, he was taking up my request to speak with him, and it sounded like he was ready to spill his guts—but this time not in a deposition he calculated would get him a plea deal, but because he wanted to let the world know what he had done. What I concluded was that Glen was telling me he wanted to get the truth on the record before he died, and he was saying he was ready to tell me the truth.

Glen kept his word. He did start talking to me and the mystery around Nicole finally started unraveling. But, again, I can't promise you the story is going to be pretty. I'm sure you've already figured out that everybody in the story had a backstory, and the backstories all seemed to intersect on drugs, sex, rock-and-roll, complicated broken-up families—people were so messed up, they were beyond repair. In listening to Glen and exploring what he was really telling me, I found the final solution added racial prejudice and official criminality to the mess. I guess I shouldn't have been surprised.

With this chapter the solution to the double-murder mystery begins. But the solution does not make things simpler. The solution, it turns out, is the strangest ride of all.

What Was Glen Rogers' Relationship to Nicole?

In all these letters Glen Rogers sent me and from the other letters I collected that Glen had sent members of his family, he was adamant that he knew Nicole, and he knew her well. Glen told me that he was painting Nicole's house and that he was dating her. Redd, the anonymous informant we met in Chapter 6, confirmed to me that Glen Rogers would call him from various nightclubs in Los Angeles, telling him that he was with Nicole, or that he was with Nicole and Faye Resnick. "It was no secret around the time Nicole was killed that Glen Rogers was hanging around with her," Redd said. "But everybody at that time knew Glen Rogers as James Peters, the alias Glen Rogers was using at the time." I knew Redd was right. I remember what Witness #1 told us about that night she and her two friends were at The Gate with Dodi Fayed. Glen Rogers was the sandy blonde guy who was with Nicole that night.

As we discussed in Chapter 6, Glen sent his mother a photograph of him and Nicole together. Glen wrote his mother when he sent her that picture, and he asked his mother, "Guess who I'm hanging out with?" Glen described Nicole as his "new girlfriend." He asked his mother, "Ain't she pretty?" Redd said he saw the picture of Glen and Nicole together, but at the time, he didn't know who Nicole was. "She was obviously a very attractive woman," Redd said. "At the time, I didn't recognize Nicole was the pretty lady with Glen Rogers in that photograph, but I know now that's who it was—the same guy who was going around posing as James Peters, an alias he stole from that older gentleman, Mark Peters, who Glen had allegedly killed back in Ohio in 1993."

So, now I didn't have to rely on Witness #1. I had Glen's statement that he knew Nicole and I had Redd's confirmation. Redd was an eyewitness who could vouch for the fact Glen Rogers and Nicole were together. But that photograph of Nicole and Glen Rogers together is now long gone. Redd claimed the FBI came and took everything—letters, tapes, photographs—everything—the police and the FBI impounded everything, and we never got the picture back again. That's why today nobody has any photograph of Glen and Nicole together.

But if Glen Rogers was dating Nicole around the time of her death, he was coming in and out of Nicole's house. I knew that was the way it had to have been. Glen was no stranger to Nicole. He was very familiar with Nicole, with her house, and with the grounds. Now, I wouldn't expect Glen Rogers had a key to Nicole's home. But he would have had a way to get in and get out of Nicole's home in Brentwood. But if O. J. had a key, that would give Glen Rogers access to Nicole's home. Provided, that is, that O. J. knew Glen Rogers at the time. I surmised this had to have been the case because otherwise in that short note Glen wrote me from prison on February 13, 2013, he would have said he made no deal with O. J. to harm Nicole because he didn't know O. J. then. But if Glen Rogers knew Nicole, it was a sure bet he also knew O. J. After that family vacation in April 1994 over Easter, the vacation Robert Kardashian was not invited to attend, O. J. and Nicole were attempting to reconcile.

The FBI Raid

On November 23, 2014, 20 years after the murders, I put out a $100,000 reward.[71] Specifically, I asked for information about what had gone on in Las Vegas when O. J. was arrested. But I never gave up on the 1994 murders and I wanted to hear from anybody who knew anything about those murders.

So, this investigator in Minnesota had been accumulating all this evidence on O. J. Simpson in boxes. I called him up, and I said, "I need this information you've been accumulating." Some thirty minutes later, the FBI along with the Minneapolis Police Department raided his office with a SWAT team and took everything he had on O. J. Simpson, leaving behind everything else.

The police broke down the office doors and broke locks using ram, crowbars, and bolt cutters, when the manager of that office would have unlocked the doors, if the Minneapolis Police Department had first presented a search warrant. The FBI threw flash grenades into

---

71   "O. J. Simpson's Manager Offers $100,000 Reward to Prove Defense Attorney Is to Blame in Simpson's Las Vegas Trial," RadarOnLine.com, October 31, 2014, https ://radaronline.com/exclusives/2014/10/oj-simpson-manager-reward-lawyer-involved -robbery/.

the office that blinded everyone. The SWAT team dressed all in black came into the office armed with automatic weapons. The FBI took all the employees outside and set them down on their knees. The police forced everybody to board a city bus where they swabbed each person in the mouth to collect DNA. The FBI claimed they were there to raid a non-existent "High Stakes" poker game, but what they did was to pry open with a crowbar the private locked office. In there, the FBI took away everything on the shelves that had O. J. Simpson's name on it. The boxes on those two or three shelves contained all evidence we had collected on O. J. Simpson after that award was announced. I don't know how the O. J. Simpson material the FBI confiscated pertained to suspicion of illegal gambling. An attorney sent a letter to the FBI demanding the return of the O. J. Simpson files that were taken, but the FBI never returned anything to us.

That raid in 2014, occurred minutes after my phone call to Minnesota asking for the O. J. material that we had received on the reward offer to be sent to me. So, even two decades after the murder of Nicole Brown Simpson and Ron Goldman, the FBI was still monitoring anybody looking into the O. J. Simpson case. I believe the FBI wanted to make sure nothing on Glen Rogers came out in that case and I am confident the FBI knew that I was corresponding with Glen Rogers in prison. The FBI wants the entire O. J. Simpson case to remain hidden. I know that because of all the sealed files that I kept finding in my investigations. There is a deep, dark secret at the heart of the Nicole Brown Simpson and Ron Goldman murders, and I believe the secret is the LAPD and the FBI were probably both involved in the drug trade. We know Glen Rogers was working with the LAPD because he entered into a plea deal with Los Angeles County District Attorney Gil Garcetti. I know Glen Rogers was working with the FBI because he told me he was working with the FBI.

But the FBI did not know what I was getting after I posted that reward. That's what scared them. It also scared O. J. because O. J. did not know what I was accumulating. Nobody on this planet put a $100,000 reward out on the O. J. Simpson case except for me. I'm the only one who ever put out a reward for O. J. Simpson stuff. The FBI raided that office to get their hands on the information I was getting on O. J. after I offered that reward.

Let's understand that in the police investigation of the Nicole Brown Simpson and Ron Goldman murders, the LAPD and the District Attorney Garcetti wanted Glen Rogers to go away because he was a serial killer, and as soon as the jury knew a serial killer was painting Nicole's house and dating her, you would probably destroy the case against O. J. Simpson. O. J. did not want to admit he knew Glen Rogers. "You don't want to have anything to do with that guy," O. J. told me. "Stay away from that guy." Then, when O. J. figured out that I was getting letters Glen Rogers sent me from prison, he got mad. "I told you to stay away from that guy." O. J. knew I was getting close to Glen Rogers and he figured out I was getting close to figuring out the murders.

That's why O. J. and I started fighting when O. J. was in prison for the Las Vegas kidnapping and robbery. When O. J. was in prison, I sent him that first letter that Glen Rogers had sent me. Remember, Glen Rogers asked me in that letter to "please tell O. J. Simpson that I'm very sorry for the death of his wife." So, I sent O. J. that letter. That's when O. J. went ballistic. "I don't know you anymore," O.J, said to me because of that letter. "I told you to stay away from that guy." That was the last time I talked with O. J. Simpson. It was obvious to me that O. J. knew all about Glen Rogers and the role Glen Rogers had played in the murders, and O. J. went ballistic over me talking to Glen Rogers. After some twenty years of being O. J.'s confidant, this one letter—the first one Glen Rogers wrote me from prison—was all it took for O. J. to distance himself from me completely.

LAPD: The Rampart Scandal

The Rampart Scandal was triggered when LAPD officer Rafael Perez decided to become a whistleblower. He charged that dozens of his fellow police officers of the CRASH anti-gang unit (Community Resources Against Street Hoodlums) working in the LAPD Rampart Division in the 1990s were corrupt. Perez claimed the Rampart CRASH unit "was filled with drug-dealing rogue cops who were shaking down gang members and framing people."[72] Perez accused the Rampart CRASH unit of harassing and shaking-down suspects, manufacturing evidence, falsifying reports, and making false arrests while these same LAPD officers were controlling and profiting from the drug trade.

On June 30, 2009, a global civil settlement paid $20.5 million to the victims of the Rampart Scandal. On November 3, 2000, the City of Los Angeles and the Department of Justice entered into a consent decree under which the DO. J. would oversee the operations of the LAPD for five years.[73] Whistleblower Perez claimed the police officers in the Rampart Division CRASH program mimicked the gangs by wearing skull tattoos, as well as dressing and displaying the mannerisms of gang members. Before the LAPD Rampart Scandal was done, some 100 criminal cases were overturned, and Los Angeles paid upwards of $100 million for the indiscretions of the Rampart Division of the LAPD.[74]

LAPD: Mark Fuhrman Racial and Sexual Slurs

On Tuesday, September 5, 1995, at the O. J. Simpson murder trial, the defense played for the jury a tape of former LAPD officer Mark Fuhrman uttering racial slurs that he had previously under oath denied doing over the past decade. Fuhrman had been one of the LAPD officers who had been most active at the Nicole Brown Simpson and Ron Goldman murder crime scenes. It was Fuhrman who found the bloody glove at Simpson's estate that matched the bloody glove found at the scene where Nicole and Ron were killed.

The O. J. defense also called to the stand that day two other witnesses to testify that Fuhrman had not only used racial slurs, but also

---

72 "The Rampart Scandal," PBS.org, no date, https://www.pbs.org/wgbh/pages /frontline/shows/lapd/scandal/.

73 "Good Cops Get Justice—The Untold Story of the Rampart Scandal," InsiderExclusive.com, no date, https://insiderexclusive.com/good-cops-get-justice-the -untold-story-of-the-lapd-rampart-scandal/.

74 Renford Reese, Cal Poly Political Science Department, "The Multiple Causes of the LAPD Rampart Scandal," *Journal of Interdisciplinary Studies*, Spring 2003, https ://www.cpp.edu/~rrreese/nonfla/RAMPART.HTML.

indicated he wanted to see the black race obliterated.[75] Taking the stand the next day, Fuhrman asserted his Fifth Amendment rights against self-incrimination, refusing to answer questions posed by the defense lawyers who charged that Fuhrman framed O. J. Simpson. "Have you ever falsified a police report?" defense attorney Gerald F. Uelmen asked Fuhrman on the stand. "Did you plant or manufacture any evidence in this case?" Fuhrman did not respond, passing the opportunity to refute or deny the accusation.[76]

The defense attorneys created what many consider a key turning point in the O. J. Simpson murder trial questioning Fuhrman and raising the possibility the LAPD had biased the evidence as part of a racially motivated plot to plant or otherwise alter evidence so as to get a guilty verdict in the O. J. murder case. The Rampart Scandal strongly suggests ethnic and racial prejudice existed in the LAPD in the 1990s, with evidence LAPD corruption extended to direct LAPD participation in the drug trade. Fuhrman's tape-recorded rantings made public in 1997 also provided evidence Fuhrman allegedly played a leadership role in "Men Against Women" (MAW), an all-male club of LAPD officers who wore hoods, Ku Klux Klan style, to preside at beer-fueled mock trials held in the dead of the night at a baseball field. LAPD officers participating in MAW promoted sexual as well as racial discrimination, with MAW aimed at driving women off the force.[77]

The Night of the Murders: A Planned Event

Remember, O. J. is not a jealous person. He's not that way. I've seen him with his other girlfriends. The one girl allegedly had a lot of sex with the football players all around the neighborhood in Miami when

---

75 United Press International (UPI), "O. J. Jury hears Fuhrman tape," Tuesday, September 5, 1995.

76 Stephanie Simo, Henry Weinstein, and Andrea Ford, "Fuhrman Invokes 5th Amendment, Refuses to Testify," Los Angeles Times, September 7, 1995.

77 Michelle Caruso, "Fuhrman Led 'Klan' vs. Female Officers on Tapes, O. J. Cop Tells of 'Tribunals.'" New York Daily News, April 28, 1997, https://www.nydailynews.com/archives/news/fuhrman-led-klan-female-officers-tapes-o-trial-tells-tribunals-article-1.757959.

O. J. was with her, and he didn't seem to mind. O. J. didn't object, "Oh my God, she had sex with all these football players, get rid of her." This is the stupidest thing in the world for people to say, "O. J. went into a jealous rage and started killing people." No. You start killing people because you go insane and you start killing people. The events that night appeared to be planned.

What I think happened started when O. J. went to his daughter's recital. He had missed too many events with his children, and he felt he had to be at his daughter's recital. O. J. stayed at the recital for a while but ended up leaving before Nicole and her mother, Mrs. Juditha Brown, left with the kids. At about 6:30 p.m., Nicole and her mother took the kids to Mezzaluna for dinner. O. J. and Nicole were obviously having problems. There are 911 calls to support that. But we saw those photographs in Chapter 3 when weeks before the murders, Nicole and O. J., along with the entire Kardashian family, were on Easter vacation together, in April 1994. Kris Jenner was there with her new husband, Bruce Jenner, and everyone was there except Robert Kardashian. At that time, it appears Nicole and O. J. were again trying to make their relationship work. Two months later, Nicole was dead.

So, on the night of the murder, Nicole and her mother go out to dinner with Nicole's kids, and they leave the Mezzaluna around 8:30 p.m.. Mrs. Brown loses her glasses but doesn't realize it when she leaves the restaurant. When she gets to her home in Dana Point, she calls the Mezzaluna, looking for her eyeglasses. From there, Nicole and the kids stop for ice cream. After that, Nicole and the kids went home, where Nicole put her ice cream in the freezer. The kids ate their ice cream. She put the kids to sleep.

Enter Kato Kaelin

In 1994, Kato Kaelin was staying at the guest house on O. J. Simpson's Rockingham estate. Faye Resnick and Nicole met Kato when they went to Aspen, Colorado, for New Year's 1992–1993. In her 1994 book, *Nicole Simpson: The Private Diary of a Life Interrupted*, Resnick claimed Kato and Nicole did not have a sexual relationship. "He was sweet but had minimal sex appeal," she wrote. Faye

Resnick characterized Kato as "a jester" and "a would-be comedian." She said Kato, another aspiring actor or model, arrived in Los Angeles with no place to stay. Nicole let Kato move into her guest house when she was living at Gretna Greene, in exchange for Kato babysitting the kids. When Nicole moved to the Bundy Drive condo, there was no guest house for Kato. So, O. J. offered to move Kato into his guest house at Rockingham, in exchange for working as a caretaker.[78]

(VIDEO STARTS)

> **[We see O. J. walking down a hall, talking. O. J. is being taped from behind and we don't see the face of the person walking alongside him.]**
>
> **O. J.:** What people don't understand, Kato—I can count on my fingers the number of times I have seen these people. When Nicole was divorced, these were the party group people they were running around with. Now Nicole, she makes these people my best friends

(VIDEO OFF)

O. J. needed Kato out of the house at Rockingham, so at 9:15 p.m., on Sunday, June 12, 1994, Simpson leaves with Kato to go to McDonald's. At O. J.'s murder trial, there is testimony by the housekeeper that O. J. left the gate to his property open when he drove Kato to the McDonald's.

What made this story strange for me is that O. J. never ate at McDonald's. When we were on tour and I took O. J. to all these different places, McDonald's is the only restaurant O. J. never ate at. I know this because we got lost once. We were somewhere in North Carolina. Not only did we never find the hotel room, but we also never found anything. We were just riding aimlessly. So,

---

78 Faye D. Resnick with Mike Walker, *Nicole Simpson: The Private Diary of a Life Interrupted*, op.cit., pp. 74-80.

about two or three o'clock in the morning, O. J. finally blew up and
said, "Remember what I said about McDonald's. Fuck it! Take me
there. I'm hungry." But this was a rare event, because in all the time
I spent with him, O. J. did not like to go to McDonald's, so I was
surprised he took Kato there.

(VIDEO STARTS)

> [It's a rainy night. Norman is taking his video from his
> usual back seat position.]
> **Norm:** Just drive to the drive-through. We'll get us a hamburger
> to take to the hotel. Get a whole bunch of them. **[Laughter]**
> **O. J.:** **[More Laughter]** Get me a Burrito Supreme . . . **[More
> Laughter]**
> **Driver:** This ain't Taco Bell N****r **[More Laughter]**

(VIDEO OFF)

That's the point. O. J. wanted a Burrito Supreme because he never
ate at McDonald's. But yet, the night of the murders, he took Kato
to McDonald's. So, that threw up a flag in my mind. Why would you
take someone to McDonald's, if you never go to McDonald's because
you don't even know McDonald's serves hamburgers?

To return to the night of the murders, at 9:30 p.m., the housekeeper
at Rockingham reports hearing someone in the garage. The housekeeper, Rosa Lopez, a Spanish-speaking woman born in El Salvador,
worked and lived next door to the O. J. Simpson mansion. She testified that while her employers were in Europe, her main task the
evening of June 12, 1994, was to take their golden retriever outside periodically. Lopez testified that when she took the dog out at
approximately 8:15 p.m. that night, she saw O. J. Simpson's white
Bronco parked in the street "a little bit crooked." At about 9:00 p.m.,
she saw a black car that she assumed was O. J.'s Bentley leave his
estate next door and head toward Sunset Boulevard. She noted that
O. J. had a blond-haired person in the passenger seat. This testimony

appeared to corroborate Kato Kaelin's testimony that O. J. drove him to McDonald's at approximately that time.

Then about 9:30 p.m., Lopez testified that she heard footsteps coming from O. J. Simpson's property and she became frightened. She "ducked down" in her bedroom but she felt better when she heard O. J. Simpson's voice a few minutes later after the footsteps. The footsteps she heard indicated to her that the person was going toward her garage. She testified she heard O. J. return about 9:45 p.m., and she heard O. J. talking to someone. Lopez testified through an interpreter and her answers about times were rarely precise. She said she took the dog for a walk about 10:00 p.m., but it might have been 10:15 p.m., or as defense attorneys insisted, perhaps even 10:20 p.m. or 10:30 p.m.. Lopez repeatedly said, even under cross-examination, that it was "after 10:00 p.m." that she saw the Bronco still parked there. This seemed to coincide with her testimony that she saw the white Bronco still parked in the street when she took the dog out for the 10:00 p.m. walk. This testimony gave prosecutors trouble because 10:15 p.m. was the time the prosecutors had pegged for O. J. to be at Brentwood, killing Nicole and Ron Goldman.

The prosecutors insisted that "*No me recuerdo*," Spanish for "I don't remember," became the mantra for Rosa Lopez's testimony.[79] Still, Lopez remained insistent that in the time O. J. Simpson was gone from his estate, taking Kato to McDonald's, she heard footsteps "by the garage" and somebody rustling around the garage that scared her. Several times, she described this person as a "prowler," but that seemed to reflect that she felt so frightened hearing the footsteps that she appears to have hidden in the bedroom. She had no idea who this person was or what they were doing, but she feared for her life hearing this "prowler."

Listening to Rosa Lopez testifying in Spanish made clear how taxing the extensive cross-examinations by the prosecutors were on her. The prosecutors were determined to break her testimony because if her testimony stood, the defense had an alibi. So, Cristopher Darden

---

79 Jessica Seigel, "L.A. Latinos tun into Lopez drama," *Austin American-Statesman*, Austin Texas, March 5, 1995.

and Marcia Clark ground every detail trying to raise doubt about the accuracy and truthfulness of what she said. Rosa did not speak English and she resented the distrust and harassment. Her main job that night was to take the dog out, yet she was alone in that house and worried something could go wrong. She was fearful of intruders.

In the end, all Rosa wanted to do was to go back to El Salvador. She accused the prosecutors of racism and she was more correct in that assessment than she possibly ever knew. Rosa was clearly losing patience with the detailed, repetitive, insistent questioning. Consider this exchange, when Darden was exploring to see if someone paid Lopez to testify as she did:

> **Darden:** You didn't then receive $5,000 from the *National Inquirer* for your story?
> **Rosa Lopez:** (laughing, as though the question were foolish) No, sir. With $5,000, I would no longer be here, sir.
> **Darden:** But what if you got paid $5,000 to stay here?
> **Rosa Lopez:** (laughing nervously) I'm not planning on staying here, I'm planning on getting lost in some other part the world God knows where.

Then a couple of minutes later, this exchange occurred:

> **Darden:** Do you remember telling Silvia Guerrero that she would also get paid $5,000 if she said she saw the Bronco.
> **Rosa Lopez:** (grim faced, tense) I don't remember having said that, sir.
> **Darden:** So, you could have told her then.
> **Rosa Lopez:** I don't remember having said it, sir.

What followed was Darden asking her over and over again if she told Guerrero that she could get paid $5,000 if she supported the possible O. J. alibi that she too saw the Bronco parked there after 10:00 p.m.. To every question, Rosa Lopez answered she didn't remember. Darden asked Judge Ito to instruct the witness to answer the question directly. Ito, losing patience, explained flatly to Darden that she had answered his question, and she said she didn't remember. Darden resumed by asking Lopez if she understood he was asking if anyone had bribed her for her testimony, and if she understood how serious that was. She understood.

But Darden wouldn't let go of this:

Darden: Have you ever been a witness before?
Rosa Lopez: No, sir, and perhaps this will be the last time.

The prosecution was never able to prove Rosa Lopez was paid a penny for her testimony.

When Lopez finally got back to El Salvador, television news in the United States sent camera crews and reporters to El Salvador to set up their cameras in the bed of a pickup truck to follow her driving around on the dirt roads where she lived some fifty miles south of San Salvador, the capital city.

In her confusing and often contradictory testimony, further complicated by her need to communicate through a translator, the key points remained: namely, that she heard a prowler when O. J. was gone with Kato, that the footsteps came from O. J.'s property, and that she heard noise she associated with the garage, and she became so frightened that she "ducked down" in her bedroom. Also clear was that a short time later, she heard O. J.'s voice and "after 10:00 p.m.," when she again took the dog for a walk, she saw O. J.'s white Bronco still parked on the street where she had seen it earlier that evening. O. J.'s defense team wanted to move the time Lopez took the dog for a walk closer to 10:30 p.m. because that created an alibi for O. J. What Lopez said over and over was "after 10:00 p.m.." If the dog walk had been closer to 10:30 p.m., I would have expected her to say, "shortly before 10:30 p.m.."

What I concluded from Lopez's testimony, that it was possible O. J. took Kato to McDonald's to get Kato out of the house, so some-one could come in the estate to pick up the keys Nicole reported missing from her home. O. J. knew he didn't have much time to waste that evening. O. J. had scheduled a limousine to be at his Rockingham mansion at 10:30 p.m. that night to take him to the airport (LAX), because he was on an 11:45 p.m. American Airlines flight leaving LAX that night on a flight for Chicago. I believe O. J. left the gate at his estate open when he took Kato to McDonald's because that was the time that he was expecting someone to come into his property to get something.

Because the housekeeper heard footsteps she associated with the garage, my theory is that O. J. had in the garage a set of keys to Nicole's gate. O. J. staged the "McDonald's run" to provide a window for someone to come into his property and get those keys. You needed a key to the gate at Brentwood to get into Nicole's house. Before the murder, Nicole had reported a set of keys to her home were missing a few weeks before the killings. The LAPD found two sets of keys to Nicole's condo in O. J.'s possession. Despite the confusion in Rosa Lopez's testimony, I believe the footsteps Lopez heard were Glen Rogers coming to get the keys so he could let Ron Goldman into Nicole's property without calling her on the intercom to open the gate.

When O. J. got back to Rockingham from McDonald's with Kato, somewhere between 10:00 p.m. and 10:15 p.m., that's when O. J. got in the white Bronco and left Rockingham to head over to Nicole's home on Bundy.

O. J. Confronts Ron Goldman

O. J. got involved with Glen Rogers, a real bad guy, as we now know—a serial killer who was hanging out in L.A. a painter, operating under an alias from a guy he had murdered in Ohio. But O. J., like everybody who knew Glen, knew he was the quiet guy who didn't say much, but they had to understand Glen had a hard edge to him.

So, what I think happened, and this is my opinion, is that O. J. in his mind was doing the same thing he did in Las Vegas. What O. J. really wanted back in Las Vegas was not the sports memorabilia, but some treasured photographs he couldn't replace, family pictures of his first daughter and his mother who were now deceased. It wasn't the sports memorabilia. O. J. didn't need sports memorabilia. O. J. could always create sports memorabilia whenever he wanted to, especially since his signature was still very much desired as a collectible, and he could always find a football to sign.

The mistake O. J. made in Vegas was the same mistake O. J. made in the Nicole Brown Simpson case. In Vegas, O. J. brought a couple of guys to go with him as muscle. His mistake in Las Vegas was that the thugs going with O. J. to the memorabilia dealer's hotel room brought guns with them. The mistake O. J. made in Brentwood was to bring Glen Rogers with him as muscle, with O. J. probably not knowing Rogers was a serial killer who was an expert with a knife. Glen Rogers tended to kill people by strangling them or by using a knife.

What O. J. was thinking is pretty typical for O. J. He thought, 'We're just going to go over there, to Nicole's home in Brentwood, and we are going to thug Ron Goldman, scare him a little bit, and get him to stop dealing drugs to Nicole.' Remember, O. J. had been determined to get Nicole's notebook that had the phone numbers of her contacts, as well as a record of her activities. O. J. had to have seen Ron Goldman's name all over that notebook. O. J. was determined to get the drug dealers out of Nicole's life, not because he disapproved of Nicole doing drugs, but because Nicole's life with Faye Resnick had gotten out of control. Nicole was holding wild drug-induced sex orgies in the living room of her Brentwood home when O. J.'s children were asleep in the bedrooms upstairs.

In Chapter 7, we went over Ron Goldman's background and his association with Marvin Glass, including Marvin Glass's involvement with the Colombian drug cartels and the importing of cocaine into the United States. From the sealed records in Ron Goldman's LAPD files, he was probably a drug user turned drug informer. The way I read Glen Rogers short note of February 13, 2013, the "contract" he had with O. J. was not to kill or hurt Nicole, but Glen did agree to accompany O. J. when O. J. needed him if the opportunity arose to make it clear to Ron Goldman that O. J. wanted him to stop dealing drugs to Nicole.

Glen Rogers was a drug user and a hardened habitual killer. It is possible, if not likely, that Glen knew if Ron Goldman had drug ties through Marvin Glass. It is likely Marvin Glass never quit his involvement with the Colombian drug cartels. Given his involvement with Marvin Glass in Chicago, Fred Goldman could have known too. Fred Goldman's shadowy past raises questions if he derived income working with Marvin Glass in the drug business. But if there were two people in the world who may have wanted revenge for losing their wives, Marvin Glass may have joined Robert Kardashian on that list.

That's what I think happened. I don't think O. J. and Glen Rogers going over to Brentwood that evening really had anything to do with Nicole. O. J.'s target was Ron Goldman. When Glen Rogers told O. J. that Ron Goldman asked him to drive Goldman to the Baha Cantina in Marina Del Rey, making a quick stop at Nicole's place to drop off her mother's eyeglasses that she left at the Mezzaluna, Glen Rogers knew he had his chance. Even though O. J.'s time that evening was short because of the 11:45 p.m. flight to Chicago, there was enough time for the confrontation to occur so O. J. could make his point with Ron Goldman.

My conclusion was that O. J.'s intention the night of June 12, 1994 was to confront Ron Goldman. I believe Glen Rogers was the person who went to pick up those keys at O. J.'s estate, and I believe O. J. took Kato to McDonald's that night to allow Rogers time to slip into O. J.'s Rockingham estate and pick up the keys. After he got the keys, I believe Rogers then drove over to Ron Goldman's apartment to pick him up. Ron left the Mezzaluna wearing black trousers and he was wearing jeans when he was murdered. So, I believe Ron Goldman may have walked home to his apartment to change clothes. With Ron in the car, Glen Rogers drove over to Nicole's home.

From the way I have it figured, between 10:00 p.m. and 10:15 p.m., O. J. drove his white Bronco to get there before Glen Rogers showed up with Ron Goldman. This way, O. J. was standing inside the gate on Nicole's Brentwood home when Rogers arrived with Ron Goldman. Ron went through the gate unsuspecting, basically expecting to make a short stop just to give the eyeglasses to Nicole. Ron Goldman would have wanted to make the drive to Marina Del Rey before it closed that night. Very possibly, Goldman had a drug deal waiting for him with the "guys" he was expecting to meet then, or maybe Ron was planning to sell drugs at the Baha Cantina that night. Ron Goldman was seen by Karen Crawford leaving the Mezzaluna just before 10:00 p.m.. This puts the time of his confrontation with O. J. at Nicole's Bundy address at approximately 10:20 p.m..

So, when Glen Rogers arrived with Ron Goldman, O. J. was already inside the gate, sitting on the steps. O. J. had bad knees from getting beat up all those years playing football. He was always sitting down when he could. Glen Rogers was behind Ron Goldman coming onto the property. That's how Ron Goldman got cornered. If you look at a map of Nicole's house, you can tell Ron had to go back there into the bushes. Coming through the gate, Glen Rogers was behind Ron Goldman, blocking Ron's possible escape back out that gate. When O. J. saw them come through the gate, he stood up by the steps, in front of Ron. O. J. blocked Ron's escape out of the other gate. So, Ron Goldman couldn't go up the stairs there because that is where O. J. was, and he couldn't go back through the gate they used to enter the property because that is where Glen Rogers was. So, Ron Goldman backed up into the bushes.

O. J. started yelling at Ron Goldman, like O. J. always does, pointing his right index finger, shaking it in front of Ron Goldman's face. O. J. was trying to intimidate Ron Goldman, to make Goldman understand that he was serious about ordering Goldman to stay away from Nicole. "I want you to stop dealing drugs to Nicole . . . blah, blah, blah," O. J. would have been demanding with that finger O. J. wags at you when he was angry. O. J. was just making clear to Goldman that Goldman had better hear and understand what O. J. was telling him he had to do. I think what happened is that O. J. and Glen Rogers scared Ron Goldman. Think about it—O. J. and Glen Rogers have Ron Goldman cornered in the bushes. O. J. is getting up in Ron Goldman's face, wagging his finger at him, speaking in a demanding way that Ron Goldman has to quit dealing drugs to Nicole. What do you think Ron Goldman is going to do? He's going to feel scared, threatened. 'What's O. J. or Glen Rogers going to do next?' he has to be wondering.

Ron Goldman has a knife with him, and he pulls it out. He starts telling O. J. to back off, but O. J. doesn't stop. Ron slashes with the knife and gashes deeply O. J.'s right index finger, the finger O. J. has been pointing at Goldman's face. Blood begins spouting out from the deep cut on his finger. At that point, O. J. himself panics and takes off. O. J. high-tails it back to the white Bronco and drives back to his estate at Rockingham. So, basically, what I believe happened is that O. J. took off, running like a baby once the fight starts. His finger is bleeding badly, and the limousine is going to be at his Rockingham estate at 10:30 p.m. to take him to the airport. O. J. has an airplane to catch and he has to get the bleeding on his finger stopped before he gets into that limo. O. J. is rapidly running out of time.

The limo arrives at the Rockingham estate to pick up O. J. at 10:25 p.m.. The limousine driver, Allan Park, begins buzzing O. J.'s intercom at 10:40–10:50 p.m.. At 10:55 p.m., Park calls his boss and tells him O. J. isn't home. His boss instructs Park to wait there until 11:15 p.m. since O. J. is always late. Finally, O. J. opens the door at 11:05 p.m., explaining that he overslept. They arrive at LAX just in time for O. J. to check in at the ticket counter at 11:33 p.m.. He boards the American Airlines flight just in time to make the scheduled 11:45 p.m. departure. These are hard timestamps documented by Allan Park's phone calls to his boss.

Imagine how Ron Goldman's fight with Glen Rogers must have gone. If I'm stuck in a corner, the way Ron Goldman was, pushed back into a little hole where an adult man had no room to maneuver, and there's two people in front of me, I'm going to defend myself. Ron pulls a knife. He swats at O. J. pointing a finger in his face. A switch goes off in Glen's head and O. J. runs away. It's a bad idea to pull a knife on a serial killer, but Ron Goldman that night probably knew Glen as James Peters, a painter, not as Glen Rogers, a serial killer.

Our anonymous informant Redd, who we have called Witness #2, had direct contact with Glen Rogers in prison. Redd confirmed to me that this is what happened. "Ron Goldman was a pretty tough guy," Redd explained to me. When that switch went off in Glen's head, he and Ron Goldman fought each other viciously. Ron Goldman's corpse showed extensive bruising, with the fingers and knuckles of his hands badly damaged.

You remember that letter we saw in Chapter 6, from the William J. Galvin Custom Painting Company, the painting company Glen Rogers worked with in L.A., under the alias James Peters. That letter that James Peters missed work on June 14, 1994, explained by a ceiling that fell on him that Monday, June 13, 1994. Glen

Rogers too must have been badly beat up after his encounter with Ron Goldman—so beat up that the painting company wrote him a letter documenting his pay had to be cut because he missed work that day.

"Glen Rogers showed up there that night with a knife," Redd told me. "But in the fight, he managed to get Ron Goldman's knife away from him." Redd insisted that rather than use the knife Glen Rogers had brought with him, Glen used the knife he took from Ron Goldman to slash Ron's throat and kill him. "Ron Goldman was a pretty tough guy," Redd insisted. "Glen kept hitting Ron Goldman, but Ron kept getting right back up. Glen wanted to make sure Ron stayed down. That's why Glen Rogers stabbed him so many times."

Ron Goldman cut O. J. and that is why O. J.'s blood was found from the crime scene to his estate at Rockingham. That was O. J.'s blood, but when Goldman cut O. J.'s finger, O. J. ran. "O. J. ran off with his finger bleeding," Redd confirmed. "O. J. just left Glen Rogers there to deal with Ron Goldman on his own." When O. J. left, Glen Rogers jumped up, got into a struggle with Ron that ended up with Glen Rogers killing Ron. The time Ron Goldman was killed was around 10:28 to 10:30 p.m. that night.

This has not gone the way O. J. planned. The confrontation with Ron Goldman went wildly wrong, with Goldman reacting aggressively, not submissively like O. J. had imagined. O. J. leaves before anyone is killed. In the air to Chicago, O. J. has no reason to suspect any harm will come that night to Nicole. I've seen O. J. do that finger-pointing in-your-face number many times. O. J. and I would get into an argument sometimes, and I would even try to make O. J. so angry that he would take a swing at me. O. J. would get so mad that he couldn't see straight, but he would always back off, shaking his head and calling me a "crazy motherfucker."

(VIDEO STARTS)

Note: O. J. is in the passenger seat in the front and Norm is in his usual spot, the back seat behind the driver.

O. J.: (shouting back over his left shoulder to Norm) Shut the fuck up, Norm. You don't even know what the fuck you're talking about.

Norm: I read it in the papers, and I talked to one of the guys, the promoters.

O. J.: (shaking his head, looking back at Norm) Norm, look at you. I don't care what you looked at . . .

> Note: O. J. starts aggressively attacking Norm, but he backs off immediately, once Norm answers him back. That's the first time in the interaction that O. J. looks at Norm, only after O. J. has decided to drop it.

(VIDEO ENDS)

O. J. would get mad, but he wasn't a fighter. As I commented earlier, when O. J. was a kid, he was in a gang, but O. J. wasn't a fighter, he was a leader. That gang mentality never left O. J. He's good at getting people around him to protect him. O. J. let the other guys do his dirty work. That's why I knew O. J. did not kill Ron Goldman or Nicole. It was not in his nature to be jealous and that night O. J. did not expect violence. O. J. might have asked Glen Rogers to help O. J. set things right, but Glen Rogers was correct in that his deal to help O. J. with Goldman did not involve bringing any "harm" to Nicole.

Quite the contrary, O. J. must have told Glen Rogers that by getting Ron Goldman out of Nicole's life he was helping Nicole. O. J. would have known about who Ron Goldman was, just like Glen Rogers would have known. Glen would understand that by getting Ron Goldman to back off, he would have cut off any ties with Marvin Glass and the Colombian drug cartels. O. J. would not have wanted Marvin Glass and the Colombian drug cartels hanging around Nicole in the background, especially if O. J. knew about Ron's family ties and that Fred Goldman married Patti Glass and took Marvin's kids with her.

When O. J. takes off, Glen Rogers finds himself confronting Ron Goldman, a guy Rogers knows to be a karate expert. Goldman's mistake was pulling that knife. Glen Rogers takes one look at Ron Goldman standing there with a knife in his hands and adrenalin pumping through his veins. That's all it takes for a switch to flip in the serial killer's head.

At the O. J. Simpson murder trial, Eva Stein, a neighbor of Nicole, testified that she heard a dog barking very loud at 10:15 p.m.. "I tried to go back to sleep, and I couldn't because the dog barking seemed very, very persistent, non-stop and very, very loud."[80] This clue marks the time O. J. confronted Ron Goldman, when O. J. ran, and serious blows started being exchanged as Ron Goldman fought Glen Rogers for his life. As you might expect, the serial killer won.

The Bloody Glove

"When Ron Goldman got to Nicole's, he would have had a knife on him, most people dealing drugs do," Redd, our Witness #2, told me. "But when Ron Goldman pulled that knife, he had no idea who he was dealing with. Glen took Ron's knife and killed Ron Goldman with it. Glen was so beat up he didn't go to work the next day." What about the bloody gloves? I asked Redd. "Glen had those leather gloves on that night. He was wearing them when he picked up Ron Goldman to drive him to Nicole's and to the Marina Del Rey." Where did Ron get those gloves? I asked Redd. "From Dodi Fayed," Redd answered. "Dodi got those gloves at Harrod's in London. He liked to hand them out to his henchmen, and Glen Rogers was the type of guy who fit Dodi's profile for his henchmen." But didn't Witness #1 say Glen came to that club, the Gate, with Nicole? "Yes, but Dodi knew that Glen might have been one of Nicole's boyfriends, but Dodi also could have saw a value to a guy like Glen that had more to do with his potential value as a henchman," Redd explained.

So, what happened next that night was that after Glen killed Ron Goldman, the gloves were bloody, so Glen took them off and threw them on the pavement there. Only one glove was found by Ron Goldman's body. What happened to the other glove? "After he

---

80 Greg Lefevre, "Simpson Testimony Concentrates on Body's Discovery," CNN News, February 9, 1995.

killed Ron Goldman, Glen started to walk away," Redd explained. "But he stopped and went back to pick up one glove. Glen Rogers was pissed O. J. ran away and he thought to himself there was no way that n***er was going to leave him holding the bag—a murder O. J. put in motion but then didn't commit because he ran away." That was my conclusion, that O. J. would just let Glen Rogers hold the bag. That's how O. J. works. But I knew O. J. was not innocent—he never was innocent of anything. That's power.

O. J.'s blood that was found proves O. J. was there that night, but he was only there to confront Ron Goldman, not to kill him. O. J. did not participate in or witness the killings of either Ron Goldman or of Nicole. The LAPD never found blood from any victim on O. J., not on his clothing, or his shoes, or in his shower. The prosecutor Marcia Clark had her whole case based on one person's testimony on DNA saying the blood was O. J.'s. She threw out all the evidence that didn't fit that theory. That was pure stupidity. O. J.'s blood was at the murder scene, but that's because O. J. got cut there. So, because O. J.'s blood was at the murder scene, Marcia Clark thought in her mind that O. J. had to be the murderer. Yes, O. J.'s blood was there. There was no EDTA preservative found in any blood drops from the Nicole Brown Simpson condo to the Simpson estate. Those were not blood drops planted by the police. So, O. J. Simpson jumped in his Bronco and drove back to his house, all the way dripping blood, dripped blood all the way up to his bedroom. That's where O. J.'s blood comes from—the cut on his finger.

So, O. J. gets back to Rockingham at approximately 10:50 p.m. and he is out front with the limousine at 11:15 p.m.. But while this is going on, Kato Kaelin, who lived there in the back of O. J.'s mansion, hears this noise, this loud thump on the outside wall of his room. That was about the same time O. J. was getting back home. "What happened," Redd said, continuing to explain, "was that Glen Rogers picked up a bloody glove, and headed back to Rockingham to collect some money from O. J. But O. J. wasn't there. What Kato heard, was the noises of Glen Rogers throwing the bloody glove over the gate and the glove landing where it hit the house where Kato's room was located." Redd's explanation made clear that LAPD officer

Fuhrman did not plant the bloody glove there, but the glove landed there, oddly placed nowhere near the blood drops from O. J.'s cut finger, when Glen Rogers threw it over the wall. "Glen Rogers ran up the embankment and threw the glove over," Redd said. "Glen told me he threw the glove over because that n***er wasn't going to leave him holding the bag." It's the only thing that makes sense why the glove was there. The glove was found there because Glen Rogers threw it there.

Nicole Was Alive at 11:00 p.m.

Nicole's mother, Juditha Brown, first said that the last time she spoke to Nicole was when she called her at 11:00 p.m.. But that did not fit the prosecution's timeline. From the start, the prosecutors assumed Nicole and Ron Goldman were there together and that O. J. killed them both at the same time. But that isn't how it happened. Nicole and Juditha Brown spoke on the telephone at 11:00 p.m., and Nicole had to explain to her mother that she did not have the eyeglasses yet because Nicole was still waiting for Ron Goldman to show up. The LAPD and the prosecutors appeared to have doctored the phone records; you can see that by looking at the entries and seeing calls marked "p.m." but the placement on the phone bill was where the "a.m." calls were listed. Juditha Brown told the truth the first time, proving Nicole was alive at 11:00 p.m. that night. Juditha Brown kept backing up the timing of that phone call. She said it was at 10:30 p.m., then she came back and said she talked with her daughter at 9:40 p.m..

Glen Rogers was not done that night. But Nicole was not killed at the same time Ron Goldman was killed. They were killed anywhere from one hour to two hours apart. The melting ice cream proves that, but we are going to save that for the next chapter. If you get rid of all the smoke and mirrors from the prosecution lying and rigging the evidence to prove O. J. was the killer, the evidence tells the same story Glen Rogers told. That's what the next chapter is all about. Even Glen Rogers was astounded by how little the LAPD cared about the truth, even after he told them in his 1995 deposition that he killed Ron Goldman and Nicole Brown Simpson. That was the story that nobody wanted to believe. The LAPD, instead of indicting Glen Rogers for the murders, gave him a plea deal and let him go. In one of his letters, Glen expressed how even he couldn't believe it. "So, it's okay for the LAPD to charge a black guy who didn't do it but refuse even to try to convict a white guy who says he did it," Glen wrote.

"The more Glen Rogers thought about it, the angrier he got," Redd continued. "So, he calls Nicole and tells her he has some 'nose sugar'—some cocaine—to bring her. Glen had done some drug deals before and he worked at Nicole's house, so she knew he had done drug deals in the past. Glen knew Nicole would have money and O. J. had stiffed him." Glen told Nicole to get the money ready and he would bring some 'nose sugar' over to her." Redd said that when Glen got to Nicole's house she stepped outside because she didn't want to be doing a drug deal with the kids sleeping upstairs. Glen met Nicole at the door with the cocaine in one hand and a knife in his other hand behind his back. Nicole came out and she led him around the corner so they would be out of sight. Nicole did not even know Ron was lying there dead until she went around the corner. Back in the bushes where Ron Goldman died, nobody could see the body. That's why the witnesses who said they passed Nicole's house at 10:30 p.m. and did not see any blood or bodies were telling the truth.

Here's what I think happened. When Nicole got down the pathway, she saw some blood and a body in the bushes. She probably even then did not know it was Ron Goldman. I believe she freaked out and said something like, "What's that?" At that moment, Glen grabbed her throat, sliced her throat with the knife, and threw her down the stairs. Those two murders happened totally apart from each other. "Glen basically took Nicole around the side of her house where Ron was dead, already murdered," Redd told me. "Then he grabbed her from behind, slit her throat, and dropped her down the stairs." Nicole's body can be seen from the street. I believe she was murdered around midnight and it didn't take ten minutes for a neighbor to discover something was really wrong and to find the bodies.

Glen Rogers Takes the Money and Steals Nicole's Jewelry

At the time the bodies were found, Nicole had on her wristwatch, but Nicole's jewelry was not on her. "Glen used the jewelry for currency and that's what he ran around with," Redd said. "I think it eventually ended up in a pawn shop in Salt Lake, Utah."

Then, Glen wrote another letter, and I knew immediately what had happened to at least one piece of the jewelry Nicole was wearing the night she died. In one of his letters, Glen mentions there is a picture of his mother sitting in a courtroom. "This is the truth," Glen wrote. "Mom has on a black vest top. Pinned to it is a gold angel with a diamond in its hand. I sent that to mom the day after the situation in Brentwood, and I know where it is now, it can be traced back to Brentwood." So, I asked myself, 'Why is this angel pin so important to Glen?'

The answer came in the next few sentences. Glen continued, writing the following: "The pin can be traced back to Brentwood. It is something everyone missed. I need you to show O. J. the picture of that pendant or, better yet, show his children. They'll be able to identify it and where it came from." I found the picture of Edna Rogers sitting at one of Glen's first-degree murder trials. "That's right," Redd affirmed. "When he killed Nicole, Glen Rogers took from her body a very distinctive gold angel pin with diamonds and the diamond earrings she was wearing that night. O. J.'s kids would recognize that pin because the kids bought it for Nicole."

With that letter, Glen was giving us proof he murdered Nicole Brown Simpson. He stole that pin the night of the murder. He mailed it to his mother who was photographed with it sitting in the public gallery of one of Glen's murder trials. The photograph clearly showed Edna Rogers wearing the golden angel pin with diamonds that O. J.'s children had given their mother, Nicole. I remembered that when Nicole's sister, Denise Brown, showed up at the O. J. Simpson trial, she was wearing a small white button that read: "Remember Nicole Brown and Ron Goldman," as well as a gold angel that Nicole Simpson's family members had been wearing in memory of her.[81] Now

81 Andrea Ford, "Nicole Simpson's Sister Questions Defense Actions," *Los Angeles Times*, October 6, 1994.

that all made sense. The gold angel pin with diamonds was a piece of jewelry that Nicole treasured and when Glen Rogers stole Nicole's life that tragic night, their golden angel was stolen out of the family's lives.

This is what I came to understand about Glen that took me a while. He not only committed those murders, but he also wanted to brag about them. Here he was, Glen Rogers, a notorious and famous serious killer. Slitting the throat of Nicole Brown Simpson had been his Mona Lisa, and sitting in prison on Death Row, Glen Rogers wanted the world to know Nicole Brown Simpson's murder was his doing—his *pièce de résistance*, his masterpiece. That's why Glen mailed the golden angel pin with diamonds to his mother the day after he killed Nicole, and why Edna Rogers was wearing the golden angel pin in public at her son's murder trial—that pin was a prize, and after Glen stole it from Nicole, he awarded it to his mother.

Since 1995, Glen Rogers had been confessing because he wanted credit, admitting he was the Nicole Brown Simpson murderer even to District Attorney Gil Garcetti, willing to be convicted of first-degree murder because he told the truth. And all Glen Rogers got for it was a lousy plea deal. In his mind, it just wasn't fair. There was something wrong here. As twisted as Glen Rogers was in his murder-crazed mind, he was right about that. Wait until we examine the crime scene evidence in the next chapter. That's when you will appreciate how really messed up everything was in the O. J. Simpson murder trial.

CHAPTER 9

Crime Scene Evidence Speaks Loud and Clear

It should be clear by now that the prosecution in the O. J. murder trial had a narrative. Their narrative pegged O. J. as the murderer and went like this: O. J. Simpson went on a jealous rage and he killed his ex-wife and her young friend who was just doing her a favor with the eyeglasses. Except for the unfortunate bad timing that evening, Ron Goldman was not a target of O. J.'s rage.

The LAPD could not switch gears after Glen Rogers confessed in that 1995 deposition. The LAPD couldn't say, "O. J. went on a rage, but he had somebody with him at the time of the killings, so we have to change around our theory of the case." That's not what the LAPD did. The LAPD just fixed stuff to make it match up. If the LAPD had just left this case alone, the way it was supposed to be, this case would not have been hard to solve.

But the LAPD had racist cops who thought they were above the law. The LAPD didn't collect the evidence honestly. The LAPD didn't let the investigation play its course. The rules are simple: Just let the facts play their course. Do the investigation the honest way. Don't use false footprints. Don't talk about Bruni Magli shoes. O. J. Simpson was put through that ordeal because the LAPD was still in the throes of the Rampart Scandal and allegedly all cops like Fuhrman acted like neo-Nazis.

The Bruno Magli Shoes

One shoe print found near where Ron Goldman's body lay was identified at the O. J. murder trial to be a specialty Bruno Magli shoe of the Italian shoemaker's Lorenzo model, of which only two hundred had been imported into the United States at the time of the killings. By the size of the pavement tiles the exact shoe was found to be a Bruno Magli Size 12 Shoe with a European 46 sole. The prosecution considered this ironclad proof O. J. was the killer given that O. J. Simpson wore size 12 shoes. A photograph of O. J. Simpson wearing Bruno Magli shoes did not surface until O. J.'s civil trial. During the civil trial, the photograph of O. J. seen wearing Bruno Magli shoes while announcing a Buffalo Bills football game was widely published. During the murder trial, O. J. denied owning or wearing these Bruno Magli shoes. No Bruno Magli shoes were ever found to be in O. J.'s possession during the murder trial or afterwards.[82] The LAPD never recovered the shoes, or any other clothing worn by the murderer. The FBI was unable to find any evidence O. J. purchased a pair of Bruno Magli shoes in 1991 or 1992, the years in which this particular style was sold.[83]

In 2002, investigator T. H. Johnson conducted extensive research into the Bruno Magli shoe controversy. He contacted the Italian manufacturing company, Silga Gomma, that sold shoe soles to Bruno Magli. Silga Gomma is located in Civitanova, Marche, Italy, on the Adriatic Sea. Johnson paid the Italian company to send him samples from its U2887 rubber mold. Johnson received the size 46 (alleged size 12) shoe sole from Silga Gomma in 2002, and it measured 12 and ¼ inches. In 2014, when O. J. was imprisoned in the Lovelock Correctional Institute in Nevada, serving his thirty-three-year sentence for the kidnapping and robbery in Las Vegas, Johnson finally got O. J. to give him a foot tracing.

---

82   Allie Fasanella, "People Are Still Talking About the Infamous Shoes from O.J. Simpson's Trial More than 20 Years Later," FootWearNews.com, October 3, 2018, https://footwearnews.com/2018/shop/shoes/oj-simpson-shoes-bruno-magli-1202691446/.

83   Renee Montagne, "Footprint Expert Testifies at O. J. Simpson Trial," *NPR Morning Edition*, June 20, 1995.

The tracing of Simpson's foot measured 12 and $^1/_{16}$ inches in length, just $^3/_6$ inch shorter than the toe of the unattached shoe sole. "Both the small toe and large toe of the green tracing of Simpson's foot extend outside the Silga U2887 size 46/size 12 shoe sole, as well as on both sides of the arch of the shoe sole," Johnson wrote. "The comparison of the foot tracing in green overlaid on top of the red outline of the Silga shoe, one can see, would be an extremely uncomfortable fit as the rest of the padded shoe top are not attached or even taken into consideration."[84] Johnson concluded that O. J.'s normal shoe size was size 13, based upon the dimensional length and width of his foot.

Subsequent research found Silga Gomma sold soles made from its U2887 rubber mold to many different shoemakers, such that the identical sole could be found on many different shoes using that same sole Silga Gomma made from its U2887 rubber mold. Manufacturers of shoe soles typically sell the same sole to multiple shoemakers to get the sales volume to make the manufacturing profitable. Subsequent research also proved that the bloody footprint found at the Ron Goldman murder site was a partial footprint that did not include arc of the sole where the Bruno Magli logo was placed.

At the O. J. murder trial, the LAPD had given FBI special agent William Bodziak, an expert in footprint impressions, some thirty different LAPD photographs of shoeprints at the crime scene to review. Bodziak identified some of them as Bruno Magli impressions. All the shoeprints were partial impressions and of mediocre quality. "If I were a juror, I would be reluctant to rely on a shoe identification based on these types of incomplete," researcher Michael T. Griffith wrote in 2019. "I would be even more reluctant to do so if I learned that the person doing the identification apparently searched only among expensive shoes made by Italian shoe companies and did not consider shoes made by American or other foreign shoemakers who sold less expensive, copycat versions of expensive Italian shoes

---

84 T. H. Johnson, *The People vs. O. J. Simpson: Hidden Truths*, a revised update of T. H. Johnson, *Pursuit of Exhibit 35 In the O. J. Simpson Murder Trial and its Hidden Secrets*, op.cit. This revised version is in a text file also titled *Serpent's Rising*.

or knockoffs of other high-end casual shoes."[85] In his 1999 second
edition to his college textbook on footwear impression evidence,
Bodziak admitted in his chapter about the O. J. Simpson case that
Silga Gomma had provided the same U2887 shoe soles to Lord, a
company who provided the U2887 shoe soles to twenty other brands
Lord owned around the globe.[86]

Johnson took the Bruno Magli shoe investigation one step further
when he got Glen Rogers, who was then in prison, to make a tracing
of his foot. What Johnson found was that Glen's foot fit inside the
Silga U2887 comfortably. Johnson commented that identifying the
brand of the shoe as Bruno Magli was problematic, given how the
brand identity plug was placed on the U2887 shoe sole immediately
in front of the raised heel, an area of the shoe that does not touch the
ground. "That particular area of the shoe remained unsoiled by the
blood, and thus not clearly distinguishable regarding what brand was
worn that left the bloody shoes at the (Nicole Brown Simpson and
Ron Goldman) murder site," Johnson wrote.

Remember also that Witness #1 made a special point of saying
that the sandy blonde hair guy sitting with Nicole and Dodi Fayed
at the nightclub that night, who I believe to have been Glen Rogers,
was wearing "very special, expensive Italian shoes with pointed toes."
She described the Bruno Magli design in detail. That description fit
the Bruno Magli Lorenzo brand shoes in question at the O. J. murder
trial.

The O. J. defense claimed O. J. was wearing a pair of Reebok 384
tennis shoes that evening. There were no bloody prints of a Reebok
384 tennis shoe anywhere found at the crime scene, in the Bronco,
on the pavement leading into O. J.'s estate, or within O. J.'s home
that night. The LAPD and the FBI spent a fortune in time and money
trying to prove O. J. owned the Bruno Magli shoes. If the LAPD and

---

85 Michael T. Griffith, "The Bruno Magli Shoe Evidence: Does It Prove that
O. J. Simpson is Guilty?" Second Edition, 2019, https://miketgriffith.com/files
/brunomaglishoes.pdf.

86 William J. Bodziak, *Footwear Impression Evidence: Detection, Recovery, and
Examination* (New York: CRC Press, 1999, Second Edition), Chapter 15, "The Footwear
Impression Evidence in the O. J. Simpson Trial."

the FBI had accepted as the truth O. J.'s statement he was wearing tennis shoes that night, the LAPD and the FBI would have known there is no way O. J. had been there at the crime scene when Nicole and Ron Goldman were murdered in such a bloody manner.

Foot Impression Evidence at Crime Scene Fails to Prove O. J. Guilty

On June 19, 1995, William Bodziak, on the witness stand under oath at the O. J. Simpson murder trial, was questioned by defense counsel if there were any shoe prints on the Bronco carpet that were consistent with the Bruno Magli soles. "No," Bodziak responded, but he hedged his answer, knowing this testimony was damaging to the prosecution. He tried to explain there would be movement in the feet in the Bronco that would not give clarity to the footprints. "But there is also the phenomenon of when you get into a Bronco that is rather high and you step into it with your shoe, there is going to be some movement in getting into a vehicle and because of the thick nature of this carpeting, I wouldn't expect to see, necessarily, a clear rendition of—at that point of the shoe," he said, in a long, but unconvincing explanation tarnished by his contorted logic and twisting language.

The point is that the FBI's footprint impression expert could not find a Bruno Magli shoe impression in the Bronco, or at the O. J. estate, or within O. J.'s home. That there are no bloody footprints in the Bronco or at the O. J. estate should have confirmed to the LAPD that O. J. was not in Nicole's condo grounds the night of the murder when the blood started flowing. The footprint was bloody, so the murderer had to step into the blood. Yes, O. J.'s blood was found in the Bronco and dripping on the pavement as he entered his mansion, but that could have come from the cut we described earlier on his finger. No blood was found in the Bronco or at O. J.'s estate that came from the blood spurting out after Nicole's and Ron Goldman's necks that were slit from side to side, leaving gaping wounds.

Besides, there was only one clear "Bruno Magli" footprint on the pavement tile, and that was the footprint found by Ron Goldman's body. A close examination of that footprint would have showed Nicole's blood flowed over the top of the footprint. This was a clue the LAPD should have picked up that the Bruno Magli footprint impression was made when Ron Goldman was killed, and that Nicole was killed after Ron Goldman. Good police work should also have established that a second set of bloody footprints were found heading out of the grounds of Nicole's condo, heading away from the stairs where the bodies were found. If you look closely at the footprints heading away from the stairs, they are not pigeon-toed. O. J. Simpson, as we established earlier, was advantaged as a football running back because he is pigeon-toed. The LAPD should have realized the footprint impression evidence does not confirm their theory of O. J. being the murderer. The blood evidence shows O. J. was wounded that night and that would explain his cut finger. But the footprint impression evidence at the crime scene was never tied to O. J. in any way.

The LAPD should have realized there were two people at the Nicole Brown Simpson and Ron Goldman murder scenes, and they should have known Glen Rogers was the second person. It amazes me how determined Glen Rogers was to take credit for killing Nicole and Ron and how little the law enforcement officers in the case cared. Glen confessed to being the murderer in his 1995 deposition to the California DA and even went as far as to allow an impression to be made of his foot when he was in prison. Glen Rogers had followed the O. J. murder trial well enough to know that the foot impression taken in prison would tie him to the Bruno Magli shoe and identify him as the murderer.

The defense attorneys also interviewed Glen Rogers, and Robert Shapiro and Johnnie Cochran turned him down, just as Garcetti had done. Shapiro and Cochran probably made a good decision not bringing Glen Rogers into the case. O. J. might have been convicted of being an accessory to the murders of Nicole Brown Simpson and Ron Goldman, but Garcetti's team did not have the evidence to convict O. J. of being the murderer. O. J. should have been tried as an accessory to murder and he probably would have been convicted if the LAPD and Garcetti's office had done an honest job, but in my opinion they did not do so. The truth is the defense did an excellent job at the O. J. murder trial of impeaching all the evidence the prosecution entered in their flawed attempt to advance their racially biased "Othello jealous rage" narrative in their failed attempt to convict O. J. of first-degree murder.

The truth is there was no attempt made whatsoever by the LAPD or by Garcetti's office to find the truth. When the LAPD first impounded the Bronco, the LAPD said there was no blood in the Bronco anywhere. It was two weeks later before the LAPD found some blood drops in the Bronco. Finally, the LAPD had to admit there was 1.5mL of O. J.'s blood assumed missing from a vial of evidence. The LAPD never effectively countered arguments of "planted evidence" after the defense team found EDTA in the samples of blood that were found at the crime scene. EDTA is an anticoagulant blood fixer used in crime labs to be mixed with collected blood samples taken by police.

The defense team also learned Simpson's Bronco was entered at least twice by unauthorized personnel when in the impound yard. And earlier we covered that one of the lenses was missing from Mrs. Juditha Brown's eyeglasses while it was in the LAPD facility. When Detective Fuhrman, known by some as an alleged neo-Nazi racist, was asked under oath at the O. J. murder trial if he had doctored evidence by falsifying police records or by contaminating critical evidence with Simpson's blood, or otherwise planting evidence, he invoked his Fifth Amendment privilege against self-incrimination.[87] There were no cuts in the bloody gloves found, yet the LAPD assumed O. J. wore those gloves committing the murders and the blood drops found in the Bronco and at O. J.'s home came from a cut O. J. had suffered in the act of committing the knife murders of the two victims.

Photographs published after June 12, 1994, show blood all over the pavement tiles outside Nicole's home where the murders had occurred. But again, the confusion of multiple bloody footprints and the spread of blood evidence throughout that area resulted from sloppy LAPD forensic work at the crime scene. The LAPD did not

---

87 "Forensics at the O. J. Simpson Trial," CrimeMuseum.org, no date, https://www .crimemuseum.org/crime-library/famous-murders/forensic-investigation-of-the-oj -simpson-trial/.

cordon off the crime scene, allowing reporters and others to contaminate the scene. The LAPD did not wear foot booties or exercise any kind of chain-of-custody rigor in examining and documenting the two bodies or the blood and other debris that was caused by Ron Goldman's struggle to defend himself or by the vicious nature of the large, gaping slash wounds to their throats that took their lives. Put simply, by the time the LAPD were finished trampling around in the crime scene, there was little or no crime scene evidence that should have been permitted to be entered as exhibits during the murder trial.

From 12:10 a.m. on June 13, 1994, the first moment the double homicide was found—some ten minutes after Glen Rogers killed Nicole—the LAPD appeared to have just presumed O. J. committed the murders and fled. Why conduct an honest investigation when the police have already identified the killer with certainty in their own prejudiced minds? The day after Nicole Brown Simpson and Ron Goldman were killed in cold blood, the LAPD was doing what the LAPD was good at: namely, framing an innocent black man of a crime he did not commit, while ignoring all evidence, including a confession, that should have easily proved a white man—a serial killer already on the FBI most wanted list—had been forgiven of the crime and given a plea deal to go free. There are many tragedies in the Nicole Brown Simpson and Ron Goldman murder case, and we have already mentioned one of the saddest tragedies of all. More people died because Glen Rogers was set free in 1995, while the O. J. murder trial was yet in progress.

Drug Angle Ignored

The elephant in the room in the O. J. Simpson case was drugs—an issue that screamed for attention but was totally ignored by the LAPD, the District Attorney, and by the FBI. Nicole Simpson and Faye Resnick (living with Nicole at that time but in drug rehab on the night of the murders) were open about their use of drugs, especially marijuana and cocaine. Glen Rogers had to have been an informant to get his plea deal. We have speculated Glen Rogers could have fingered Ron Goldman as a drug user or dealer, revealing his father Fred's long-standing ties to Marvin Glass. Patti Glass, who appears to have been Fred Goldman's half-sister, became Fred's wife after Marvin Glass was sent to prison for helping the Colombian cartels import cocaine into the United States. Fred and Marvin both ended up in Los Angeles but had started their association in Chicago. The Los Angeles-to-Chicago route was one of the routes used by the Colombian cartels to bring their product from the Mexican border east into the country.

Then too, Robert Kardashian met William Wasz over drugs, as Wasz too was a criminal supplier of even more exotic drugs, like crack cocaine. The LAPD knew Wasz was in possession of Nicole's notebook/address book at the time he was arrested driving the car he had stolen from Paula Barbieri, O. J.'s on-and-off-again girlfriend. O. J. had taken that book from Nicole the day of that famous 911 call. O. J. wanted that book to get his hands on the contact information of the drug dealers and prostitutes who were profiting from her profligate sex/drug lifestyle that threatened O. J.'s children. Drugs were everywhere I looked in this case, yet the LAPD didn't seem to care.

At one point during the O. J. murder trial, Johnnie Cochran elaborated to the press that Nicole Brown Simpson and Ronald L. Goldman were not the victims of a jealous former husband but of irate drug dealers who had set out to kill one of her friends—one of their customers—instead. In March 1995, during the O. J. murder trial, the *New York Times* published the following two paragraphs—one advancing Cochran's theory, and the other explaining why the LAPD wasn't interested:

> Continuing his effort to offer some plausible alternative to the prosecution's case, Mr. Cochran suggested the very brutality of the killings indicated that the perpetrators were drug dealers out to collect a debt, and that the real target was Faye Resnick, who was living with Mrs. Simpson, and taking drugs, around the same time.
>
> In yet another round of questions for the detective, Tom Lange, Mr. Cochran implied that the police had turned a "blind eye" to any

theories that could have cleared Mr. Simpson of the crimes. He also hinted that Mr. Lange implicated Mr. Simpson last June because Marcia Clark, the chief prosecutor in the case, already had.[88]

Clearly in his deposition with the LAPD and in his interviews with Shapiro and Cochran, Glen Rogers filled them in on the drug aspects of the double murder case. After all, when Glen Rogers went back to kill and rob Nicole that night, he enticed her to get her money ready and come outside by telling her he had some "nose sugar" he wanted to deliver to her in person.

When Johnnie Cochran questioned Detective Lange on the stand, the New York Times reported the two "continued their seemingly endless fencing match today, delving into topics like the rate at which ice cream melts and the murder methods used by Colombian drug lords." Cochran asked Lange "whether he had ever heard of two ways drug dealers disposed of drug users in arrears: a 'Colombian neckless,' slang for murder by a slashed throat, and a 'Colombian necktie,' a variation in which the victim's tongue is pulled through the slit."[89] As I commented earlier, Glen Roger's *modus operandi* was typically to kill his victims with a knife or by strangulation. But generally, Glen liked to stab his victims repeatedly, often letting them bleed out in a bathtub. With Nicole and Ron Goldman, the slit throats may have just been done to get it over with because he was out in the open where someone might see, or perhaps Glen deviated from his knife routine because he too was thinking about the Colombian drug cartels and their involvement in this case.

Corruption Abounds in the O. J. Simpson Murder Saga

But what exactly was the participation of the LAPD and the FBI at that time in the Colombian drug cartel's importation and distribution of drugs in Los Angeles and throughout the United States? We know from the Rampart Scandal that rogue elements of the LAPD were not

---

88 David Margolick, "Simpson's Lawyer Hints Slayings Were Mistake by Drug Dealers," *New York Times*, March 9, 1995.

89 Ibid.

averse to taking over for themselves the operation of the drug trade in L.A., while framing blacks and Hispanics for their crimes.

We also know that to run an international drug trade, drug cartels must have the cooperation of international banks. After all, there is a limit to what anyone can do with a warehouse full of the street cash used to transact the drug trade in a major U.S. city like Los Angeles. Driving around semi-trucks full of $100 bills is no way to run a business. The drug trade depends upon money-laundering to transform a cash business into a useful international business transaction. Various federal agencies monitor all wire transfers and several multi-national banks have been found guilty of federal crimes laundering money in the United States for foreign drug cartels.

It is also preposterous to think an addict strung out on drugs can still figure out where to make the next drug buy, but law enforcement agencies of the caliber of the LAPD and the FBI are unable to investigate and prosecute the drug cartel operatives, or to track the street operatives back to their organized crime bosses.

In framing O. J. Simpson as the murderer, who was District Attorney Garcetti protecting? That's one of the real questions here. I think the answer lies in that Garcetti was protecting himself. That's why the LAPD records on Glen Rogers are sealed. Garcetti knew he had a racist, drug-dealing police department on his hands, with officers allegedly dressing up in Ku Klux Klan hoods and getting tattoos on their bodies just like the Hispanic and black gangs they had come to imitate. Glen Rogers knew too much. Being in the L.A. drug scene, he got to know Nicole Simpson. That put him in touch with O. J. Glen Rogers was smart enough to figure out the backstory to Robert Kardashian, and after he met Ron Goldman, to figure out the Marvin Glass saga. Glen came on the scene to replace William Wasz, and in the final analysis, Glen completed the job. He slashed the throats of Nicole Simpson and Ron Goldman with the style that would have done a Colombian drug cartel kingpin proud.

The California DA appeared to have heard Glen Rogers out, including how Glen committed the murders and why Glen committed the murders. The better part of valor for the DA was to let Glen go. Eventually somebody else would catch Glen Rogers for one murder or another. That was not the DA's concern. And if the American public heard the real O. J. murder story, there was a lot of corruption in L.A. that would be laid at the California DA's doorstep. In the final analysis, there was nobody clean in this entire sad and tragic saga.

Left-Handed Glen Rogers Was Adept at Using a Knife

In one of his letters from prison, Glen Rogers explained that he learned to use a knife harvesting tobacco as a field worker. Here is how Glen explained it:

> I cut tobacco for years. 1,000 sticks a day, that's 6,000 stacks, because there's 6 stacks to a stick. I always stopped at 1,000 sticks. A hundred bucks a day at 10 cents a stick. I always finished before 12 noon, only because I cut left-handed. A left-handed cutter on his hands & knees can cut and spear each stack as he goes. A right-handed cutter can't. They cut, then go back & spear all 6 on a stick. I'm just telling you this as proof I always used both hands. I was nicknamed lefty by the crop owner.

Glen continued to say there were three in the family who were left-handed, including his father and himself. He was not sure about the others, but he remembered his dad had perfect shooting scores with a pistol in each hand.

He added:

> But it's a trick of the trade in the business. Right now, my left hand is messed up from years of abuse using it cutting tobacco in the field, left-handed tobacco knife. My hands were the same equal strength. But for years my left was stronger.

The question of whether Glen Rogers was right-handed or left-handed was relevant after the Deputy Los Angeles County Medical Examiner Dr. Irwin Golden, who performed the actual autopsies on Nicole Simpson and Ron Goldman, made public descriptions of the wounds on Nicole's neck. The claim was that it was improbable a right-handed assailant plunged 4 deep single-edge stab wounds into the left side of Nicole's neck.

This was another threat to the prosecution's attempt to frame O. J. as the murderer because O. J. is right-handed. To counter Golden's testimony, Deputy District Attorney Brian Kelner stood behind the opinion of the coroner, Dr. Lakshmanan, who came public with his supposed conclusion the killer was right-handed. The coroner alleged the right-handed assailant, O. J. Simpson, stabbed Nicole four times in the left side of the neck before turning to kill Ron Goldman with the same right-handed attack from behind. The coroner's hypothesis was that after killing Ron Goldman, Simpson then turned to slit Nicole's throat.

Again, if the conclusion of the medical examiner conducting the autopsy had not raised this issue, the government would not have had to find a coroner who would refute the left-handed assailant theory that was most likely correct, to find a coroner who would put the fatal knife in the right hand of the presumed killer, O. J. Simpson. This is another example where the evidence is consistent with Glen Rogers's various confessions that he was the killer, not O. J. Glen Rogers just turns out to be left-handed, a relatively rare condition, given that only about 10 percent of all Americans are born left-handed.[90]

As investigator T. H. Johnson pointed out, "Dr. Lakshmanan Sathyavagiswaran, then the Chief Medical Examiner-Coroner for the County of Los Angeles, however, never participated in the autopsies, and was brought in to testify during the actual Simpson criminal trial instead of Dr. Golden." The medical examiner, Dr. Golden, had given his opinion during the preliminary hearings ten months earlier held to determine whether or not Simpson should stand trial. During Golden's testimony in the preliminary hearing, the killer used two distinctive knives that night, a single-edge knife and a double-edged knife or daggers. Again, this is consistent with Glen's confession that he brought a knife to Nicole's home when he took Ron Goldman

---

90 Christopher Ingraham, "The surprising geography of American left-handedness," *Washington Post*, September 22, 2015, https://www.washingtonpost.com/news/wonk /wp/2015/09/22/the-surprising-geography-of-american-left-handedness/.

over there, with O. J. waiting inside the property, sitting on the steps, waiting to confront Ron over the drug issue. Glen Rogers also said that in the struggle with Ron Goldman, he managed to get ahold of the knife Ron had pulled on O. J., cutting O. J.'s finger. Glen also claimed that after taking Ron's knife from him, Glen used Ron's knife to kill him.[91]

The Ice Cream that Didn't Melt

LAPD Officer Robert Riske was the first police officer on the scenes of the murders in the O. J. Simpson case. Early in O. J.'s murder trial, on Tuesday, February 14, 1995, Riske testified that he found an ice cream cup from Ben and Jerry's partially melted on the bannister inside on the staircase near the front door of Nicole's condo. The key part of his testimony about the ice cream was that he found the ice cream there about 12:30 or 12:40 a.m. on June 13, 1994. This was more than two hours after the prosecution had pegged the time of death for both Ron Goldman and Nicole Simpson, who the LAPD assumed had died at approximately the same time together.

I tested how long it took ice cream to melt and I found it takes about 45 minutes to one hour for ice cream to completely melt at that time of night, with June temperatures in Los Angeles ranging from highs of 79 degrees to lows of 62 degrees. If the ice cream that Riske found on the bannister was not yet melted, that meant whoever brought that ice cream outside had to be alive at 12:00 a.m. midnight, or possibly even 11:30 p.m. that evening.

To me, that melting ice cream pegged the time of Nicole's death right where I thought it would be—an hour and a half, give or take, after Ron Goldman died. I believe Juditha Brown was telling the truth when she said the first time that she spoke to Nicole over the phone was at 11:00 p.m. that night. I peg the time Glen Rogers called

---

91   This and the previous three paragraphs on the left-handed versus right-handed issue are drawn from the same source: T. H. Johnson, *The People vs. O. J. Simpson: Hidden Truths*, a revised update of T. H. Johnson, *Pursuit of Exhibit 35 In the O. J. Simpson Murder Trial and its Hidden Secrets*, op.cit. See also: Seth Mydans, "Simpson Prosecutors Decide Pathologist Won't Testify," *New York Times*, June 13, 1995.

Nicole to say he was coming over with some "nose sugar" for her at 11:10 p.m. that night.

Nicole was not expecting any trouble that night, and she didn't eat her ice cream when the kids ate theirs, right after dinner. Nicole probably put her ice cream in the freezer and was eating it when Glen Rogers arrived. Office Riske also noted that a pink plastic spoon was found on the ground by the bannister where the melting ice cream cup was found. Prosecutor Marcia Clark commented that the pink plastic spoon had fallen out of the ice cream as it was melting.

This was likely not the first time Nicole bought drugs from Glen. Expecting just to pay Glen for the drugs and that Glen would then leave, Nicole was relaxed. The evidence suggests Nicole placed her ice cream on the bannister as she went outside to lead Glen Rogers around the side of the condo.

That's when everything went terribly bad. Nicole was startled to see a body there, and she may have recognized the body as Ron Goldman. She suddenly may have understood why Ron Goldman had not arrived with the eyeglasses earlier, and she may have felt frightened at that instant for her own life. But she didn't have time to scream because nobody reported hearing a scream that night. That's when Glen Rogers grabbed her from behind and slit her throat.

This time of death for Nicole also rules out O. J. as the murderer. The limousine driver has precise timestamps, in part because his activities on the road were monitored by his boss. A limousine service depends on pick-ups and deliveries being made at the right time. O. J. got in the limo just after 11:00 p.m., and O. J. was checking into LAX by 11:30 p.m. that night. O. J. could not have been committing a murder at Nicole's condo at those times, because the LAX and American Airlines timestamps are as reliable as the limo driver timestamps.

A few other details Officer Riske gave on the stand were important. Riske saw the bloody footprints leaving Nicole's property through the other gate from where Ron Goldman's body was, now joined by Nicole's body. One bloody footprint was pointed toward Nicole's door on the Bundy side of the house.

Here I remembered a detail Redd had added. "After he killed Nicole, Glen Rogers thought about going into her condo and stealing some more," Redd had commented. "But he thought better of doing that. The kids might wake up and he had enough with Nicole's cash and the jewelry she was wearing to compensate for O. J. stiffing him. He decided he better get out of there before he was caught." The evidence again confirmed Redd's story. I was certain Glen Rogers had killed Nicole second and she was unsuspecting, not knowing Ron Goldman was already dead.

Officer Riske also found Nicole had drawn a bath and lit candles for a late night, candle-lit bath. Nicole obviously had no reason to think June 12 was going to be her last evening alive.[92]

O. J.'s Missing Golf Clubs

In Chicago the early morning of Monday, June 13, 1994, O. J. Simpson checked into a hotel. Upon learning Nicole had been murdered, O. J. returned to ORD to catch a flight back to Los Angeles. O. J. got back to his L.A. mansion around noon that day. The LAPD waiting there for him handcuffed him and took him to the police station where he was questioned for hours. Instantly, O. J. was suspected of the murders. The suspicion deepened when the LAPD realized O. J. had left his golf clubs in Chicago. O. J. had taken the golf clubs to Chicago and the LAPD suspected O. J. had hidden the bloody clothes and the knife used to commit the murders in the golf bag. That's how police explained the fact they found no bloody clothes or murder weapon when they searched the mansion at 10:30 a.m., after the LAPD got a judge to issue a search warrant.

As we discussed earlier, in Chapter 3, Robert Kardashian was filmed bringing to O. J. Simpson's home the Louis Vuitton garment bag O. J. had taken with him. As we commented there, the LAPD suspected that bag may have contained the bloody clothes and murder weapon. Kardashian had picked up O. J. at LAX when he arrived

---

92 Linda Deutsch, "Simpson Defense Zeroes in on Melting Ice Cream, Nicole's Bath Water," *Associated Press* (AP), February 14, 1995, https://apnews.com/article /c031673be23c4b7eb3e8d9c5ea397985.

at noon from ORD. Kardashian went back a second time to pick up O. J.'s golf bag. Kris Kardashian said, "They were more worried about the golf clubs than they were about Nicole getting killed." I think in the golf clubs were other things way more valuable. O. J. told me one day that his golf clubs were more valuable than my house. So, I think there was something way more valuable than a bloody knife in those golf clubs.

The golf clubs had gone missing by 2003, when Robert Kardashian died of cancer. On March 4, 2014, when burglars broke into the home of Khloe Kardashian and Lamar Odom, there was suspicion the burglars were after O. J.'s golf clubs.[93] Today, I'm not sure those golf clubs were ever found. I have come to suspect O. J. may have been carrying drugs in those golf clubs. You can put a lot of cocaine in the hollowed-out shafts and in the heads of those golf clubs and O. J. may have just been delivering cocaine as the real reason he took those golf clubs with him on that trip. The point is that the golf clubs were never really found. If the golf clubs came back, they were never seen again. No bloody clothes or murder weapon was ever produced by the LAPD to prove O. J. committed the crime.

It's a very simple thing. Let's go back to this: O. J. got tired of paying for Nicole's drug deals. But if those pictures Nicole had in the safe of her beat up in that argument with O. J. from 1989 had surfaced, O. J.'s career would have been over, done. But, at the same time, those pictures in the safe deposit box would have been a good way for Nicole to say, "Hey, O. J., I need $50,000 for some drugs. You know those pictures could be a problem if I don't get my money." So, O. J. had to pay the bills. Like we've said, O. J. just got tired of paying. That's why he took Nicole's notebook with the phone numbers. O. J. gave that book to Robert Kardashian, who gave it to William Wasz. Wasz followed Nicole around for a week or two, got into a

---

93 Luke Kerr-Dineen, "Weird Golf News of the Week: Did burglars steal a set of golf clubs linked to the O. J. murder case?" *Golf Digest*, March 11, 2014, https ://www.golfdigest.com/story/weird-golf-news-of-the-week-did-burglars-steal-a-set -of-golf. See also: "Was Kloe Hiding Evidence? Recent Break-in at Kardashian's Home linked to Simpson's Hidden Property, Jailed Star's Manager Claims," RadarOnLine.com, March 11, 2014, https://radaronline.com/exclusives/2014/03 /khloe-kardashian-break-in-oj-simpson-memorabilia/.

car accident and the book got impounded by the LAPD. We have been over that part of the story before. But what's new here is the golf clubs. I don't rule out that O. J. was making some good money delivering drugs in those golf clubs to Chicago. That's probably why O. J. thought that those golf clubs were so valuable.

Everybody in this story seemed to be dealing drugs. Robert Kardashian met Wasz in the L.A. clubs where Wasz was selling drugs. Wasz claimed he set the price to Kardashian so Kardashian could make some good money reselling the drugs to his friends. Even Nicole in that meeting at the club with Dodi Fayed told Witness #1 and her three friends that a trip to London on Dodi Fayed's private airplane would be *carte blanche*, all expenses paid, even shopping expenses. In the club that night, Witness #1 said Nicole told her and her friends that she was going to Washington to pick up drugs. Since Dodi Fayed had diplomatic immunity to travel feely without having to go through customs, ferrying drugs on his private airplane would easily pay for the girls to spend freely in London. As Witness #1 told the story, the free trip to London was all about party time and drugs. Yet, District Attorney Garcetti and the LAPD did everything possible to keep drugs out of the O. J. murder trial, including releasing Glen Rogers from custody on a plea bargain.

Fred Goldman and O. J.'s Rolex

Fred Goldman was ruthless in his pursuit to grab O. J. Simpson's assets to fulfill the judgment Goldman held against O. J. from the wrongful death civil suit. One of the stranger episodes in that long saga involved O. J. Simpson's Rolex watch. On October 3, 2007, California Superior Court Judge Gerald Rosenberg ordered O. J. to turn over to Fred Goldman three assets: (1) future royalties from a videogame in which O. J. appeared; (2) any of the then-disputed memorabilia O. J. could prove was his after Las Vegas police seized that property when they arrested him the previous month on kidnapping and robbery charges; and (3) O. J.'s Rolex watch. At that time, Simpson attorney Roland Slates questioned whether O. J.'s Rolex watch was a fake, claiming the watch in question sells for

$125.00. Fred Goldman's attorney David Cook contested that, claiming he saw O. J. wearing the watch posted on a celebrity website, estimating the value of the Rolex to be between $5,000 and $22,000, provided it was a real Rolex.[94]

Three days later, on October 6, 2007, the same judge ordered Simpson's watch returned to him, after it was determined to be a knockoff made in China. Goldman's attorney David Cook had argued to Judge Rosenberg that Goldman had a buyer who would pay as much as $10,000 for the Rolex because it belonged to O. J. Simpson. Simpson's lawyer Ronald Slates countered that if Rosenberg allowed Goldman to sell that watch, Goldman would try to go after other O. J. possessions, claiming he could sell them too at a huge markup. "We don't want to create a precedent where Fred Goldman can do that and we're forever faced with it," Slates countered. Judge Rosenberg agreed with Slates, so he ordered Fred Goldman to return the $125.00 Rolex back to Simpson.[95]

This one puzzled me. Can you imagine somebody chasing O. J. around for a $100 watch? To start with, if you believed O. J. had just killed your son, why would Fred Goldman want to wear anything O. J. had on his person? Fred Goldman just wanted money. I've always questioned whether Fred Goldman cared about his son, despite all the theatrics in the courtroom when O. J. was acquitted. We know Fred Goldman did not get along all that well with Ron because the two of them used to get into fist fights. Then, the second time Ron Goldman was arrested, Fred refused to come bail him out, insisting that being in jail would teach Ron Goldman a lesson. I don't think Fred and Ron Goldman were close by any means. Fred and Ron Goldman appear to have been constantly bickering. Then, when Ron was murdered, it seems to me Fred Goldman was more interested in money than he was in his own kid. There were so many records about Fred Goldman that appear to be gone, including simple records

---

94 "Goldman awarded Simpson's Rolex," HollywoodReporter.com, October 3, 2007, https://www.hollywoodreporter.com/news/goldman-awarded-simpsons-rolex-151546.

95 "O. J. Simpson's Rolex Found To Be Fake, Ordered Returned," Cleveland19News .com, October 6, 2007, https://www.cleveland19.com/story/7177815/oj-simpsons-rolex -found-to-be-fake-ordered-returned/.

that should readily be available, like birth certificates, information about how Fred Goldman earned a living. I was shocked and it was mind-twisting when I figured out Patti Glass could have possibly been both Fred Goldman's sister and his wife.

The Mysterious Goldman Family Car Accident

In 1985, Kim Goldman, Ron Goldman's sister, was involved with the family in a horrific car crash. She claims the accident did the following: "permanently scarred my barely fourteen-year-old face, with braces cutting into my lips, my eyes without vision, and battery acid burning an imprint on my soul."[96] Like everything involving the Goldman family, the details of this car accident are hard to document and nearly impossible to figure out. To begin with, the accident happened in a parking lot. How do horrific accidents happen in a parking lot? The accident was on day two of what was supposed to be a two-week vacation in sunny Ft. Lauderdale, with her father, Fred Goldman, her brother, Ron Goldman, and her "soon-to-be stepmother," Patti Glass, in the car.

What was Fred Goldman doing riding around Ft. Lauderdale with Marvin Glass's wife in the front seat, when the Goldman family at that time lived in Chicago, and Marvin Glass was wearing a wire for the FBI in Operation Greylord, informing on the mob and crooked Cook County judges? Marvin Glass was arrested that year, in 1985, charged with helping the Colombian drug cartels import cocaine into the United States. At the time of that accident, Patti Glass was still married to Marvin Glass.

But back to the horrific car accident in the Ft. Lauderdale parking lot. Kim Goldman has claimed that the Goldman family station wagon was "at the mercy of a drunk driver who lost control of his car," such that the drunken driver had "a tire blow, causing him to swerve, hitting a nearby tree, and forcing the battery from his automobile to catapult across the median into our car, breaking off into tiny pieces,

---

96 Kimberly Goldman, "The other night that changed my life," KimberlyGoldman .com, December 21, 2001, http://kimberlygoldman.com/2011/12/night-changed-life/.

spewing acid, glass and chaos everywhere."[97] All of this is supposed to have happened in a parking lot, and batteries do not generally fly out of a car's engine under the hood, from the impact of hitting a tree.

Was that really a car accident or was that because of Fred Goldman's and Patti Glass's backgrounds? Marvin Glass at that time was wearing a wire against Ronald Ofshe, a drug dealer in close proximity, arrested in Miramar, Florida, for possession with intent to distribute four and a half pounds of cocaine and snitching on the mob and corrupt judges in Chicago, to get favorable treatment on the money-laundering and distribution efforts he had been making on behalf of Colombian drug cartel godfathers. Usually, the cartel does not take kindly to informants, and Colombian drug cartel gangsters do not take kindly to their accountant and chief marketing officer in the United States being under investigation by the FBI.

I've never been 100 percent certain that someone didn't just throw that battery into the Goldman's windshield to kill the whole family. Then too, Marvin Glass had no problem putting out $2,500 to put a hit job to kill an ex-partner, I can only imagine what he would do to somebody who was taking his wife. In this so-called "accident," what are the odds of a drunken driver on the road blowing a tire and running into a tree, such that their battery flies out from under the hood, flies through the air, crashes into the windshield of a car in a parking lot, throwing glass and battery acid all over, and burning her face? There's something wrong with that story.

Maybe the 1985 car accident that ended up disfiguring Kim Goldman's face was just a shot over the bow. It could have been that whoever threw that battery into the windshield that day was sending a warning to Fred Goldman. By messing with Patti Glass, Fred Goldman was getting himself into a world of hurt. Marvin Glass may have wanted revenge because Fred Goldman was dating his wife when his problems with the FBI were mounting. The Columbian drug cartels and the Chicago mobs may have wanted revenge because Marvin Glass was snitching on their $100 million dollar drug-smuggling racket. Fred Goldman should have known that if the Colombian drug

---

97   Ibid.

cartel and the Chicago mob wanted to destroy Marvin Glass, they would do so by destroying Marvin Glass's family. After that bizarre car accident, Fred Goldman should have realized how dangerous it was for him to be messing with Patti Glass, especially when it appears that she may have been his sister and you are thinking about making her the stepmother to your young son and daughter.

But this is why a lot of people suspect Ron Goldman's killing had to do with Fred Goldman's background. Fred Goldman's background may have brought this whole thing together such that the murders never had anything to do with anybody but him. Ron Goldman's killing may have had nothing to do with O. J. Simpson. O. J. was sort of in the middle. But when Fred Goldman started messing with the wife of the Colombian drug cartel's money man in Chicago, who appeared to be his sister, what do you expect to happen? Marvin Glass informed on the Cook County mob and on the Colombian drug cartel in Chicago.

If the mobsters want revenge, who do they go after? Marvin Glass or his family? So, even if Marvin Glass didn't want Ron Goldman killed, the Colombian mobsters might have wanted him killed. That's why a lot of people think Ron Goldman's murder was due to Fred Goldman's background.

Fred Goldman's entire family nearly got killed from a flying battery in a parking lot, but you go ahead and marry Patti Glass. After Fred Goldman married Patti Glass, Ron Goldman became an alleged drug dealer. Arrested by the LAPD, he gets himself out and his criminal files sealed by informing on drug dealers in L.A. Then when Ron Goldman connected with Nicole, that would have brought the mobs thirst for revenge against Marvin Glass into O. J.'s house.

Truthfully, it's hard to figure out whose family is more screwed up, Fred Goldman's family or Robert Kardashian's family. Think about it. O. J. ruined Kardashian's marriage by having sex with his wife Kris Kardashian. That sex, complicated by the size of O. J.'s organ, turned out to be so violent that Kris, a few hours later, needed to go to the hospital. But when she asked O. J. to take her, O. J. told Kris to have her husband take her to the hospital because he was going to stay in bed. Next, Kris Kardashian divorces Robert Kardashian and marries

Bruce Jenner, who is now a female with a new name, Kaitlyn Jenner. Kris and Bruce vacation with Nicole and O. J. over Easter in 1994, who are at that time, happily back together, attempting to reconcile. A couple of months after that happy family vacation to which Robert Kardashian was not invited, Nicole gets her throat slashed "Colombian necklace" style by the exact same serial killer who had just an hour or two earlier slashed Ron Goldman's throat in the same manner.

Sounds pretty normal to me, but then, what do I know? I'm just a country boy.

Glen Rogers Does Contract Killing Jobs for the Mobs

You probably won't find it surprising to learn Glen Rogers admitted in his documents that he did hits for the mobsters and the drug cartels. In Las Vegas, Glen Rogers claimed to have killed two people for the Gambino family and buried them behind the Greyhound bus station. In the world where the Colombian drug cartel operated, Glen Rogers was known to be a hit man. Glen was the perfect mob hit man. He was not part of the mob and he enjoyed killing people. The mob paid well and getting paid to kill people would have made his work as a serial killer even more pleasurable for Glen. As we saw when Glen went back to Nicole's after O. J. stiffed him that night, Glen liked to get paid for his handiwork.

But the question here is a difficult one to answer with certainty. Who was Glen Rogers working for that night? For Robert Kardashian, who may have wanted revenge on O. J. for having sex with his wife, Kris Kardashian, and wrecking his marriage and family? For Marvin Glass, who may have wanted revenge for Fred Goldman wrecking his marriage with Patti Glass and breaking up his family? For the Colombian drug cartels, who may have wanted revenge on Marvin Glass for being an informer and turning state's evidence against the Chicago mob, threatening a $100 million drug-smuggling business? Was he working that night as a serial-killer hitman, or was he only expecting to be the muscle for O. J. confronting Ron Goldman? If Glen Rogers was not working for someone other than O. J. that night, maybe it was O. J. Simpson who should have brought and won the wrongful death civil suit against Robert Kardashian, Fred Goldman, and Marvin Glass for getting Nicole killed and ruining his family.

On the night of June 12, 1994, O. J. was about to mess up his marriage to Nicole and his life permanently. But the truth is that Robert Kardashian, Marvin Glass, and O. J. Simpson had already pretty much messed up their lives and their marriages all by themselves. Kris Kardashian, Patti Glass, and Nicole Simpson were all unfaithful to their husbands before their marriages to Robert Kardashian, Marvin Glass, and O. J. Simpson broke up. In O. J.'s case, he and Nicole were "open marriage" swingers virtually the entire time they were together.

In all these marriages, drugs were involved, one way or another. Ron Goldman was not an innocent victim killed because his timing doing a favor was horribly unfortunate. For all we know, Ron Goldman was headed to Marina Del Ray to do a drug deal. Ron Goldman had not achieved the heights Marvin Glass achieved with the drug lords, but it looks like he could have been following in Marvin Glass's footsteps. Ron, with a sealed LAPD criminal record and a history of getting out of jail as an informer, was openly dealing drugs working. Far from being just another aspiring actor failing in L.A., Ron was handsome enough to pull off being a Gigolo waiter in a trendy eatery, who amused himself dating attractive women, like Nicole, who may well have picked him up in the steamy hot party clubs popular among the Hollywood-Beverly Hills glitterati.

Had Nicole fixed the candle-lit bath expecting to have sex with Ron Goldman when he finally got there? Or was Ron just bringing Nicole her mother's eyeglasses—eyeglasses found lying somehow unnoticed in the valet parking street outside the restaurant—which were missing a lens when introduced as evidence in the O. J. murder trial?

We may never know, at least not for sure. But my goal from the beginning was not to tell you with certainty how the O. J. Simpson murder case was to be solved. My goal was to give you the facts as I have found them after twenty years investigating and to show you what I learned—new revelations in a story that was as much about drugs and revenge as it was about sex and marriage. The true backstory here was racism that framed O. J. as the Othello-motivated murderer. The even truer backstory was a possibility of a corrupt District Attorney and police department more interested in running the drug trade than solving crimes. You now know what I conclude.

In this tragic, sad saga, where all the principal actors were living lives messed up beyond repair. But in my opinion the guy who killed Nicole Brown Simpson and Ron Goldman was Glen Rogers. As twisted and as evil as all these people may have been, nobody but Glen Rogers had ever actually killed anybody, at least not so far as we know.

That the serial killer murdered Nicole Brown Simpson and Ron Goldman was a fact the LAPD and O. J.'s "Dream Team" defense knew but chose to forget about. How Glen Rogers managed to pull this all off to leave L.A. and go on killing was the question I came away from this twenty-year quest determined yet to figure out.

CONCLUSION:

The Sequel Yet to Be Written:
Who Is Glen Rogers?

―――――

When we began this book, I said I wasn't going to solve the O. J. Simpson murder mystery for you. Well, I don't think I have solved the case. I'm pretty sure I'm right that Glen Rogers was the one who killed Nicole Brown Simpson and Ron Goldman.

I challenge you to come up with a different, better solution. Whatever you come up with as your solution, make sure you don't commit the same error the District Attorney Garcetti and the LAPD committed. Don't develop a narrative you want to be the solution. Don't jam the facts into your solution until they fit. The challenge here is to come up with the truth. You will know we have arrived at the truth when we let the facts of the case, the evidence, speak for itself.

I say I haven't solved the case yet because I have not answered the most important and at the same time most basic question of all: Who really hired Glen Rogers? And who really is Glen Rogers? I'm not asking that question in a superficial way. Yes, we know a lot about Glen—but we have not even begun to get down to figuring out who Glen Rogers was really. I mean in his mind. Why did Glen kill Ron Goldman? Well, probably because Ron Goldman pulled a knife on him. Why did he kill Nicole? Well, probably because he wanted to get paid, and after Ron Goldman was killed, Nicole had to be killed too. She knew too much.

But that explanation is too simple. Glen Rogers may not be edu-
cated, but he is by no means stupid. He is highly intelligent, and
complex. Why did he kill all those people? Even more interesting is
this: Did he intend to get caught? If he didn't intend to get caught,
why does he keep confessing to all those murders? We have not even
begun to explore the depths of that mystery.

What was it that brought Glen Rogers to Los Angeles at that time
and something in his mind brought him to Brentwood that night?
This is the question that is at the heart of the crime and we haven't
even begun to explore the depths of where the answers are going to
take us.

Glen Confesses to Multiple Murders

Through his many various letters from prison and with the help of
anonymous informants like Redd, our Witness #2, I have come to
learn of the many murders Glen Rogers is claiming to have committed. Sometimes, Glen explains that he just wants to "set the record
straight" by "taking responsibility" for his crimes by letting families
know what happened to loved ones who disappeared. Mostly, I have
come to believe, Glen exhibits one of the somewhat surprising char-
acteristics common to many serial killers. Clearly, confessing that you
have committed a murder is like sentencing yourself to the death
penalty. What rational person would ever do that? But then, I make
no claim to suppose serial killers are rational or responsible. I think
Glen's real urge is what I have suggested earlier. He knows he is on
Death Row and Glen hates the idea nobody knows he may be the
most notorious serial killer since Jack the Ripper.

I have also been following up on clues that Glen Rogers have
been dropping about the Oakland County Child Killer—Glen claims
to know the identity of the killers and what the case reveals about
the Oakland County Child Killer is fascinating. It is tied to the letters sent anonymously to a psychiatrist who worked on the Homicide
Task Force that was unable to solve the case. Those letters were
written by "Allen," who claimed to be the roommate of the killer.
"Allen" identified as a slave of the killer, "Frank," whom he identified
as the "OCCK." In the next book, we will de-code that case like

we did in this book with the O. J. Simpson murder mysteries. Glen Rogers knows as much about the children killed in Oakland County, Michigan back in the 1970s as he does about the murders of Nicole Brown Simpson and Ron Goldman.

After all, as I pointed out earlier, Glen has claimed to have killed some seventy people—that's a lot of corpses that have never been found and a lot of families who have led tormented lives searching and hoping to find closure on what happened to beloved friends, lovers, or family members they lost, without knowing what happened or why.

What I found out to my surprise is that Glen has revealed a lot and the anonymous informants have affirmed I should pay attention. "What Glen is saying you can generally believe is true," Redd insisted. "Glen had this diary book, and he recorded the names of his killings, even had some hair samples in there." Redd warned me Glen's diary is very disturbing. "It contained a lot of information about children he and his partner killed," Redd explained. "There were other killers too, working along with Glen." That continues to bother me—all these other people Glen killed and they're just sitting there, ignored. We've got records where Glen has told us he's buried bodies. But the police don't want to know about the other bodies. I bet it's going to be up to me to go dig up the bodies. It's hard to imagine the amount of damage Glen Rogers has done to the families of those victims. These were evil killings and the families deserve to know the truth.

But the truth in Glen's case is very disturbing. Consider this, for example: Redd has informed me that Glen is talking about a woman he killed who was involved with Glen when Glen murdered Mark Peters in 1993. "Glen told me that he killed and buried a woman behind a Greyhound Bus Station in Las Vegas, Nevada," Redd said. "Glen told me the police knew all about it, but they never looked for the body. Glen told me exactly where he buried the body, and he said the woman he killed there was with him when he robbed the Mark Peters house after he killed him." Glen did a lot of riding around the country in a Greyhound bus—that is, when he didn't manage to steal the identity and the car of someone who he killed, for instance, like that kindly gentleman Mark Peters who was just trying to help

Glen so he could make a favorable impression on Glen's mother—the woman who got Nicole's golden angel pin with diamonds.

Again, I didn't promise any of this was going to be pretty. "There's two people Glen Rogers killed that you could find in a gorge in Lee County Kentucky, probably near that back-woods farm the bootlegging Rogers family had," Redd continued. "His father was an original Kentucky hillbilly and I have no idea how many people his father and brothers could have killed and buried on that farm, but Glen tells me it was a lot. There's another body in Wyoming, another one in Texas. Glen goes on and we get to fifteen bodies pretty soon."

Redd insisted there was not much logic to why Glen killed people, but he liked to kill a certain kind of woman and was known as the "Casanova Killer" as well as the "Cross-Country Killer." Sometimes Glen killed a whole family. "He told me that in Grant County, there's a family killed, and kids disappeared," Redd continued. "Glen said to me that he wants to put that one to rest—he went on to make me believe there was some kind of sick sex thing involved in killing that family. I don't even want to imagine what that might mean."

The Sequel: Who Is Glen Rogers?

So, if Redd and the other informants keep coming forward, I don't think my quest to investigate is over. I may not be able to redress the horrific crimes Glen Rogers has committed, but I'm going to continue investigating. Now that I'm putting the O. J. Simpson story to bed with everything that I've told you in this book, I'm sensing my next quest will be to investigate Glen Rogers. Justice needs to be done there too. And I would like to help Glen bring closure to his troubled life, before the state of Florida executes him for killing Tina Marie Cribbs in Florida, slowly stabbing her to death in a motel bathtub in early November 1995—just one of the murders Glen Rogers committed after Los Angeles District Attorney Garcetti let him go loose with a plea deal despite his confessing that he was the true killer of Nicole Brown Simpson and Ron Goldman.

That is the sequel to this book. As I see it, Glen Rogers was the killer who never showed up in the O. J. murder trial. But now my question was what was going on in Glen's head? He was a serial killer on a rampage who wanted to be known as famous. This book accomplishes that for Glen Rogers. But this book leaves open an even more intriguing question. What kind of pathology was going on in Glen's mind that put him in Brentwood the night of June 12, 1994, and on Death Row in Florida today? That is going to be a dark and dangerous ride. We will have to explore the depths of homicidal psychosis to understand who Glen Rogers really is.

What makes this next project interesting, the sequel of the O. J. Simpson murder mystery, is that I think Glen Rogers still wants to talk, especially if he thinks talking will keep him alive a few days longer. As much as Glen might be mad at me for not getting him out, I suspect he won't be able to resist answering the questions I'm thinking about asking. There is a sequel to this book that I am planning to write next. I'm going to take Glen's diary, his letters, what informants like Redd have to say, and I'm going to go out there and see if we can dig up those bodies. Yes, I plan on writing more letters to Glen, asking Glen to explain to me what this serial killing was all about.

I don't know for sure that Glen will answer, but I plan on asking him the questions I come up with, and I'm asking you to come along for the ride. I can't promise it will be pretty, but I have no doubt it will be interesting, and strange—probably more bizarre than you and I can imagine right now.

At any rate, my quest continues and now I am on to the Glen Rogers story: Who really is Glen Rogers? That's what I plan on finding out next.

About the Author

Norman Pardo was O.J. Simpson's right-hand man, his confidant, the keeper of his secrets, and his business manager for nearly twenty years. He is the founder of the Urban Core Institute and regarded as a pioneer of the web. His adventures have garnered him international recognition and he has had the honor of appearing on almost every wmajor network, magazine, and newspaper around the globe. As an actor, producer, and director, he has created and distributed numerous films while working with some of the most distinguished film directors and celebrities in Hollywood, even appearing in Oscar-winning films like *O.J.: Made in America*.